A GLOSSARY OF
SUFI
TECHNICAL TERMS

A GLOSSARY OF

SUFI
TECHNICAL TERMS

COMPILED BY

'Abd al-Razzāq al-Qāshāni

TRANSLATED FROM THE ARABIC BY

Nabil Safwat, M.A., Ph.D.

REVISED AND EDITED BY

David Pendlebury

THE OCTAGON PRESS LTD
LONDON

Copyright © 1991 The Sufi Trust

All rights reserved
Copyright throughout the world

No part of this publication may be reproduced or transmitted in any form or by any means, electronic, mechanical or photographic, by recording or any information storage or retrieval system or method now known or to be invented or adapted, without prior permission obtained in writing from the publishers, The Octagon Press Ltd., except by a reviewer quoting brief passages in a review written for inclusion in a journal, magazine, newspaper or broadcast.

Request for permission to reprint, reproduce, etc., to:
Permissions Department, The Octagon Press Ltd.,
P.O. Box 227, London N6 4EW, England

Published with the aid of a subvention
from The Sufi Trust

ISBN 0 863040 32 2

Published 1991

Photoset, printed and bound in Great Britain by
Redwood Press Limited, Melksham, Wiltshire

CONTENTS

Foreword xv

Part 1: English Translation

Introduction 1

LETTER ALĪF 3
1 *Alīf*
2 Union
3 Connection
4 The One
5 Oneness
6 The Unity of Union
7 Enumerating the Names of God
8 States
9 Charity
10 Desire
11 The Thrones of Unity
12 The Name
13 The Essential Names
14 The Greatest Name
15 The Technical Term
16 The Heights
17 Established Essences
18 Isolated Individuals
19 The Visible Horizon
20 The Supreme Horizon
21 Sainthood
22 The Trusted Ones
23 The Two Imams
24 The Mother of The Book
25 The Eternal Present
26 Egoism
27 Selfhood
28 Agitation
29 The Severance of Union
30 The Mainstays
31 The Foremost Names

LETTER BĀ' 9
32 *Bā'*
33 The Door of Doors
34 The Glimmer
35 Nullity
36 The Substitutes
37 Corpulence
38 Lightning
39 Intermediate World
40 The Universal Interval
41 Expansiveness (also 42)
43 Discernment
44 The Cow

v

A GLOSSARY OF SUFI TECHNICAL TERMS

45 Intuitive Impulses
46 The House of Wisdom
47 The Sacred House

48 The Sacrosanct House
49 The House of Glory

LETTER JĪM   12
50 Attraction
51 The Ringing Bell
52 The Body
53 Clarity
54 Clarification
55 Splendour
56 Beauty
57 Combination
58 Union
59 Union of Union
60 The Paradise

61 The Paradise of Inheritance
62 The Paradise of Qualities
63 The Paradise of the Essence
64 The Honourable Ones
65 The Two Aspects of Limitation and Expanse
66 The Two Aspects of Desire
67 The Jewels of Science, Prophecy and Deep Knowledge

LETTER DĀL   16
68 The West Wind

69 The White Pearl

LETTER HĀ'   17
70 *Hā'*
71 He
72 Dust
73 Far-reaching Ambition
74 Disdainful Ambition

75 Noble-minded Ambition
76 Craving
77 Suggestions
78 Attacks
79 Primordial Matter

LETTER WĀW   19
80 *Wāw*
81 Oneness
82 The One
83 Incoming Thought
84 Event
85 The Mediator of Grace and Assistance
86 The Odd Number
87 Existence
88 The Two Aspects of Providence
89 Unconditional and Conditional
90 The Face of Truth
91 The Goal of All Servants
92 The Record Sheet
93 Behind the Outer Covering

94 The Essential Attribute of Truth
95 The Essential Attribute of Creation
96 Reunion
97 The Reunion of Separation
98 Reunion of Reunion
99 The Fulfilment of the Covenant
100 Keeping the Covenant of Conduct
101 Moment of Time
102 Eternal Time
103 The Halt
104 Authentic Undertaking
105 The Friend of God
106 Sainthood

CONTENTS

LETTER ZĀ' — 25
107 The Reprover
108 The Glass
109 The Emerald
110 Duration of Time
111 The Flowering of Information, Knowledge and Reunion
112 The Olive Tree
113 The Oil

LETTER ḤĀ' — 26
114 The Mystical State
115 The Demonstration to Mankind of the Truth
116 The Veil
117 The Letters
118 The Sublime Letters
119 Freedom
120 Burning
121 Keeping The Covenant
122 Keeping the Covenant of Lordship and Service
123 The Reality of Realities
124 The Reality of Muhammad
125 The Realities of the Names
126 The Truth of Certitude
127 Wisdom
128 Explicit Wisdom
129 Tacit Wisdom
130 Unknown Wisdom
131 Universal Wisdom

LETTER ṬĀ' — 30
132 Rising Stars
133 The Pure
134 The Outwardly Pure
135 The Inwardly Pure
136 The Secretly Pure
137 The Secretly and Overtly Pure
138 Spiritual Medicine
139 The Spiritual Physician
140 The Way
141 Effacement

LETTER YĀ' — 32
142 The Red Ruby
143 The Two Hands
144 The Day of Assembly

LETTER KĀF — 33
145 The Clear Book
146 The Totality
147 The Word
148 The Word of the Presence
149 The Hidden Treasure
150 The Ungrateful
151 Fission
152 The Morning Star
153 Alchemy
154 The Alchemy of Happiness
155 The Alchemy of The Masses
156 The Alchemy of the Elect

LETTER LĀM — 35
157 The Sign
158 Divine Nature
159 The Kernel
160 The Kernel of Kernels
161 Disguise
162 Eloquence
163 The Tongue of Truth
164 Subtlety
165 The Human Subtlety
166 The Tablet
167 Signs
168 Rays
169 The Night of Power

LETTER MĪM — 38
170 The One Who Holds, The Thing Held, and For Whom it is Held
171 Sacred Water
172 The Original
173 (There is no entry bearing this number)
174 Starting Points and End Results
175 The Foundation of Sufism
176 The One who is Confirmed in Truth
177 The One who is Confirmed in Truth and Creation
178 The Attracted
179 The Universal Manifestations
180 The Manifestation of the Active Names
181 The Meeting of the Two Seas
182 The Meeting of Desires
183 The Meeting of Opposites
184 Genuine Love
185 The Protected
186 External Obliteration
187 Inward Obliteration
188 The Obliteration of True Union
189 The Obliteration of Service and of the Individual Servant
190 Eradication
191 Audience
192 Facing
193 The Conversation
194 The Retreat
195 Sustained Existence
196 The Universal Ranks
197 The Mirror of Being
198 The Mirror of Existence
199 The Mirror of the Two Presences
200 The Evening Talk
201 The Paths of Total Praise
202 The Abode of the Greatest Name
203 The Basis of Deep Knowledge
204 The Consumed
205 The Obscure Issue
206 The Relaxed One
207 Dawnings of Victory
208 Dawnings of the Sun of Reality
209 The Dawning of Inner Minds
210 The Correspondence between Qualities and Realities
211 The Correspondence between the Presences and Creation
212 Insight
213 The Point of Departure
214 Signs Identifying the Qualities
215 The First Teacher and the Teacher of the Angels
216 The Setting of the Sun
217 The Key to the Secret of Destiny
218 The First Key
219 Release from Sorrow and Anxiety
220 The Bestower
221 The Stage
222 The Stage of Divine Descent

CONTENTS

223 The Exalted Position
224 Fraud
225 The Kingdom
226 The Heavenly Kingdom
227 The King of the Kingdom
228 The Enlarger of Aspirations
229 Equity
230 The First Way
231 Utter Separateness

232 Ultimate Knowledge
233 The Essential Relationship
234 The Enraptured
235 Death
236 The White Death
237 The Green Death
238 The Black Death
239 Balance

LETTER NŪN 55
240 Prophecy
241 The Noble
242 Breath
243 The Breath of The Merciful
244 The Self
245 The Commanding Self
246 The Accusing Self
247 The Serene Self
248 The Chiefs
249 The Connubial Bond Diffused through all its Issue

250 The End of the First Journey
251 The End of The Second Journey
252 The End of the Third Journey
253 The End of the Fourth Journey
254 The Gift
255 Letter *Nūn*
256 Light
257 Light of Lights

LETTER SĪN 59
258 The Precedent
259 The Wayfarer
260 Floating
261 The Veil
262 Screens
263 Veils
264 The Adoration of the Heart
265 Crushing
266 The Final Lote Tree
267 The Secret
268 The Secret of Knowledge
269 The Secret of a State
270 The Secret of Reality
271 The Secret of the Illuminations

272 The Secret of Destiny
273 The Secret of Deity
274 The Secret of the Secret of Deity
275 The Secrets of the Traces
276 The Last Night of the Moon
277 The Abundance of the Heart
278 Journeys
279 The Abolition of Viewpoints
280 The Sesame Seed
281 The Request of the Two Presences
282 Blackness of Face in the Two Abodes

LETTER ʿAĪN 64
283 The World
284 The World of Power
285 The World of Command, the World of the Heavenly Kingdom and the Invisible World

286 The World of Creation, the World of the Kingdom and the Visible World
287 The Wise
288 The Learned
289 The Common People

ix

A GLOSSARY OF SUFI TECHNICAL TERMS

290 The Great Reproach, and the Thing Greatly Hated
291 Worship
292 Servants of God
The Servant of:
293   God
294   The Compassionate
295   The Merciful
296   The King
297   The Holy
298   Salvation
299   The Faithful
300   The Protector
301   The Mighty
302   The Almighty
303   The Haughty
304   The Creator
305   The Maker
306   The Fashioner
307   The Forgiving
308   The Vanquisher
309   The Munificent
310   The Provider
311   The Opener
312   The Knower
313   The Constrainer
314   The Expansive
315   The Humbler
316   The Exalter
317   The Strengthener
318   The Humiliator
319   The Hearer and the Seer
320   The Judge
321   The Just
322   The Gentle
323   The Adept
324   The Clement
325   The Glorious
326   The Pardoning
327   The Thankful
328   The Most High
329   The Great
330   The Preserver
331   The Nourisher
332   The Reckoner
333   The Sublime
334   The Generous

The Servant of:
335   The Liberal
336   The Vigilant
337   The Responsive
338   The All-embracing
339   The Judicious
340   The Loving
341   The Illustrious
342   The Reviver
343   The Witness
344   The Truth
345   The Guardian
346   The Powerful
347   The Firm
348   The Patron
349   The Praiseworthy
350   The Quantifier
351   The Initiator
352   The Restorer
353   The Quickener
354   The Mortifier
355   The Living
356   The Eternal
357   The Finder
358   The Glorious
359   The One
360   The Unique
361   The Everlasting
362   The Masterful
363   The Potent
364   The Promoter
365   The Restrainer
366   The First
367   The Last
368   The Outward
369   The Inward
370   The Ruler
371   The Supreme
372   The Pious
373   The Relenting
374   The Avenger
375   The Pardoner
376   The Benign
377   The Lord of the Kingdom
378   The Most Majestic and Noble
379   The Even-handed

CONTENTS

The Servant of:
- 380 The Universal
- 381 The Independent
- 382 The Benefactor
- 383 The Preventer
- 384 The Harmful and the Beneficial
- 385 The Light
- 386 The Guide
- 387 The Creative
- 388 The Enduring
- 389 The Inheritor
- 390 The Mature
- 391 The Patient
- 392 The Admonition
- 393 The Eagle
- 394 The Cause
- 395 Clouds
- 396 Spiritual Pillars
- 397 The '*Anqa*' Bird
- 398 The Major Element
- 399 The Worlds of Apparel
- 400 The Established Essence
- 401 The Essence of Things
- 402 The Eye of God and the Eye of the World
- 403 The Essence of Life
- 404 The Recurring Feast

LETTER FĀ'   89
- 405 Loosening
- 406 Openings
- 407 Imminent Victory
- 408 Manifest Victory
- 409 Absolute Victory
- 410 Cooling Off
- 411 The First Separation
- 412 The Second Separation
- 413 The Proof
- 414 The Separation of Union
- 415 The Separation of the Qualities
- 416 The Difference between the Emulator and the Verifier
- 417 The Difference between Perfection and Honour
- 418 The Split
- 419 Thusness

LETTER ṢĀD   92
- 420 The Master of Duration and the Master of Moment and State
- 421 The Fair of Face
- 422 The Easterly Breeze
- 423 The Sincere Friend
- 424 The Authenticity of Light
- 425 Rust
- 426 The Thunderclap
- 427 The Elite
- 428 The Image of Truth
- 429 The Image of God
- 430 The Cells of Remembrance
- 431 Safeguarding the Will

LETTER QĀF   95
- 432 The First Tendency
- 433 The Tendency towards Manifestation
- 434 The Two Bow-lengths
- 435 Setting Out for God
- 436 Arising Within God
- 437 Contraction
- 438 The Foot
- 439 The Sure Footing
- 440 Nearness
- 441 The Shell
- 442 The Pole-star
- 443 The Major Pole-star
- 444 The Heart
- 445 Restraints
- 446 Resurrection

LETTER RĀ' — 99

- 447 The Shepherd
- 448 Possession
- 449 The Lord
- 450 The Lord of Lords
- 451 Classes of the Names
- 452 Binding
- 453 The Compassionate
- 454 The Merciful
- 455 Grateful Compassion
- 456 Obligatory Compassion
- 457 The Mantle
- 458 Ruin
- 459 Form
- 460 The Forms of Cognition and their Marks
- 461 Frivolity
- 462 Delicacy
- 463 The Spirit
- 464 The Greatest Spirit, the Oldest, the First and the Last
- 465 The Spirit of Inspiration
- 466 Testimony
- 467 The Gathering of Division
- 468 Roving
- 469 The Even Number
- 470 The Vision of God
- 471 The Vision of the Particular in the Universal
- 472 The Vision of the Universal in the Particular
- 473 The Evidence of Truth
- 474 The Evidence of Unity
- 475 The Evidence of the Names
- 476 Matters
- 477 Essential Matters
- 478 The Master

LETTER TĀ' — 106

- 479 *Tā'*
- 480 Familiarisation
- 481 Illumination
- 482 Primary Illumination
- 483 Secondary Illumination
- 484 Visionary Illumination
- 485 Verification
- 486 Sufism
- 487 Change

LETTER KHĀ' — 109

- 488 Idea
- 489 The Seal
- 490 The Seal of Prophecy
- 491 The Seal of the Saints
- 492 The Patched Robe of Sufism
- 493 Khidr, the Green One
- 494 Compulsion
- 495 Sincere Friendship
- 496 Seclusion
- 497 The Renunciation of Habits
- 498 Renewed Creation

LETTER DHĀL — 113

- 499 The Treasures of God
- 500 Tasting
- 501 The Man of Reason
- 502 The Man of Insight
- 503 The Man of Reason and Insight

LETTER DĀD — 115

- 504 The Special Ones
- 505 Splendour

CONTENTS

LETTER ẒĀ'   116
506 The External Aspect of Contingent Phenomena
507 The Shadow
508 The First Shadow
509 The Shadow of God

LETTER GHAĪN   118
510 The Crow
511 The Film and the Veil
512 Wealth
513 The Helper
514 The Mystery of the Essential Identity
515 The Hidden Mystery and the Guarded Mystery
516 The Error which Falls Short of Possession

Notes on the Translation   120

Bibliography   127

Note on the Translator   128

Index to the English translation   129

Part 2: The Arabic Text
(starting at the other end of the book)

FOREWORD

Although this work has been 'required reading' in Sufi circles for the last six and a half centuries, there has until now been no readily accessible translation in any Western language. With a view to filling this gap, the present work was undertaken at the behest of the Sufi Trust.

In our translation we have relied on two main sources:

1. An edition by the noted Arabist, Dr Aloys Sprenger, based on two annotated Arabic manuscripts. This was published in Calcutta in 1845, under the aegis of the Asiatic Society of Bengal. A facsimile of this edition is to be found at the 'other end' of the present book.

2. A more recent edition (Cairo 1981) by Dr Mohammad Kamal Ibrahim Ja'far, which also refers to several manuscript sources. In the main we have followed the layout and above all the numbering scheme of the Sprenger edition; so that those versed in Arabic should have no difficulty in tracing our efforts back to the original text. However, we have on a number of occasions been guided by what seemed to be a more plausible version in the Cairo edition.

'Sufi Technical Terms' is an accurate enough rendering of the Arabic title of this work. An approximate phonetic transliteration might be: *Iṣṭilaḥāt al-Ṣūfīya*. The full name of its author is: *Kamāl al-Dīn Abi al-Ghanā'im 'Abd al-Razzāq al-Qāshānī*al-Samarqandi*. For the sake of brevity we refer to him as Abdur-Razzaq al-Qashani, or, following Dr Kamal's lead, simply Qashani. As his name suggests, his forefathers came from central Asia. He died in A.D. 1330 (= 730 A.H.).

The original is divided into twenty-eight chapters, each corresponding to a letter of the alphabet. However, the ordering is not

---

*This is often spelt with a letter *kāf: kāshāni*, or even *kāshi*.

that of the modern Arabic alphabet, but follows the so-called *abjad* order. There is no strict sorting system within the chapters themselves.

Inevitably, when a dictionary or glossary is translated the order of the section headings becomes randomised, so the English speaking reader has no means of tracing a term. We were not tempted to recast our English translation into alphabetical order, since for a number of reasons we wished to keep in step with the accompanying Arabic text and avoid tampering unnecessarily with its structure. Instead of this, we have appended an index to the English text, thus actually affording the reader slightly more freedom of navigation than is available in the original.

Items in the text which have been marked with an asterisk are discussed in the notes which follow on pages 120–126. Generally these are references to the Qur'an, or other specifically Islamic knowledge. In rendering passages from the Qur'an we are indebted to the excellent work done by A. J. Arberry and Yusuf Ali. We have taken on trust the authenticity of the Traditions quoted by Qashani in his Glossary.

We have preferred the word 'glossary' to 'dictionary', since we wish to signal the fact that the subject matter contained in it is closely and coherently inter-related; and that while of course it may be consulted and 'dipped into' like any other work of reference, it is also possible and useful to treat it as a continuous text. It seems certain that its author thought so, too, since frequently a train of thought may be observed to pass from section to section.

Both of us have worked on the text for upwards of three years. Intermittently, to be sure; but then it is in the nature of such work to be intermittent. In grappling with its subtleties, we have had the satisfaction of learning a great deal about the Arabic and English languages – not least of which was an insight into how much more, vastly more, there was still to learn. However, we both feel that the time we have spent in varying degrees of proximity to Qashani's '*World of Ideas*' has brought us other, less quantifiable benefits; and it is these above all that we would wish to share with our readers.

Our preoccupation with how best to facilitate this sharing – or at least how to avoid vitiating it – has led us into many discussions, together and with associates and friends. We concluded that there is no single, inevitably correct procedure. It is as if in our travels a party

of us came upon the remains of a camp fire. Some of us might simply wish to examine it minutely, to discover what manner of people had used it – where they came from, where they were going and when. Others, on observing that some of the ashes were still warm, might be more inclined – and might even have the requisite know-how – to stir through the embers in order to kindle a flame which would form the basis of another campfire, which was no longer 'theirs, then' but 'ours, now'.

INTRODUCTION

*In the name of God,
the Compassionate,
the Merciful.*

Thanks be to God who, in the abundance of his grace, has spared our contemplative spirit from conventional scientific research,* and from the drudgery of transmitting information and deducing proofs – who has delivered us from all useless and superfluous talk and preserved us from all competitive wrangling and debate. For these things are sources of uncertainty, suspicion and doubt – causing one to stray from the right path and lead others astray. So praised be the One who has lifted from our eyes the veils of rivalry, diversity and complexity.

Blessings, too, be upon him who guided us from the darkness of the veils of majesty to the radiance of beauty: upon Muhammad, the Chosen One – and likewise upon his most excellent of families and companions.

When I had finished writing *The Stations of the Wayfarers*, a commentary dealing with Ibn Arabi's book, *Bezels of Wisdom*, I also wrote an interpretation of the *Qur'an* based on Sufi terminology. It transpired that this was unfamiliar to most proponents of the traditional or intellectual sciences; so I was asked to explain it to them. In my explanation I pointed out that the basic principles mentioned in that book for classifying people's spiritual stages may be extended to subdivide them into a thousand further stages. I alluded to the method of deriving these subdivisions, without actually stating what they were; nor did I elaborate on their branches and levels, or declare their various categories. In order to gratify such people and assist them in their enquiries, I have now undertaken to add what has

so far been omitted. I have divided this treatise into two parts. The first part, consisting of twenty-eight chapters, describes the technical terms used – with the exception of the 'Stages', as these are thoroughly explained in the subsequent text. The terms are classified in *abjad* alphabetical order, to make it easier to look up entries one by one. The second part, which explains how all the various divisions are ordered and compiled, is arranged in normal book format with chapters and sub-headings.*

LETTER ALĪF

1 **ALĪF**
This letter is used to denote the Essence of Unity, namely Truth, since this is the start of all things in Eternity-without-beginning.*

2 **UNION**
means witnessing the existence of the unique and absolute Truth, in which all things in reality exist. Thus everything is united with it, seeing that everything that exists has its being in Truth. By itself it is nothing. Nor does this mean that anything has a prior existence of its own which subsequently becomes united, for this would be an absurdity.

3 **CONNECTION**
This arises when the individual observes his essence to be intimately linked with the existence of the One, while at the same time ceasing to consider the bondage of his essence to his own existence, and dropping his attachment to the latter. Thus he is able to see the link extending throughout existence, continually and incessantly transmitting to him the Breath of the Merciful, so that he may continue to exist within it.

4 **THE ONE**
The name given to the Essence when it is considered without recourse to its manifold specific qualities and relationships.*

5 **ONENESS**
To be considered while dropping all other considerations.*

A GLOSSARY OF SUFI TECHNICAL TERMS

6 THE UNITY OF UNION
To be considered as it is, without attempting to prove or reject it, so that the relationship of the Presence of the One and the Presence of Oneness is included in it.

7 ENUMERATING THE NAMES OF GOD
This means the verification of the latter in the Presence of the One, by obliterating from the mind all worldly impressions, whilst maintaining awareness of the eternal Presence of Oneness. As for enumerating them in the sense of actually being moulded by them, that involves entering the Paradise of Inheritance through sound and obedient conduct – as is mentioned in the sublime words of God:

> 'These will be the heirs, who will inherit Paradise: they will dwell therein forever.'*

As for enumerating them in the sense of ascertaining and acting on their meanings, that involves entering the Paradise of Deeds, through a sound faith in God in the Abode of Requital.

8 STATES
Gi4fts showered upon the individual by his Lord. They either descend on him as his just entitlement for righteous acts that purify the Self and refine the Heart – or else they are sent down to him from Truth out of pure kindness. They are called States because it is by their means that the devotee evolves from the outward forms of creation and the lower depths of remoteness – to the hidden qualities and the higher stages of Nearness. That is the meaning of evolution.*

9 CHARITY
is the confirmation, through service, of the vision of the Divine Presence gained through the radiance of insight. That is: to see Truth precisely as it is represented by its very own attributes. For the devotee sees it in particulars but not in reality.* That is why the Prophet said, '... as if you saw him ...',* because the individual only sees God behind the veil of his divine qualities, and even this he does with the eye of his own specific characteristics. So 'in reality' he does not see Reality at all: it is God on High who is the seer; whilst his place is simply to describe him; and, far from being at the Stage of Testimony, he is at the Stage of the Spirit.

10 DESIRE
A smouldering ember of love in the Heart, which cannot but respond to the summons of Reality.

11 THE THRONES OF UNITY
These are the Essential Names, the primary manifestations of the Essence in the Presence of the One.

12 THE NAME
In Sufi technical usage it is not the utterance of the Name which matters, but rather the essence of the thing named – whether one is considering a substantial quality, such as the Knower or the Capable, or an insubstantial quality, such as the Holy or the Salvation.

13 THE ESSENTIAL NAMES
Names which do not depend for their existence on the existence of other Names; though they may be subjected to examination and explanation by means of the latter, as in the case of the Knower. They are also known as the Primary Names, the Keys to the Invisible, and the Master Names.

14 THE GREATEST NAME
The Name that sums up all the Names in one. It has been said by some to be the word *allah*, since this is the name of the aforementioned Essence in all its attributes. In other words, it is that to which all the other names refer. That is why 'Divine Presence' is the designation given to the presence of the Essence together with all the Names. According to us, however, it is the name for the Holy Essence just as it is – that is to say, the Absolute, the True – whether it be with all or some or none of the Names.

15 THE TECHNICAL TERM*
An infatuation that overcomes the Heart, and closely resembles being madly in love.

16 THE HEIGHTS*
This refers to the starting-point – the Stage of witnessing the Truth in every outward form that is irradiated with its qualities. It is a Stage, too, with a commanding view over the outer regions. God Most High has said:

'And on the heights will be men who know each one by his marks.'*

The Prophet said: 'For every verse of the Qur'an there is an outer and an inner meaning, a starting point and an outer boundary.'

17 ESTABLISHED ESSENCES
The realities of the possibilities of sublime Truth.*

18 ISOLATED INDIVIDUALS
These are people lying outside the scope of the Pole-star.*

19 THE VISIBLE HORIZON
The ultimate goal of the Stage of the Heart.

20 THE SUPREME HORIZON
The ultimate goal of the Stage of the Spirit: it is the Presence of Oneness, and the Presence of the Divinity.*

21 SAINTHOOD
Every Name of God added to one's material or spiritual stock.*

22 THE TRUSTED ONES
The followers of the Path of Blame, who do not display any sign in their outward behaviour of what is within them. Their students are transmuted to the stages of the noble-hearted.

23 THE TWO IMAMS
These are two persons: one of them is on the right of the Helper, that is to say the Pole-star, and his attention is on the Kingdom; the other is on his left, and his attention is on the King. The latter is on a higher level than his companion, and he is the one who will succeed the Pole-star.

24 THE MOTHER OF THE BOOK
The Primal Intellect.*

25 THE ETERNAL PRESENT
The full expanse of the Divine Presence within which Eternity-without-beginning merges into Eternity-without-end. For that which has its being in both, both are represented as in the present

time. Thus Eternity-without-beginning, Eternity-without-end and the present moment are all united within it. That is why it is called 'mystical time', and the 'source of time': for moments of time are simply patterns and alterations within it, by which its laws and forms are made manifest; while it endures exactly as it is, forever, endlessly – though it can combine with the subjective presence. As the Prophet said, 'Your Lord has no morning and no evening'.

26 EGOISM
This arises when Reality is qualified in any way, such as by saying 'myself', 'my soul', 'my heart', 'my hand', etc.

27 SELFHOOD
The verification of authentic Existence in terms of its degree of subjective identity.

28 AGITATION
The movement of the Heart towards God Most High, as a result of hearing the Warning – and heeding it.

29 THE SEVERANCE OF UNION
This is Separation after Union, with the manifestation and awareness of plurality in Oneness.

30 THE MAINSTAYS
These are four men who are situated at the four corners of the earth – north, south, east and west. Through them God protects these regions, since it is by this means that they come under his exalted surveillance.

31 THE FOREMOST NAMES
The first seven names, also known as the Divine Names. They are: the Living, the Knower, the Willing, the Capable, the Hearer, the Seer and the Speaker. They are the basis of all the other Names.

Some people, instead of the Hearing and the Discerning, have proposed two other names: the Liberal and the Just. It seems to me that these belong to the secondary Names; since liberality and justice require knowledge, will and capacity. Indeed they require all of the foregoing, in that they also depend on seeing to it that the correct

place is prepared to receive this outpouring of liberality and justice. They depend, too, on the appropriate prayer by the supplicant being heard – and answered with the word 'Be!', in a manner appropriate to the state of readiness of the person invoking these immutable essences. These two are like the names, the Finder, the Creator and the Provider, which are among the Names of Lordship.

'The Living' was placed foremost of all, because by its very nature living precedes knowledge and is a precondition of it. So naturally enough the condition should come before what is contingent on it. And yet it seems to me that 'the Knower' should have pride of place: because, just as leadership is a relative term which presupposes being followed, and it is more illustrious to lead than be led – in the same way knowledge ultimately presupposes something that is known. Life, on the other hand, requires nothing but the Living: it is the same as the Essence, in that it does not posit any related concept. So clearly knowledge is on a more exalted level of being.

That is why it has been said by some that 'the Knower' is the Primary Individuation* of the Essence, rather than 'the Living'; because 'the Knower' does not require any relationship such as existence or necessity, nor does it have to be preceded by anything such as leadership. Whereas, surely, a balanced bodily constitution is a prerequisite for life, even though life is doubtless superior to this in rank.

LETTER BĀ'

32 BĀ'
This letter is used to designate the first created things; and these belong to the second level of Existence.

33 THE DOOR OF DOORS
This is Repentance, because it is the first entrance by which one enters the presence of the Nearness of the Lord.

34 THE GLIMMER
A light reflected from the Most Holy, which quickly fades. It is one of the first stages of revelation.

35 NULLITY
This is anything other than Truth. Hence it is non-being, since there is no real existence apart from the Truth. In the words of the Prophet: 'The truest verse uttered by an Arab is that of Labid:

"Truly, everything but God is null and void".'

36 THE SUBSTITUTES
These are seven men. If one of them goes on a journey, he leaves behind a body of the same form, so that no one will know that he has gone. That, and that alone, is the meaning of the word Substitute. They are in the mould of the Prophet Abraham.

37 CORPULENCE
An epithet for the rapacious Self on the journey – the cutpurse of the waystations and stages of travellers and seekers.

38 LIGHTNING
The name given to the first appearance of that gleam of light which calls one to enter the presence of the Nearness of the Lord and to walk the path to God.

39 INTERMEDIATE WORLD
An interval is something that stands between two things.* The expression is used interchangeably with the World of Ideas: i.e. that which separates material bodies from the world of incorporeal spirits – separates this world and the hereafter. This interval is a source of illusory revelation.

40 THE UNIVERSAL INTERVAL
This is the Presence of the One – the very first rank, which is the basis of all the various intervals. Hence it is known as the Principal Interval or the Greater Interval.

41 EXPANSIVENESS (also 42)*
When this arises in the Stage of the Heart, it resembles a sense of urgent expectancy in the seat of the Self. Its arrival inevitably summons up feelings of approval, kindness, compassion and companionship. The opposite of this is Contraction*, which is felt as anxiety – as opposed to hopefulness – descending on the seat of the Self. However, when expansion arises in the Hidden Centre*, then God expands man in his external relationship with creation, whilst contracting him inwardly with compassion for creation. For God encompasses all things, while nothing can encompass him; his influence is felt in everything, while nothing influences him.

43 DISCERNMENT
A power of the Heart, when illuminated by the Sacred Light, whereby the reality and inward essences of things can be seen. It is analogous to the function of sight for the Self, by which means the shape and external form of things can be seen. It is the power which the wise have called intelligent or reflective. However, if it is illuminated with the Sacred Light, and unveiled under the guidance of Truth, then they call it the Sacred Power.

4 THE COW
An epithet for the Self when it has become ready for exercises and has developed the capacity to tame its desires – which are its very life. The Ram is another epithet for the Self in the state prior to this; while the term Corpulence is used after it has started upon the Path of Conduct.

5 INTUITIVE IMPULSES
Coming unexpectedly from the invisible, they suddenly seize the Heart and induce either Expansion or Contraction.

6 THE HOUSE OF WISDOM
The Heart which has been conquered by sincerity.

7 THE SACRED HOUSE
The Heart which has been purified from attachment to others.

8 THE SACROSANCT HOUSE
The Heart of the Perfected Man, which has become forbidden to anything other than the Truth.

9 THE HOUSE OF GLORY
The Heart which has reached the rank of Union, the state of Annihilation in Truth.

LETTER JĪM

50 ATTRACTION
This is the access granted to the seeker, in accordance with the divine favour prepared for him, to all that he needs in order to pass through the stages leading to Truth, without any discomfort or exertion on his part.

51 THE RINGING BELL
The summing up of the message in a single powerful blow.

52 THE BODY
That part of the Spirit which becomes visible and assumes a fiery or luminous form.

53 CLARITY
The manifestation of the Sacred Essence in itself to itself.

54 CLARIFICATION
This arises when the Essence manifests itself to itself in its specific characteristics.

55 SPLENDOUR
This is the veiling of Truth from us through sheer glory, so that we may not know God as he really is, in his essential 'He-ness', as he knows himself. For none but He sees his Essence for what it is.

56 BEAUTY
The manifestation of God himself to himself. When this takes place, there is a majesty in his absolute beauty which conquers everything, so that there is no one who does not see it. Such is the sublimity of

LETTER JĪM

beauty. It also has a certain affinity with us, which draws it closer to us — and that is its manifestation in all things. As Shaybani put it:

> Your beauty goes bare-faced
> In the realities of all things,
> With nothing but your glory
> To conceal it.

That is why Beauty is Splendour: it is veiled behind specific instances. Thus for all beauty there is a splendour, and behind every splendour there is beauty. Since in descriptions of splendour there is a sense of concealment and glory, this implies exaltedness and power on the part of the Divine Presence, as well as humility and awe on our part. Conversely, since in descriptions of beauty there is a sense of nearness and unveiling, this implies gentleness, mercy and affection on the part of the Divine Presence — and intimacy on ours.

57 COMBINATION
The coming together of high-minded endeavours to turn towards God and work in him and none other than him. The opposite of this is dispersal — the distraction of working within creation.

58 UNION
This is to witness Truth in the absence of Creation.*

59 UNION OF UNION
This is to witness Creation as existing through Truth. It is also known as Separation after Union.

60 THE PARADISE OF DEEDS
The outward paradise of delicious foods, wholesome drinks, and splendid women — as a recompense for good deeds. It is also known as the Paradise of Actions and the Paradise of the Self.

61 THE PARADISE OF INHERITANCE
The Paradise of Morality — the outcome of correctly following the Prophet.

62 THE PARADISE OF QUALITIES
The mystical paradise, arising from revelations of the holy Qualities and Names. It is the Paradise of the Heart.

63 THE PARADISE OF THE ESSENCE
The contemplation of the Beauty of the One. It is the Paradise of the Spirit.

64 THE HONOURABLE ONES
These are travellers journeying through the stations of their various selves, carrying as provisions their piety and devotion, until they reach the watering places of the Heart and the stages of Nearness, and their journey henceforward continues within God.

65 THE TWO ASPECTS OF LIMITATION AND EXPANSE
These are two aspects of the Essence. On the one hand this may be seen from the perspective of purifying it from all that is susceptible to knowledge and reason; i.e. in terms of the real Unity, which has no room for anything other than itself, be it physical or intellectual. This is the aspect of Limitation. As the saying goes, 'None knows God but God.' Alternatively, it may be seen from the viewpoint of its outward appearances at all levels, in terms of the appropriate Names and attributes describing its infinite manifestations; and that is the aspect of Expanse. As the poem says:

> Do not say her house is in the Eastern Highlands:
> To Amiria every highland is a home.
> Every spring is her alighting spot;
> In every derelict camp she leaves her trace.

66 THE TWO ASPECTS OF DESIRE
These are the aspects of Necessity and Contingency: on the one hand the desire for the manifestation of the Divine Names through the Established Essences, and on the other the desire for the Essences to manifest themselves through the Names. Now if the Lord shows himself in his qualities, then both wishes are granted; and they both stand out in equal dignity of rank.

67 THE JEWELS OF SCIENCE, PROPHECY AND DEEP KNOWLEDGE
These are the immutable realities which remain unaffected by vari-

ations in Holy Law among different nations and at different times. As God has said:

> The same religion has he established for you as that which he enjoined on Noah – the which we have sent by inspiration to thee – and that which we enjoined on Abraham, Moses and Jesus: namely, that ye should remain steadfast in religion and make no divisions therein.*

LETTER DĀL

68 THE WEST WIND
An impulse arousing carnal desire and causing it to predominate. It has been likened to the west wind, because it originates in the physical side of human nature – as it were, the western, twilight zone. Its opposite is the gentle breeze from the east, whose impulse arouses the Spirit and causes it to prevail. That is why the Prophet said: 'I have been succoured by the easterly breeze, just as the tribe of 'Ād was destroyed by the west wind.'*

69 THE WHITE PEARL
This is the Primal Intellect. As the Prophet said: 'The first thing God created was a white pearl.' And the first thing created by God was the mind.

LETTER HĀ'

70 HĀ'
This letter denotes the Essence in terms of appearance, presence and existence.

71 HE
This is considered from the standpoint of absence and loss.*

72 DUST
is the substance in which God first imbued the form of the world. It is that intangible material which is known as Primordial Matter.

73 FAR-REACHING AMBITION
This is the first degree of aspiring to the Path, and it leads one to renounce the transient and seek that which endures.

74 DISDAINFUL AMBITION
This is the second degree, and whoever attains to it acquires an attitude of disdaining to ask to be paid for his labours, and his heart is filled with pride in the expectation of the rewards God has promised for good deeds. Thus he never ceases to contemplate the Truth and worships God to the best of his ability. So, with his face turned incessantly towards Truth, he seeks its nearness – until he seeks nothing else.

75 NOBLE-MINDED AMBITION
This is the third degree, which is not dependent on anything except Truth and has no regard for anything else. This is the highest of all endeavours, since it is not content with the attainment of mystical states or stages of development, or with simply coming to a standstill

at the Names and the Qualities. Indeed it aims for nothing less than the very fountainhead of the Essence.

76 CRAVING
This is when the Self inclines towards its natural needs, and shuns the higher direction in favour of the baser one.

77 SUGGESTIONS
Sensual thoughts.

78 ATTACKS
These are what comes into the Heart by virtue of the time – rather than through any personal effort. They are also the Intuitive Impulses mentioned above.*

79 PRIMORDIAL MATTER
The name given by the Sufis to the thing within which the various forms are manifested. Thus, any hidden thing in which a form can appear they call Primordial Matter.*

LETTER WĀW

80 WĀW
This letter denotes the universal aspect of the whole.

81 ONENESS
This is considering the Essence from the viewpoint that the Names originate from it, and its oneness remains with it despite its manifold attributes.*

82 THE ONE
The name of the Essence when considered in this light.

83 INCOMING THOUGHT
All the various mental images that may come effortlessly into a man's Heart.

84 EVENT
Whatever comes into the Heart from the invisible world, in whatever manner.

85 THE MEDIATOR OF GRACE AND ASSISTANCE
This refers to the Perfect Man, who is the link between Truth and Creation by virtue of his affinity to both. As God has said (according to Tradition):

> 'But for you, I would not have created the heavens.'

86 THE ODD NUMBER
This means to consider the Essence on its own, dropping all other considerations, since Oneness has no relationship to anything, and nothing is related to it. For there is nothing in that presence originally.

In contrast to this, there is the Even Number, through consideration of which the Essences and the reality of the Names are determined.*

87 EXISTENCE
The realization that the Essence of Truth is in its essence. That is why the Presence of Union is called the Presence of Existence.

88 THE TWO ASPECTS OF PROVIDENCE
These are Attraction and the Path, which are the two sides of guidance.

89 UNCONDITIONAL AND CONDITIONAL
These are two ways of considering the Essence: in exclusive terms, leaving everything else out of consideration – and in terms of its own affirmation. Now the Essence of Truth is Existence, seeing that Truth itself is Existence. Viewed thus it is an absolute; that is, it is the reality which is in everything. It will not admit of any comparison; because anything other than pure Existence is sheer nothingness. So how can a thing be compared with that in which it exists and without which it is totally void and non-existent? Thus everything other than the Essence belongs to non-entity and is something other than pure Existence, for its distinctive character is of no consequence. So everything is present within absolute Existence, and the latter is present within itself.

If you place on it the restriction of absoluteness, that is, the restriction that there should not be anything accompanying it, then it is the One, which was before, unaccompanied by anything. That is why the Sufis say: 'He is now as he was before.' If, however, you stipulate that there is something with it, then precisely the same restriction applies – that this thing exists within it and is non-existent without it. Doubtless its form was made manifest, and so Existence was added to it; but if you omit the addition, it becomes essentially non-existent. That is the meaning of the Sufi saying that 'Unification is the subtraction of additions'. He was right, whoever said that existence is identical with necessary reality, and that other than reality everything is merely incidental, because it is surplus to every essential quality. Thus there is no doubt that the blackness of the

black and the humanity of the human, for example, are things that do not exist; and without existence they are nothing.

90 THE FACE OF TRUTH
The aspect whereby a thing really exists; for there is no reality to a thing except with God. This is the significance of the words, 'Whatever direction you may turn, there is the face of God'.* He is the source of the Truth which abides in all things; so whoever has seen the everlasting Truth in things sees the face of Truth in everything.

91 THE GOAL OF ALL SERVANTS
The Presence of the Divinity.

92 THE RECORD SHEET
The Universal Soul, which is the heart of the world. It is also the Preserved Tablet and the Clear Book.*

93 BEHIND THE OUTER COVERING
This is Truth in the presence of Unity prior to Oneness; because when it is in the presence of the latter, then as a consequence it becomes overlaid, first with the meanings of the Names and the realities of the Essences, then with spiritual forms, then with ideal forms, and finally with sensory perceptions.

94 THE ESSENTIAL ATTRIBUTE OF TRUTH
This is the unity of Union; also essential necessity; also independence from created worlds.

95 THE ESSENTIAL ATTRIBUTE OF CREATION
Essential potential, and essential need.

96 REUNION
This is the real Unity connecting the inward and the outward. It may be expressed as the compassion preceding affection, which is referred to in the Tradition: 'I wished to be known, so I created the creation.' It may also be expressed by the permanence of Truth in things, for this interconnects each separate part of the multiplicity, until they are all united; and by separation the sage restrains them from arising. Ja'far Sadiq said: 'Whoever can distinguish separation

from reunion and movement from rest has attained the perfection of stability in unification and has become thoroughly imbued with deep knowledge.' The purpose of movement is the Path, and that of rest is stability in the Oneness of the Essence.

The word Reunion may also be used to express the annihilation of the attributes of the individual within the attributes of Truth; and this results from verifying and interpreting the Names of God, in the course of enumerating them. In the words of the Prophet: 'Whoever enumerated them has entered paradise.'

97 THE REUNION OF SEPARATION

This is the healing of the rift, the repairing of the breach, the merging of distinctions – which is the manifestation of Unity within multiplicity. For Unity joins together its separate and scattered parts through the union of multiplicity. As the Separation of Union is the manifestation of multiplicity in unity, so multiplicity breaks up the union of unity, augmenting the manifestation of the latter through its own specific requirements, in the first stages of differentiation of the forms of a single face in different mirrors.

98 REUNION OF REUNION

The return after departure, the ascent after the descent. For each one of us has fallen from the highest ranks. It is that same Union of Oneness which is the absolute link between Eternity-without-beginning and the lowest depths of the world of warring elements. Some of us have been living in an extremely degenerate state and have fallen into the lowest of the low; while others have come back and returned to the Stage of Union by following the path to God and in God – by praising his qualities and losing themselves in them, until finally they reached true reunion in Eternity-without-end – just as they were originally in Eternity-without-beginning.

99 THE FULFILMENT OF THE COVENANT

This goes beyond what is declared by saying 'Yes indeed!' in the affirmation of Deity. When God said, 'Am I not your Lord?' they answered 'Yes indeed!'*

For the common people it means religious observance, prompted by a desire for what has been promised and a fear of what has been threatened. For people of distinction it means devoted service to the

undertaking for its own sake, staying within its limits and being faithful to what it imposes, without desire, fear, or ulterior motive. For those of especial distinction, however, it means devoted service while abjuring any claim to strength and power.* But for the Lover it means not letting one's Heart expand to anything other than the Beloved.

One of the requirements of fulfilling the covenant of service is to see that every fault that appears in oneself is due to oneself – and not to see perfection in anything save in one's Lord.

100 KEEPING THE COVENANT OF CONDUCT
This means not forgetting your own bondage and helplessness at those times when it is given to you to master and break your habits.

101 MOMENT OF TIME*
Whatever comes to mind in the Mystical State. If it derives from Truth then you should consent and submit to it, so that you may accord with the moment, with nothing else occurring to you. But if it is something related to personal gain, then you should force yourself to attend to what is more important to you. Do not occupy your mind with the past or the future: trying to remedy the past is a waste of time – and so is thinking about what is to come; because you may never attain it, and time will have simply passed you by. That is why the wise have said: 'The Sufi is the son of time.'

102 ETERNAL TIME
The Eternal Present.

103 THE HALT
This is the pause necessary between two Stages, in order to complete the remaining obligations of the first Stage and to prepare to be able to rise to the refinements of the second.

104 THE AUTHENTIC UNDERTAKING
The undertaking which has the intention of finding Truth.

105 THE FRIEND OF GOD
This is someone who is entrusted with the Truth and who protects it from subversion and would never let it or himself down, until he

reaches such perfection as is possible to mankind. As God has said:

'... and he will choose and befriend the righteous.'*

106 SAINTHOOD

This is the standing of a man in Truth when he has achieved the annihilation of his own Self such that the light of Truth is able to take possession of him and thus bring him to the ultimate stage of Nearness and Establishment.

LETTER ZĀ'

107 THE REPROVER
God's admonisher in the Heart of the believer. It is the light which comes flashing into his Heart, summoning him to Truth.

108 THE GLASS
Mentioned in the Light Verse.* The glass is the Heart, the lamp is the Spirit, the tree, from whose oil the glass is lit up – like a 'glittering star' – is the Self. The niche for the lamp is the body.

109 THE EMERALD
The Universal Soul.

110 DURATION OF TIME
This is what is added to the subjective presence; it is the Eternal Present, mentioned above in chapter *alif*.

111 THE FLOWERING OF INFORMATION, KNOWLEDGE AND REUNION
These are the sciences of the Way, for they are the most honourable and enlightened of all the sciences, and they are the pre-condition for union with Truth.

112 THE OLIVE TREE
This is the Self when it has been prepared, through the power of thought, for illumination by the Sacred Light.

113 THE OIL
This is the original light for the Self's preparation – and success lies with God!

LETTER ḤĀ'

114 THE MYSTICAL STATE
This is what comes to the Heart purely gratuitously, without any effort or inducement – in the form of sorrow, fear, expansiveness, contraction, desire or pleasure. When it appears, the characteristics of the Self go into abeyance, and the State may or may not do likewise; but if it endures and becomes a permanent characteristic, then it is called a Stage.

115 THE DEMONSTRATION TO MANKIND OF THE TRUTH
This is the Perfect Man – like Adam, in that he was a proof to the Angels, as shown in the words of God: He said, 'Adam, tell them their names.' And when he had told them their names, God said, 'Did I not tell you I know the unseen things of the heavens and earth? And I know what things you reveal and what you were hiding.'*

116 THE VEIL
The imprint in the Heart of universal forms which inhibit the revelation of Truth.

117 THE LETTERS
The elementary realities deriving from the Essences, and from such screening entities as reason and the Self.*

118 THE SUBLIME LETTERS
These are the individual qualities that lie dormant in the most hidden part of the hidden world – like the tree latent in the date-stone. It was to them that the Sheikh was referring when he said:

> We were sublime letters, till now never spoken,
> Belonging to the offspring of the highest heights.

> I am you in him,
> We are you and you are he,
> And all in him is he:
> Just ask the one who has arrived!*

119 FREEDOM
The release from enslavement to others. There are three degrees of freedom: Firstly, there is freedom from enslavement to carnal desires. Secondly, there is special freedom – from enslavement to aspirations, through the obliteration of the personal will within the will of Truth. Finally there is the most special freedom of all – from enslavement to custom and tradition, through their effacement in the revelation of the Light of Lights.

120 BURNING
A half-way stage in the process of Illumination, which draws the seeker towards annihilation. The process starts with Lightning, and ends with obliteration in the Essence.

121 KEEPING THE COVENANT
This means to remain within the limits set by God for his servants, neither omitting what is commanded nor committing what is forbidden.

122 KEEPING THE COVENANT OF LORDSHIP AND SERVICE
Not to ascribe perfection to anything but the Lord, and not to ascribe defects to anything but oneself.

123 THE REALITY OF REALITIES
The Essence of Oneness that encompasses all realities. It is known as the Presence of Union and the Presence of Existence.

124 THE REALITY OF MUHAMMAD
This is the Essence in its primary individuation, for it contains all of the Beautiful Names and is itself the Greatest Name.

125 THE REALITIES OF THE NAMES
These are the various individuations of the Essence, and their

inter-relationships. Thus they are the qualities which distinguish the Names one from another.

126 THE TRUTH OF CERTITUDE
To witness the Reality of Truth during the stage of total Union in Oneness.

127 WISDOM
This is the knowledge of the reality of things, their precise characteristics, specialities and properties, and of the connection between causes and effects, and of the secret mechanisms regulating creation, as well as the appropriate action required:

> And he to whom wisdom is granted receives indeed a benefit overflowing.*

128 EXPLICIT WISDOM
The sciences of Holy Law and the Way.

129 TACIT WISDOM
Refers to the secrets of Reality which are not understood very well by conventional scholars or the common people, and can thus be harmful and even destructive for them.

It is related that the Prophet was walking through the streets of Medina with his companions, when a woman entreated them to come into her house. They went inside and there they saw a blazing fire with the woman's children playing round it.

She said to Muhammad, 'Tell me, Prophet of God, who is more merciful: God to his servants or I myself to my children?'

'God is more merciful,' he replied. 'Truly, of all the merciful he is the most merciful.'

'Prophet of God, can you see me ever wanting to throw one of my children into the fire?'

'No.'

'Then how could God throw his servants into it, seeing that he is the most merciful of all?'

The narrator goes on to say that the Prophet wept and said, 'That is how God inspired me.'

130 UNKNOWN WISDOM
According to us, this is what has been concealed from us by the

countenance of wisdom behind the afflictions of certain people, such as the death of children, or an eternity in hellfire – for not only is belief in this required, but also acceptance of it as right and just.

131 UNIVERSAL WISDOM

This means knowing and working with Truth, and knowing and avoiding falsehoods. As the Prophet said: 'Oh God, show us the Truth as it really is, and grant us the means to follow it; and show us falsehood for what it is, and grant us the means to avoid it. Show us things as they really are.'

LETTER ṬĀ'

132 RISING STARS
The first of the illuminations of the Holy Names to appear in a person's Heart. Thus his character and qualities are improved through the irradiation of his inner self.

133 THE PURE
Those whom God has safeguarded from transgressions.

134 THE OUTWARDLY PURE
Those whom God has safeguarded from criminal acts.

135 THE INWARDLY PURE
Those whom God has safeguarded from temptations, carnal desires, and attachment to others.

136 THE SECRETLY PURE
Those who are not distracted from God for so much as the winking of an eye.

137 THE SECRETLY AND OVERTLY PURE
Those who have undertaken to fulfil the obligations of both Truth and Creation, trying to do them equal justice.

138 SPIRITUAL MEDICINE
The knowledge of the perfection of hearts – not only their afflictions and ailments, and the remedies for these, but also the directions for keeping them healthy and warding off sickness.

139 THE SPIRITUAL PHYSICIAN
The Master who has the above knowledge, as well as the power to guide and complete the treatment.

140 THE WAY
The specific course of conduct followed by seekers on their way to God, passing through various phases and rising step by step through the developmental stages.

141 EFFACEMENT
This is when the customs of the traveller pass away totally in the attributes of the Light of Lights.

LETTER YĀ'

142 THE RED RUBY
This is the Self, so called because of the blending of its luminosity with the darkness of attachment to the body – in contrast to disembodied reason, which is sometimes described as the White Pearl.

143 THE TWO HANDS
These are contrasting Names of God, such as either the Active or the Receptive. As God said to Iblis,

> 'What prevented you from bowing down before that which I created with my own hands?'*

Because the presence of the Names comprises two types of presence – the necessary and the possible – some have said that the Two Hands are indeed necessity and possibility; but in fact the contrast is more general than that. The active aspect may be compared variously with the Beautiful, the Sublime, the Gentle, the Vanquisher, the Beneficial and the Harmful; while similarly, the receptive aspect may be compared with the Friend, the Timid, the Hopeful, the Fearful, the Beneficiary and the Harmed.*

144 THE DAY OF ASSEMBLY
The time of gathering together and arriving at the Source of Union.

LETTER KĀF

145 THE CLEAR BOOK
This is the Preserved Tablet to which the words of God refer:

> 'Not a thing, whether fresh or dry, but is recorded in a clear book.'*

146 THE TOTALITY
A name for Sublime Truth, seen from the perspective whereby the presence of Divine Oneness comprehends all the Names. This is why we say 'one' for the Essence and 'all' for the Names.

147 THE WORD
The means by which to allude to every single quality, essence, reality and externally existing thing – in short to everything that is specific. Intellectual concepts, such as qualities, realities and essences, may be distinguished by means of the Essential Word; the invisible and the external by means of the Concrete Word; and the various incorporeal entities by means of the Authentic Word.

148 THE WORD OF THE PRESENCE
This refers to the word of God: 'Be!' – as shown in the words:

> 'For to anything which we have willed, we but say the word "Be!" – and it is.'*

149 THE HIDDEN TREASURE
The Essence of Oneness that is concealed in the invisible. This is the innermost secret of all.

150 THE UNGRATEFUL
In Holy Law this refers to those who have abandoned the divine

precepts. In the Way it means those who forsake excellent virtues. In Reality it is those who desire something which God does not want; since they are contending with his wishes without knowing the reality of his grace.

151 FISSION
The existence of Fission does not dissolve Union. This means that the proliferation of the one and only Truth into distinct particularizations does not imply the dispersal of the Divine Whole or of the Oneness of the Essence.

152 THE MORNING STAR
The first manifestation of beatific visions. It may also be used to indicate someone who has verified the objective reality of the Universal Soul. From the words of God:

> 'When night enveloped him he saw a star...'*

153 ALCHEMY
This is contentedness with what is present, and relinquishing the desire for what is absent. In the words of Ali, the Commander of the Faithful, 'Contentedness is a treasure which is never exhausted'.

154 THE ALCHEMY OF HAPPINESS
The refinement of the Self by protecting and purifying it from worthless things – and by seeking to acquire virtues and become adorned with them.*

155 THE ALCHEMY OF THE MASSES
This means to exchange the enduring goods of the other world for the ephemeral trifles of this world.

156 THE ALCHEMY OF THE ELECT
This is the deliverance of the Heart from creation and into the exclusive power of the Creator.

LETTER LĀM

¶57 THE SIGN
The light of Illumination, which appears and then passes away. It is also called a flash of insight or an idea.

¶58 DIVINE NATURE
The life which pervades things. Human nature is its fixed abode; and that is the Spirit.

¶59 THE KERNEL
This is the mind when it has been illuminated by the Sacred Light and freed from the external husks of delusion and fantasy.

¶60 THE KERNEL OF KERNELS
This is the divine substance of the Sacred Lights, by which the mind is strengthened, and thus freed from the above-mentioned husks, so that it attains the sublime sciences – freed from the consciousness of the Heart, which is attached to creation and prevented from understanding what is veiled from conventional knowledge. This comes about through the beauty of the former Stage leading to the goodness of the latter.*

¶61 DISGUISE
The elemental form that envelops spiritual realities. God said:

> 'And if we had made him an angel we should have sent him as a man; and we should certainly have caused them confusion in a matter which they have already covered with confusion.'*

One such guise is the clothing of real truth in the forms of humanity. It is to this that the words of God refer in the Tradition.

'My friends are beneath my domes: none knows them but myself.'

162 ELOQUENCE
This is the means whereby the divine declaration is made to attentive ears concerning those things which God wishes to teach – either by way of divine communication, or via a prophet, saint or friend.

163 THE TONGUE OF TRUTH
The human being who has verified the manifestation of the pronoun 'I', by virtue of being its object.

164 SUBTLETY
Any sign of delicate spiritual significance. When one of these appears in the understanding, its meaning cannot be encompassed by words.

165 THE HUMAN SUBTLETY
This is the Rational Soul, which Sufis call the Heart. In fact it is the descent of the Spirit to a level close to that of the Self – to which in one aspect it is related, whilst in another it is related to the Spirit. The former aspect is called the Breast, and the latter the Heart.

166 THE TABLET
This is the Clear Book, and also the Universal Soul.*

167 SIGNS
These are sometimes used to indicate what appears to the senses from the World of Ideas – as in the case of 'Umar.* This is a pictorial revelation, whereas in its original meaning it is a spiritual revelation proceeding from the Most Holy.

168 RAYS
Radiant lights which shine for those novices who are of a delicate disposition. They are reflected from the imagination to the common sense; and they then become perceptible to the external senses, so that the subject seems to see lights, like those of bright stars, the sun and the moon, illuminating all around them.* This light is either predominantly violent and threatening, taking on a reddish hue – or else it is predominantly gentle and promising – in which case it has a greenish colouring.

169 THE NIGHT OF POWER

This is a night in which the seeker is favoured with a special state of illumination, in which he learns his true potential and rank in relation to the Beloved. It is the time when the seeker begins to arrive at the Source of Union and the stage of those who are matured in deep wisdom.*

LETTER MĪM

170 THE ONE WHO HOLDS, THE THING HELD, AND FOR WHOM IT IS HELD
These are spiritual pillars; and they are also the reality of the Perfected Man. As God said:

> 'Were it not for you, I would not have created the heavens.'

Sheikh Abu Talib al-Makki writes:

> 'Truly the heavens are turned by the breath of the Children of Adam.'

And Sheikh Muhiyuddin Ibn al-Arabi writes:

> 'Praise, honour and glory be to God, who created the Perfect Man to be the teacher of the angels and caused by his breath the heavens to turn!'

Both of these refer to the above concepts.

171 SACRED WATER
The knowledge which purifies the Self from the defilement of nature and the squalor of vice. Alternatively it means to witness the Eternal through Illumination, and thus rise above the defilement of accidental phenomena.

172 THE ORIGINAL
This is an unalloyed augmentation of Oneness; seeing that the Essence of Oneness has precedence over the presence of Unity, which latter is the origin of all the designations and derivations of the Names; since their characteristics and associations are rational considerations.

173 (*There is no entry bearing this number*)

174 STARTING POINTS AND END RESULTS
The former are the devotional duties, namely: prayer, almsgiving, fasting and pilgrimage.

The outcome of prayer is complete Nearness and real communication.

The outcome of fasting is abstaining from the forms of creation and from that which reinforces them – through Annihilation in God. That is why, in the sacred words of the Tradition it is said, 'Fasting is for me, and I shall repay it.'

The outcome of pilgrimage is the acquisition of wisdom and the verification of Permanence after Annihilation. For all the ceremonies and hardships of the pilgrimage are analogous to stations of the seeker and the Stage of the Oneness of Union and Separation.

175 THE FOUNDATION OF SUFISM
According to Abu Muhammad Ruwaym, this consists of three qualities: adherence to poverty and need, the attainment of certainty through liberality and altruism, and abandoning conflict and personal choice.*

176 THE ONE WHO IS CONFIRMED IN TRUTH
Whomsoever God observes in every detail without becoming specific for him. For God is supreme: even though he may be witnessed in anything that is bound to a name, attribute, aspect, viewpoint or specification – yet he is not himself restricted or bound in any way thereby. He is the Absolutely Binding and the Binding Absolute, far above binding and non-binding, absolute and non-absolute.

177 THE ONE WHO IS CONFIRMED IN TRUTH AND CREATION
Whoever sees that every absolute in existence has an aspect of restriction, and every restricted thing has an aspect of freedom. Furthermore, he sees all of existence as a single reality, which has both an absolute aspect and a limited one subject to every restriction. Anyone who witnesses this through experience has been confirmed in Truth and Creation, annihilation and permanence.

178 THE ATTRACTED
Someone whom Truth has singled out for himself and selected for his own intimate companionship, purifying him with Sacred Water. Thus, by dint of all these favours and gifts, he has attained what is achieved in all the various stages and degrees of development, without himself going to the trouble of acquiring it.

179 THE UNIVERSAL MANIFESTATIONS
These are the outward expressions of the Keys to the Invisible, by which the gates between outward and inward existence are unlocked. There are five of them:

The first is the manifestation of the Essence of Oneness, the Source of Union, the Stage of 'Even Nearer'*, the Major Resurrection, and the manifestation of the Truth of Truths. This is the ultimate objective and the end of ends.

The second is the initial manifestation of the Intermediate World between death and resurrection, the Meeting of the Two Seas, the Stage of Two Bow-lengths, and the presence of the totality of the Divine Names.

The third is the manifestation of the World of Power and the unveiling of the Sacred Spirits.

The fourth is the manifestation of the Heavenly Kingdom and the celestial powers who uphold the divine decree in the world of the Godhead.

The fifth is the manifestation of the World of the Kingdom through visions and the wonders of the World of Ideas, and material powers in the lower world.

180 THE MANIFESTATION OF THE ACTIVE NAMES
The cosmic gradations which make up the world. Also: the records of illustrious deeds.

181 THE MEETING OF THE TWO SEAS
This is the presence of Two Bow-lengths, because of the meeting in it of the two seas of necessity and possibility.* It has also been stated that it is the presence of the totality of existence, seeing that the Divine Names and the cosmic realities are assembled in it.

82 THE MEETING OF DESIRES

The presence of absolute Beauty. For desire is attached to nothing other than the distillation of Beauty. That is why the poem says:

> Let your longing heart wander where it will,
> There is no love other than the first Beloved.

And Shaybani says:

> All of beauty is summed up in your face;
> Yet the details of it fill creation.

83 THE MEETING OF OPPOSITES

This is the Absolute Essence, which is the presence of the embracing extremities.

84 GENUINE LOVE

The love of the Essence precisely for its very own essence. Far from being a superfluous state of affairs, this is the source of all other kinds of love; and whatever love may exist between two beings has to do either with a correspondence in each of their essences – or with a concord of quality, rank, state or function.

85 THE PROTECTED

Someone whom God has preserved from delinquency, whether in word, deed or intent. Thus he does not say or do anything except what pleases God, and does not desire anything but what God desires, and does not strive for anything other than God's command.

86 EXTERNAL OBLITERATION

The elimination of habitual characteristics and reprehensible traits, countering these with the affirmation which consists in carrying out the stipulations of worship and striving to acquire laudable qualities.

87 INWARD OBLITERATION

The removal of the veil of theoretical knowledge and all its afflictions, and countering these with the affirmation of constant communion.* This is achieved by eliminating the attributes of the seeker and the characteristic habits of his nature and behaviour, and irradiating him with the attributes of Truth and its nature and behaviour. As it has been said, 'I was his hearing, by which he heard, and his seeing, by which he saw.'

188 THE OBLITERATION OF TRUE UNION
The annihilation of multiplicity in unity.

189 THE OBLITERATION OF SERVICE AND OF THE INDIVIDUAL SERVANT
This means ceasing to ascribe existence to the Essences, because these are subjective entities which have emerged in the Presence of Oneness as a result of scholarly endeavour. They are thus information devoid of any substance whatsoever. Except insofar as the existence of Truth may become perceptible in them, both they and their world are non-existent possibilities. There are, nevertheless, traces of them in external existence, as it is commonly understood.

Existence is none other than Sublime Truth itself, and no basis exists for ascribing any other connection outside this. Actions and effects are entirely subordinate to Existence. Since the non-existent has no effect, there is nothing active or present save Truth Most High alone.

For, seen in terms of his specific limitation within the form of the individual, which is a subjective matter, he is the worshipper. Seen, however, in terms of his absoluteness, he is the worshipped; while the individual himself remains non-existent. Thus both the individual servant and his service are obliterated.

As in the words of God Most High:

> 'And when thou threwest, it was not thyself that threw, but God threw.'*

or in his words:

> 'Three men conspire not secretly together, but he is the fourth of them, neither five men, but he is the sixth of them.'*

or in his words:

> 'They are unbelievers who say "God is the third of three".'*

This affirms that he is the fourth of three and denies that he is the third of three; because if he had been one of them he might have been similar to them – he who is exalted and revered far above all such things. However, if he were the fourth among them, he would remain distinct from them in terms of their reality, existence and specific nature.

LETTER MĪM

0 ERADICATION
This is the annihilation of individual existence in the Essence of Truth, just as Obliteration is the annihilation of one's own actions in the action of Truth, and Effacement is the annihilation of one's attributes in the attributes of Truth. Obliteration does not see effectiveness in anything except Truth; and Effacement does not see any quality in anything except Truth; while Eradication does not see existence in anything except Truth.

1 AUDIENCE
The presence of the Heart together with Truth amidst the profusion of the Names of God.*

2 FACING
The presence of the Heart tending towards a contemplative state that is oblivious of everything other than itself; such that it does not see any other thing, since it is so remote from everything else.

3 THE CONVERSATION
This is a message from Truth, transmitted through one of the forms of the angelic world – like the call which Moses received from the bush.

4 THE RETREAT
The place where the Pole-star is concealed from those who have attained.

5 SUSTAINED EXISTENCE
This is the attainment of all that is needed for the phenomenal to sustain its continued and uninterrupted existence. For Truth sustains existence with the Breath of the Merciful, so that its being outweighs its non-being – which latter is a requirement of its essence without its existence. This is achieved by the processes of break-down and exchange in nutrition and respiration, and derives its support from the externally perceptible air.

As for inanimate beings, celestial bodies and spiritual entities, it is the intellect which determines, through the abiding superiority of their existence, which of them is predominant; while it is the sight of God which determines, through unceasingly bringing everything possible into existence, that renewed creation unfolds.

196 THE UNIVERSAL RANKS
There are six of these:

– the Rank of the Essence of Oneness;
– the Rank of the Divine Presence, which is the presence of the One;
– the Rank of the Incorporeal Spirits;
– the Rank of Active Souls: the World of Ideas and the Angelic World;
– the Rank of the World of Power, which is the visible universe;
– the Rank of Comprehensive Being, which is the Perfect Man, the total manifestation and collective form of mankind.

But we have said that there are five Manifestations and six Ranks.* The reason for this is that the Manifestation is the external aspect in which these Ranks are revealed. Now the Essence of Oneness cannot constitute a manifestation for anything else, since there is no aspect of plurality in it whatsoever – not even in learned and scholarly circles. The other Ranks are arranged in descending order and have both an inward and an outward Manifestation. However, there is no manifestation of the Oneness of the Essence other than in the Perfect Man.

197 THE MIRROR OF BEING
This is absolute and unique Existence, for it is only in this that the various worlds with their qualities and properties appear, and its own presence is thereby concealed – just like the surface of a mirror, which becomes invisible the moment that an image appears in it.

198 THE MIRROR OF EXISTENCE
This denotes the specifications relating to inner qualities whose outward forms are created beings. For the qualities are inward, whilst the existence based on their specifications is external. Seen in this way, the qualities are mirrors for a single existence to which their specific forms are allocated.

199 THE MIRROR OF THE TWO PRESENCES
This refers to the presence of necessity and possibility, which is the Perfect Man. It also refers to the mirror of the Divine Presence, because this is the appearance of the Essence together with all the Names.

200 THE EVENING TALK
The dialogue which Truth holds with the individual in his Secret

Faculty.* It is so called because conventionally this conversation takes place at night.

1 THE PATHS OF TOTAL PRAISE
This refers to the commemoration of the Essence through full knowledge and direct vision of the essential Names, rather than by the attributive or active Names. This is because the Absolute Essence is the origin of all the Names of God. Thus of all the sublime ways of glorifying God, the most glorious is that absolute glorification which itself partakes of all his attributes; because if the one who was commemorating God were to praise him in terms of his own knowledge, generosity or capacity, then his glorification would be confined to that particular attribute. However, if he praises him using his essential Names, such as the Holy, the Glorious, the Salvation, the Most High, the Truth – and by other similar names which are the foremost of all the names – then in his glorification he embraces all of God's perfections.

2 THE ABODE OF THE GREATEST NAME
This is the temple in which Truth is housed: I mean the heart of the Perfected man.

3 THE BASIS OF DEEP KNOWLEDGE
The Presence of Oneness, which is the origin of all the Names.

4 THE CONSUMED
Someone who is annihilated in the Oneness of the Essence, so that no trace remains of him.

5 THE OBSCURE ISSUE
This is the fact that the Established Essences remain in a state of non-existence, while the Truth, by virtue of its Name, 'the Light', illuminates their forms and apparently assumes their properties. Thus it transforms them over a period of time into a new creation, by adding to them its own existence and specific make-up; while they remain in their initial state of non-existence. For if it did not hold constant sway over their existence by augmenting and developing them, then they would never have appeared at all.

This is a matter for revelation and intuitive 'taste' – something

which is repugnant to the understanding and rejected by the intellect.

206 THE RELAXED ONE
This refers to that one of God's servants, who has been acquainted with the secret of destiny. Since he can see that whatever has been decreed must take place at its fore-known time, and that whatever has not been decreed cannot happen, he is delivered from desiring or expecting things which will not occur, and from grieving over what has taken place. As God has said: 'No misfortune can happen on earth...'*

That is why Anis, a Companion of the Prophet said: 'I served the Prophet of God for ten years, and he never said, of something I had done, 'Why did you do that?' – or, of something I had not done, 'Why didn't you do that?'

Such a person is never found to be other than even-tempered.

207 DAWNINGS OF VICTORY
The manifestations of the Names, since these are the keys to the secrets of the invisible world, and the illumination of the Essence.*

208 DAWNINGS OF THE SUN OF REALITY
Illuminations of the Essence prior to total annihilation in the essential Oneness of all.

209 THE DAWNING OF INNER MINDS
This refers to those to whom God has disclosed the innermost minds of people. He has illuminated them with his Secret Name; thus they can survey people's inner natures. Sheikh abu Said ibn Abi al-Khair was one such man.

210 THE CORRESPONDENCE BETWEEN QUALITIES AND REALITIES
This is the arrangement of universal realities in accordance with the divine realities which are the Names. The Names are ordered according to the essential qualities; so that existing things are the shadows and forms of the Names, and the Names are shadows of the qualities.

LETTER MĪM

1 THE CORRESPONDENCE BETWEEN THE PRESENCES AND CREATION

This is the relationship of existing beings to the three presences – the presence of necessity, the presence of contingency and the presence of both of these together.

Any being whose relationship to necessity is stronger is of a more distinguished and elevated rank. So it has a higher spiritual reality, whether angelic, or pertaining to a celestial body.

Any being whose relationship to the contingent is stronger is baser and lowlier, and its reality is that of an inferior element or compound.

Any being whose relationship to both is equally strong is more complete; and its reality is that of humanity.

A person who is more inclined to the contingent, and in whom the characteristics of manifold contingency are present, numbers among the unbelievers.

Anyone who is more inclined to necessity, and in whom the characteristics of necessity are predominant, is foremost among men – one of the Prophets or Saints. Any person in whom both aspects are equal is a man of moderation among the believers.

As the inclination tends toward one or other of these two aspects, so do believers vary in the strength or weakness of their belief.

2 INSIGHT

This refers to the favours bestowed by Truth on the wise – either immediately, or arising from questions concerning what has happened to them. The word may also refer to the ascent into contemplative vision at the moment when this dawns.

3 THE POINT OF DEPARTURE

The Stage in which the speaker actually experiences the verses of the Qur'an which he is reciting. His speech is illuminated by the quality which is the source of that particular verse.

As Ja'far Sadiq said: 'God has made himself manifest in his words for his worshippers; but they do not see.'

One day Ja'far fell down unconscious while in prayer. Afterwards, when asked about the incident, he answered: 'I did not stop repeating the verse until I heard it spoken by its Author.'

The Great Sheikh, Shahabuddin Suhrawardi, said of this incident

that at that moment Ja'far's tongue was like the burning bush of Moses, when the call came from it, 'I am God!'

However, I wish to affirm that the meaning of the 'point of departure' is more general than this. It is the Stage of witnessing the Truth in everything that is irradiated by its qualities – of which qualities that thing is the outward manifestation. But because it was said in a Tradition of the Prophet: 'There is no verse of the Qur'an without an outward and an inward meaning; for every letter there is an end point, and for every end point a point of departure.' – the meaning has become restricted to this sense.

214 SIGNS IDENTIFYING THE QUALITIES
These are organs such as the eye, the ear and the hand; since these are the locations where the meanings and the sources of the qualities become apparent. A sign is an outward indication, like a religious emblem or a signpost on the road.

215 THE FIRST TEACHER AND THE TEACHER OF THE ANGELS
This is Adam, for God said to him: 'Adam, tell them their names.'*

216 THE SETTING OF THE SUN
The concealment of Truth within its own specific particulars, and the concealment of the Spirit within the body.

217 THE KEY TO THE SECRET OF DESTINY
The diversity of the Contingent Essences within eternity.*

218 THE FIRST KEY
This is the incorporation of all things as they are in the Utterly Concealed, which is the Oneness of the Essence – just like the tree latent in the date-stone. It is also called the Basic Root.*

219 RELEASE FROM SORROW AND ANXIETY
Faith in destiny.

220 THE BESTOWER
This is one of the names of the Prophet Muhammad, since it was he who confirmed the Names of God, and shone forth the light of

guidance upon them in all their intricate detail, and acted as their intermediary.

21 THE STAGE

This is the fulfilment of one's prescribed duties, for whoever has not fulfilled the requirements of the various Stations is not fit to progress to a higher level. Thus, anyone who has not verified the reality of Abstemiousness until he has made it his own, is not fit for the Stage of Trust; whoever has not verified Trust is not fit for Submission – and so on through all the Stages.

The word 'fulfilment' does not imply that none of the steps of the lower stage may be left incomplete before one is able to proceed to a higher one. The greater part of what has not been completed in the lower stage and its finer gradations will be rectified in the higher. Rather the intention is that one should become so solidly grounded in that particular stage that one actually becomes a part of it, and that the name associated with one's state, such as Abstinent or Trusting, is an exact description of the case. The same applies to all the stages. It is called a Stage because it is the halting place of the Seeker on the Way.

22 THE STAGE OF DIVINE DESCENT

This is the Breath of the Merciful, by which I mean the appearance of authentic existence in the ranks of specific individuation.

23 THE EXALTED POSITION

This is the rank which is closest in dignity to God. It may also be called the Place. It is referred to in the words of God Most High: 'In a sure setting, in the presence of an almighty King.'*

24 FRAUD

This is following up blessings with misdeeds, sustaining mystical states without regard for propriety, and divulging signs and miracles without authority or restraint.

25 THE KINGDOM

The visible world.

26 THE HEAVENLY KINGDOM

The invisible world.

227 THE KING OF THE KINGDOM

This is Truth, in its function of requiting what the individual has actually performed of the tasks which were required of him.

228 THE ENLARGER OF ASPIRATIONS

This is the Prophet, because he is the medium for the outpouring of Truth and guidance to whichever of his servants God chooses, and he sustains them with the illumination and strength of the verses of the Qur'an.

229 EQUITY

This is justice, by which I mean fair dealings both with Truth and with creation

230 THE FIRST WAY

The diffusion of Oneness from essential Unity, and the manner in which all the Qualities and the Names evolve in the ranks of the Essence. Whomsoever God has shown the arrangement of the Names and the Qualities in all the ranks of the Essence has been set on the shortest route to the First Way.

231 UTTER SEPARATENESS

This is the Collective Presence, in which there is not so much as a trace of any other thing. Thus it is the place where all separateness ceases, the very Union of Oneness. It is also known as Implicit Separateness, or the Presence of Existence, or the Presence of Union.

232 ULTIMATE KNOWLEDGE

This is the Presence of the One and it is called the starting point of the 'straight and even path'* – in view of the quickening Breath of the Merciful, from which spiritual forms become manifest in existence. It is known as the Station of Abasement, in which the descent of Truth takes place into the forms of creation; it is also known as the Station of Drawing Near, since within it creation draws near to the Truth. Another name for it is the Fountainhead of Liberality, since it is the source from which pours forth the generosity of Truth; and there are yet other names for it.

33 THE ESSENTIAL RELATIONSHIP

This is the relationship between Truth and the individual, and it may take one of two forms.

On the one hand the specific properties of the individual and the multiplicity of his attributes may have no effect on the fixed requirements of Truth and its unity; rather it is a case of him being influenced by the latter, and the darkness of his multiplicity being imbued with the light of the Unity of Truth.

Alternatively, the individual might acquire the attributes of Truth and verify all its Names. If these two alternatives are in harmony with each other, such a person is precisely the perfected individual that is being aimed for. If only the first alternative occurs without the second, then it is known as the Beloved Companion. Acquiring the second alternative without the first is an impossibility. In both alternatives, however, there are many gradations.

Concerning the first case, this is the result of the strong dominance which the light of Union exercises over the weakness of multiplicity – as well as the power of the properties of Necessity over the much weaker properties of Contingency.

As for the second alternative, this depends on the extent to which the individual is able to encompass both his verification of all the Names and his own incapacity to verify only some of them to the exclusion of others.

34 THE ENRAPTURED

These are angels in ecstatic contemplation of the Beauty of Truth – who are unaware that God has created Adam, so intense is their absorption and involvement in witnessing Truth. They are those exalted ones who were not required to perform the prostration, due to their absence from everything save the Truth, and their passion for the light of Beauty; and hence they seek nothing apart from that.*
They are also called Cherubim.

35 DEATH

In Sufi usage this is the taming of selfish desire, since the latter is what constitutes life. It is precisely towards this self-love that all lusts and natural bodily needs incline. If the Self inclines towards a lower level, it pulls the Heart, which is the Rational Soul, down with it towards its centre; and thus the Heart dies to the real life of learning which belongs to it by right, and lives instead a life of ignorance.

However, if the Self is tamed and dies to its own lusts, then the Heart proceeds on its natural way of Genuine Love to its own world: the world of holiness, light and essential life, which is not susceptible to death at all.

It was to this kind of death that Plato was referring when he said: 'Die to desire and you will live according to your nature.'*

The impeccable Ja'far Sadiq said: 'Death is repentance.' And in the words of God,

> '... now turn in repentance to your Creator, and slay yourselves.'*

He who has repented has killed his own Self. That is why, when Sufis put Death into categories, they classify thwarting the Self as 'the Red Death'.

When the Prophet Muhammad returned from holy war against the infidel and said, 'We have returned from the lesser holy war to the greater' – they asked him what the 'greater holy war' might be. He replied, 'It is the struggle against the Self.' In another Tradition it is said: 'The holy warrior is he who has waged war against his own Self.'

He who is dead to his desire lives through right guidance far from error, and through knowledge far from ignorance. When God Most High says: 'He who was dead, and we gave him life...'* he means 'dead' through ignorance, and 'we gave him life' through knowledge.

They have also called this death, Universal Death, to stand for all the various kinds of death.

236 THE WHITE DEATH

This is hunger, and it is so named because it illuminates the inward and brightens the face of the Heart. Thus any follower of the Path who does not assuage his hunger will die the White Death. In so doing he will revive his intelligence; for overeating kills intelligence, and whenever a person's gluttony dies, his astuteness is restored.

237 THE GREEN DEATH

This is the wearing of the patched garment made of discarded and worthless rags. If one is content to give up beautiful clothes for this, and merely limits oneself to a decent covering sufficient for the performance of prayers, then one has died the Green Death. The life

of such a person has become green through his abstemiousness and the blooming of his countenance in the verdant grace of the essential beauty within which he lives. As the poem says:

> As long as his honour is unstained,
> Whatever cloak he wears is fair.

Once when Shaf'i was seen dressed in shabby, worthless clothes, some ignorant people criticised him for it. He replied with these verses:

> What if my shirt is not worth a penny?
> I have beneath it a soul of priceless love.
> Your garb is a sun: beneath its radiance – darkness;
> Mine is black night, beneath which lies – a sun.

38 THE BLACK DEATH

This is enduring the suffering occasioned by people. One is not oppressed by the harm they do, and is not hurt, but rather takes pleasure in it as something coming from the Beloved. In the words of the poem:

> Sweet is the blame for desiring you;
> So let them blame me for my love of your memory.
> Seeing myself to be just like my enemies,
> I made up my mind to love them, too;
> May I fare as well with you
> As I have fared with them!*
> You belittled me, so I made myself small;
> But who is more honoured than one thus scorned?

Such a person has died the Black Death and is annihilated in God, since he sees all the abuse inflicted on him from a viewpoint in which all actions are annihilated in the one action of his Beloved; and, what is more, he sees himself and others all annihilated in the Beloved. Henceforth he lives by the existence of Truth, sustained by the presence of absolute liberality.

39 BALANCE

The means by which man arrives at correct views, apt sayings and fair deeds, and is able to distinguish these from their opposites.

It is that kind of justice which is the shadow of the real Unity

comprising the knowledge of the Holy Law, the Path and Reality. These are only verified by someone who has gone through the realisation of the Stage of Oneness of Union and the Stage of Separation.

The Balance of the people of externals is Holy Law; the Balance of people of inwardness is a mind illuminated by the Sacred Light; the balance of the exceptional is the Path; while the balance of the most select of all is Divine Justice, which is not realised except in the Perfected Man.

LETTER NŪN

240 PROPHECY
This is information concerning the divine realities – the knowledge of the Essence of Truth, its Names, Qualities, and Decrees. It consists of two parts: the prophecy of exposition, and the prophecy of legislation. The first comprises statements about the knowledge of the Essence, the Qualities and the Names. The second, in addition to the foregoing, involves the communication of the decrees, the inculcation of morality and wisdom, and the administration of government. The latter applies particularly to the prophetic mission.

241 THE NOBLE
These are forty persons whose charge it is to rectify the affairs of the people and bear their burdens. They are none other than the administrators of the rights of mankind.

242 BREATH
The soothing of the Heart by the subtleties of the invisible world. For the Lover it is companionship with the Beloved.

243 THE BREATH OF THE MERCIFUL
This is the existence of the One God, augmented in its reality by the spiritual forms which are the Essences and their states in the Presence of Oneness.

It is called thus as an analogy to the way in which human breath may be varied to produce vocal sounds. Although in itself it is simply air, the intention is to animate and release the inner Names that come under the domain of the Name of the Merciful. It is made up of the things that are in these names, and they have their being through its power, just as human animation is the result of breath.

244 THE SELF

This is the term for that subtle, ephemeral substance which is the vehicle for the vital energy, the senses and the voluntary bodily movements. The wise call it the Animal Soul. It is the intermediary between the Heart, which is the Rational Soul, and the body. It is referred to in the Qur'an as the Olive Tree '... the blessed tree, neither of the east or of the west...' – by which the human race and its blessings will increase.* Thus it is neither of the 'eastern' world of incorporeal spirits, nor of the 'western' world of physical bodies.

245 THE COMMANDING SELF

The Self which inclines towards bodily nature, and commands one to sensual delights and lusts, pulling the Heart downwards. Thus it is the abode of evil, the fountainhead of reprehensible morals and wicked deeds. God says: 'The self commands what is evil.'*

246 THE ACCUSING SELF

The Self which has been illuminated by the light of the Heart, to the extent that it becomes aware of its habitual heedlessness. Thus it awakens and begins to improve its condition, vacillating between Godliness and its natural state; so that whenever a misdeed occurs through its natural propensity towards evil, it is corrected by the divine admonitory light, and it starts to blame itself and turn in repentance to the door of the Forgiving, the Merciful. This is why God expressly mentions it in oaths: 'No! I swear by the accusing self!'*

247 THE SERENE SELF

The Self whose enlightenment has been completed by the light of the Heart, so that it has divested itself of base qualities and has been moulded by laudable moral conduct and orientated toward the way of the Heart, generally following it closely and progressively rising to the sacred world – free from sin, assiduous in its devotions, rising step by step, until its Lord addresses it in these exalted words:

> 'O serene self, return unto thy Lord, well-pleased and well-pleasing: enter among my servants, enter Paradise!'*

248 THE CHIEFS

Those who have ascertained the Inner Name, and have thus seen into

the inwardness of people and discovered their secret thoughts. For them the veils have been drawn back from the faces of the secrets. There are three hundred such individuals.

249 **THE CONNUBIAL BOND DIFFUSED THROUGH ALL ITS ISSUE**
This is the favour of the Living God, alluded to in his words: 'I was a hidden treasure and I wished to become known.' The words 'I was a hidden treasure' indicate that the priority of hiddenness and absoluteness, over manifestation and specific individuation, is an eternal and essential precedence. The words 'and I wished to become known', indicate a fundamental inclination and an essential love, which is the link between the hidden and the manifest, the latter being indicated by the words 'to become known'. It is this connection which is at the root of the notion of 'the Connubial Bond diffused through all its issue'.

The single requirement of love is the appearance of the characteristics of Oneness, diffused throughout all the levels of ordered individuation – all of it in the minutest detail, leaving nothing out. This is what preserves the unity of multiplicity, in all its forms, from division and dispersal. Thus the connection of that unity with multiplicity is the Connubial Bond. This may be seen firstly on the level of the Presence of the One, with the Oneness of the Essence in the forms of individuation and the oneness of the totality of the Names; then with the oneness of secondary existence on all its levels and the worlds which arise on its account; and then even in producing an outcome in terms of teaching and learning, feeding and eating, male and female. This love that requires both affection and lovableness – indeed this knowledge that requires both capacity to learn and informedness – this is the first flowing of unity into multiplicity, and the appearance of the triad of impact, receptivity and activity, which is the source of existence; and this is what is meant by the Connubial Bond diffused through all its issue.

250 **THE END OF THE FIRST JOURNEY**
The raising of the veils of multiplicity from the face of Unity.

251 THE END OF THE SECOND JOURNEY
The raising of the veil of Unity from the multiple facets of inner knowledge.

252 THE END OF THE THIRD JOURNEY
The cessation of the limitation of the two opposites, the outward and the inward, through the attainment of the Source of Union.

253 THE END OF THE FOURTH JOURNEY
This occurs upon the return from Truth to creation, in the Stage of Uprightness. It is the Oneness of Union and Separation, while witnessing the diffusion of Truth within creation and the disappearance of creation in Truth, so that the Essence of Unity may be seen in the forms of plurality, and, conversely, the multiplicity of the forms may be seen in the Essence of Unity.

254 THE GIFT
Anything that is bestowed by Truth on the People of Nearness, such as robes of honour. Every such robe conferred by God upon someone may be called thus. It may also mean special honours bestowed upon individuals.

255 THE LETTER *NŪN*
This occurs in God's exalted words: '*Nūn*: by the pen...'.* *Nūn* is concise knowledge in the Presence of Oneness, and the Pen is the presence of the full details.

256 LIGHT
One of the Names of God. It is his radiant manifestation in his Outward Name, by which I mean external existence in all its cosmic forms. It may be applied to anything that unveils the concealed aspects of the sciences of the Essence and the divine events that banish the world from the Heart.

257 LIGHT OF LIGHTS
Truth Most High.

LETTER SĪN

58 THE PRECEDENT
This is the eternal providence, referred to in the Qur'an in the words:
'... and give good tidings to the believers, that they have a sure footing with their Lord.'*

59 THE WAYFARER
Someone who is travelling towards God. While he continues on his journey, he is halfway between the aspirant and the one who has arrived.

60 FLOATING
This refers to those fine particles known as Primordial Matter. They are extremely obscure, and have no existence in themselves other than the forms which they assume.

61 THE VEIL
This is anything that screens you from what is important to you – like the veil of existence, or holding to conventional customs and acts.

62 SCREENS
The forms of the worlds, and the outward manifestations of the Divine Names, which are to be discerned behind them. As Shaybani put it:

> You have become manifest to the worlds from behind their screens: So you revealed only what those screens could grasp.

63 VEILS
This term is applied especially to the human bodily forms flowing between the visible and the invisible worlds.

264 THE ADORATION OF THE HEART
The annihilation of the Heart in Truth, such that while this illumination is being experienced, nothing may occupy it or divert it from its total absorption.

265 CRUSHING
This means the wasting away of the devotee through grief.

266 THE FINAL LOTE TREE
This is the Greater Intermediate World, which is the ultimate conclusion of everyone – and of all that they do and know.* It is the last of the designatory ranks, and there is no rank higher than this.

267 THE SECRET
This is what is characteristic of everything belonging to Truth in its creative aspect – as is referred to in the words of God:

> 'For to anything which we desire we but say the word "Be!" – and it is.'*

Hence the saying that none may know Truth except Truth, and none seek Truth except Truth, and none love Truth except Truth – because the secret is precisely the seeker, lover and knower of the Truth. As the Prophet says: 'I knew my Lord through my Lord.'

268 THE SECRET OF KNOWLEDGE
This is the reality of knowledge; because in reality knowledge is tantamount to Truth – only seen from a different perspective.

269 THE SECRET OF A STATE
What may be gathered from it concerning God's intention.

270 THE SECRET OF REALITY
Whatever does not conceal any of the reality of Truth in all things.

271 THE SECRET OF THE ILLUMINATIONS
This is the witnessing of everything in everything; and it takes place through the unveiling of the Primary Illumination in the Heart, so that it may witness the oneness existing collectively among all the Names. For every name is an attribute of all the other names, by

virtue of their unity in the Essence of Oneness; and their distinctness is the result of appearing in the world of specific instances, which are their forms. Thus everything is witnessed in everything.

272 THE SECRET OF DESTINY
This is what God discovers about every individual in Eternity, concerning which of the states that he experienced during his existence have made an impression on him. For God does not pass judgement on anything other than that which he has personally ascertained in its eternal condition.

273 THE SECRET OF DEITY
The fact that Deity depends on that which is deified. This is because it is a relationship with Eternity which has to have two components. One of these component parts is the deified, which is none other than the Established Essences – themselves in non-being. Now that which depends on the non-existent is itself non-existent. That is why Sahl said:

> 'There is a secret to Deity: if it became apparent, Deity would become null – due to the nullity of that on which it is dependent.'

274 THE SECRET OF THE SECRET OF DEITY
This is the appearance of the Lord in the forms of the Essences, so that the latter subsist through him and exist through his existence, by virtue of being the object of the self-subsistent Lord manifesting in his individuation. They are, in this respect, deified servants, and their Lord is the Truth. Thus in fact Deity never occurs except in the Truth, and the Essences are non-existent by themselves in Eternity. So the secret of Deity has a secret of its own, which is manifest and not void.

275 THE SECRETS OF THE TRACES
The Divine Names, which are the inner aspects of the created worlds.

276 THE LAST NIGHT OF THE MOON
The obliteration in Truth of the follower of the Path at the moment of his final arrival. It is to this that the saying of the Prophet refers:

> 'With God I have a time...'*

And in another Tradition God says:

> 'My friends are beneath my domes – none knows them but myself.'

277 THE ABUNDANCE OF THE HEART
The verification by the Perfected Man of the reality of all the intermediate worlds of contingency and necessity. For the heart of the completed man is indeed this intermediate world. Hence the Tradition:

> 'Neither my earth nor my heavens can contain me; yet I am contained in the heart of my faithful servant.'

278 JOURNEYS
This refers to the orientation of the Heart towards Truth. There are four such journeys.*

The first is the journey towards God from the Stations of the Self until the Visible Horizon is reached – which is the final Stage of the Heart and the commencement of the various illuminations of the Names.

The second is the journey within God, assuming his qualities and verifying his Names, until the Supreme Horizon is reached. This is the end of the Stage of the Soul and the Presence of the One.

The third is the ascent to the Essence of Union and the Presence of Oneness. This is the Stage of Two Bow-lengths, so long as duality remains; but if the latter is removed, then it is the stage of 'Even Nearer', which is the end of sainthood.*

The fourth journey means travelling in God and through God, which is the stage of Permanence after Annihilation, and Separation after Union.

279 THE ABOLITION OF VIEWPOINTS
This is the viewpoint of the Oneness of the Essence.

280 THE SESAME SEED
Knowledge too subtle for expression.

281 THE REQUEST OF THE TWO PRESENCES

This is the request arising from the presence of Necessity, in the language of the Divine Names, seeking from the Breath of the Merciful to be manifested in the forms of the Essences. Likewise it is the request arising from the presence of Contingency, in the language of the Essences, seeking to be manifested in the Names. The Breath of the Merciful always lends its support by answering their requests.

282 BLACKNESS OF FACE IN THE TWO ABODES

This is total annihilation in God, such that the subject has no existence either inwardly or outwardly, in the visible or the invisible world. This is authentic poverty – returning to the original non-existence. Hence the saying: 'If true poverty is perfected, then it is God.' And God is the Guide.*

LETTER 'AĪN

283 THE WORLD
This is the Second Shadow – which is none other than the Existence of Truth made visible in all its contingent forms. Because of its appearance in these specific particulars, it is termed both uniform and diverse.

When we consider Truth's augmentation of the contingent, the latter has no existence except by dint of this one relationship. Otherwise existence would be identical with Truth; and in the science of Truth the non-existence of the contingencies is established as being their essential characteristic. For the World is a form of Truth; and Truth is the essence and spirit of the World. These specific elaborations in the single existence of Truth are properties of its outward Name, and this in turn is the revelation of its Inward Name.

284 THE WORLD OF POWER
The world of the Divine Names and Qualities.*

285 THE WORLD OF COMMAND, THE WORLD OF THE HEAVENLY KINGDOM AND THE INVISIBLE WORLD
The world of spirits and spirtuality, since these exist by the command of Truth, without any material or temporal intermediary.

286 THE WORLD OF CREATION, THE WORLD OF THE KINGDOM AND THE VISIBLE WORLD
The world of bodies and mass: that which exists subsequent to the command of substance and time.

287 THE WISE
This refers to those for whom God has made visible his Essence,

Qualities, Names and Actions. For deep knowledge is a condition that arises through personal experience.

288 THE LEARNED
People whom God has informed of everything mentioned above, but through conviction rather than personal experience.

289 THE COMMON PEOPLE
This refers to those whose knowledge is limited to Holy Law. The learned among them are termed 'experts of customary form'.

290 THE GREAT REPROACH, AND THE THING GREATLY HATED
This is breach of trust, either by saying what one does not do, or by making a promise which one does not keep. In the words of God Most High:

> 'Very hateful is it to God, that you say what you do not.'*

He also said:

> 'Will you bid others to piety, and forget yourselves while you recite the book? Do you not understand?'*

The words, 'Do you not understand?' imply that they are ignorant – which is a great reproach.

291 WORSHIP
For the common people this is the utmost self-abasement.

For the Elect – those who have corrected their relationship to God – their veneration lies in the sincerity of their intent and the manner in which they follow his Path.

For the Elect among the Elect – those who have experienced themselves established in him in their adoration – they worship him for himself in the Stage of the Oneness of Union and Separation.

292 SERVANTS OF GOD
People who have been illuminated by the Divine Names. If they have verified the reality of one of the names, and have been imbued with the quality which is the reality of that name, they become related to God through the adoration and contemplation of its

divinity. The adoration of Truth from the standpoint of its divine sovereignty is by virtue of the perfection of that special Name. Thus one such person is called the 'Servant of the Provider', and another the 'Servant of the Mighty', and yet another the 'Servant of the Benefactor' – and so on.*

293 THE SERVANT OF GOD
The man whom Truth has illuminated with all its Names, so that there is no devotee of Truth who is in a more exalted stage than he is. This is due to his having ascertained the Greatest Name of God and acquired all its qualities. That is why our Prophet was especially distinguished by the bestowal of that Name. In the words of the Qur'an:

> 'When the servant of God stood calling on him, they were well-nigh upon him in swarms.'*

Actually this name should only be used for him, and for the Pole-star of each ensuing age, from among the heirs to his succession; however others have, as it were figuratively, been called Servant of God. The characteristic of every one of God's Names is in all of the names taken together, by virtue of the oneness and the unity of all the Names.

294 THE SERVANT OF THE COMPASSIONATE
epitomises the name of the Compassionate and is a mercy to all the world in general. Thus no one with the capacity for this is excluded from his compassion.

295 THE SERVANT OF THE MERCIFUL
exemplifies the name of the Merciful, and bestows his mercy particularly upon the pious, the virtuous and those with whom God is pleased. But he is vengeful towards those with whom God is angry.

296 THE SERVANT OF THE KING
Whoever masters himself and others by acting according to God's wishes and commands. And he is the severest of God's creatures upon his own nature.

297 THE SERVANT OF THE HOLY

The person whom God has exempted from being veiled, since his Heart has no room in it except for God. It is the person whose Heart is able to encompass the Truth. As God says in the Tradition: 'Neither my earth nor my skies can contain me; yet I am contained in the heart of my faithful servant.' It is through its own vastness that Truth is purified of everything else; for when Truth has become manifest nothing else remains. Thus nothing may contain the Holy except the Heart that has been purified of the worlds.

298 THE SERVANT OF THE SALVATION

Someone to whom the Truth has made itself manifest in the name of the Salvation, so that it preserves him from any misfortune, blemish or fault.

299 THE SERVANT OF THE FAITHFUL

The person whom God has safeguarded from punishment and calamity, and to whom the people have entrusted their persons, their property and their honour.

300 SERVANT OF THE PROTECTOR

Someone who with great vigilance witnesses the emergence of Truth. Thus he attentively observes himself and others, whilst the Truth is fulfilled for everyone who is entitled to it; since he is the one who embodies the name of the Protector.

301 THE SERVANT OF THE MIGHTY

This is whomsoever God has irradiated with his power, so that no misfortune in the world may overcome him, and he conquers everything.

302 THE SERVANT OF THE ALMIGHTY

restores whatever is broken or defective; because the Truth has restored his state and subjected him to the irradiation of this name, putting every situation right and mastering it.

303 THE SERVANT OF THE HAUGHTY

The person whose pride has been annihilated in his humility before the Truth, until the grandeur of God constitutes the stage of his pride and through Truth he comes to feel superior to all others and refuses to abase himself before them.

304 THE SERVANT OF THE CREATOR
Determines things according to the purpose of Truth, since this has been revealed to him in the course of appraising the characteristics and organisation of creation. Consequently he will not ordain anything except by God's decree.

305 THE SERVANT OF THE MAKER
This is close in meaning to the preceding entry. It refers to someone whose work has become free from contradiction and disagreement; so that he will not do anything which does not befit the presence of the Name of the Maker: balanced, appropriate, free from contradiction – as in the words of God Most High:

> 'Thou seest not in the creation of the All-Merciful any imperfection.'*

This is because the name 'Maker', with which this person has been illuminated, is one branch of the many subdivisions of the Names which come under the Name of the Merciful.

306 THE SERVANT OF THE FASHIONER
neither visualises nor fashions any image, unless it corresponds to the Truth and conforms to its likeness. This is because his actions have their origin in the creativity of God Most High.

307 THE SERVANT OF THE FORGIVING
forgives whatever wrongs may be committed against him, and veils in the behaviour of others what he would wish to be concealed of his own behaviour. God has concealed his misdeeds and irradiated him with his forgiveness; so he treats others in the same way that God has treated him.

308 THE SERVANT OF THE VANQUISHER
Someone whom God has made successful by backing up his efforts to subdue his own Self. He has been irradiated with the name of the Vanquisher and is thus able to overpower anyone who is hostile to him and defeat anyone who fights against him. He influences existence without himself being influenced by it.

LETTER 'AIN

09 THE SERVANT OF THE MUNIFICENT
Someone whom Truth has irradiated with the name of the Generous, so he gives what ought to be given to whom it ought to be given in the manner in which it ought to be given, without seeking recompense and without any ulterior motive. He simply extends assistance to the worthy people of God, because he is the instrument and manifestation of God's generosity.

10 THE SERVANT OF THE PROVIDER
A person whose livelihood God has enlarged; so he uses it to influence God's servants, spreading it before whomsoever God chooses; since it was God who laid this wealth and blessing at his feet. Thus he cannot fail to arrive at a place where blessings and benevolence are showered upon him.

11 THE SERVANT OF THE OPENER
Someone whom God has given the knowledge of the secrets of the keys in all their variety, unlocking for him all controversies and vexed questions. God sends down to him the triumphs of mercy and such blessings as he is able to grasp.

12 THE SERVANT OF THE KNOWER
This refers to anyone to whom God has imparted mystical revelations – intuitively, not through study or thought, but merely through natural clarity and the support of the Sacred Light.

13 THE SERVANT OF THE CONSTRAINER
God has seized hold of such a person, causing him to restrain himself and others from what is unseemly for them. Nor is he extravagant with God's wisdom and justice, but rather holds back from devotees whatever is not appropriate for them. For they are held tightly in his restraining hands.

14 THE SERVANT OF THE EXPANSIVE
Someone whom God has caused to be delighted with mankind. With God's permission he lavishes on them whatever of his own self and substance will gladden them and make them happy. This is in keeping with God's command, for he has illuminated him with the Name of the Expansive; and hence it is not contrary to Holy Law.

315 THE SERVANT OF THE HUMBLER
abases himself before God in all things. He lowers himself thus because he sees that the Truth is in God.

316 THE SERVANT OF THE EXALTER
looks down on all things, because he sees them with other eyes, raising himself above his own level because he operates from within Truth, which is the supreme level.

However, it may be the reverse of this. Firstly, when, through the manifestation of the Name of the Humbler, the individual puts himself below everything else, in view of his own absolute non-existence and nothingness. Or, in the second instance, the illumination of the individual with the Name of the Exalter causes everything else to be elevated because he sees the Truth in it. The latter, in my opinion, is worthier, since the wise man seeks compassion in order to acquire that quality himself. Thus he becomes merciful, as opposed to pitiable – the latter mode of compassion being the lot of the ordinary person.

317 THE SERVANT OF THE STRENGTHENER
Someone whom Truth has irradiated with the Name of the Strengthener, so that he lends strength to those among his friends whom God has supported with his might.

318 THE SERVANT OF THE HUMILIATOR
The manifestation of the attribute of humiliation. Thus Truth humbles into abasement all those of his enemies whom God has disgraced, in the Name of the Humiliator, by virtue of which such a person has been illuminated by God.

319 THE SERVANT OF THE HEARER AND THE SERVANT OF THE SEER
Someone who has been irradiated by these two Names, so that he has acquired the quality of hearing and seeing the Truth. As is said in the Tradition: 'I was his ears with which he heard, and his eyes with which he saw.' Thus he hears and sees things with the ears and eyes of Truth.

320 THE SERVANT OF THE JUDGE
Whoever judges God's servants by the divine verdict.

321 THE SERVANT OF THE JUST

acts justly with the people in accordance with the Truth, since he is the manifestation of God's justice. However, justice is not identical with equality, as the ignorant imagine. Rather it is the fulfilment of the right of everyone who is entitled to justice, and the provision of it for him in accordance with his deserts.

322 THE SERVANT OF THE GENTLE

is kind to God's servants, because he has insight into the occasions for kindness, due to the delicacy of his perception. Thus he is able to perceive inner states, and form a channel for the subtlety of Truth to reach its servants, and provide a support for them without their knowing it; and this by virtue of the gentleness which he acquired through the manifestation of the Name of the Gentle. This is something beyond the reach of perception.

323 THE SERVANT OF THE ADEPT

God has exposed to him the knowledge of things before and after they come into existence.

324 THE SERVANT OF THE CLEMENT

is not in any haste to punish those who do him wrong. Rather he shows patient forbearance, and endures both the injuries of those that harm him and the impudence of the foolish. Thus he wards off sin with something better.

325 THE SERVANT OF THE GLORIOUS

Truth has irradiated him with all its majesty; and he abases himself in utter humility before it. God glorifies him in the eyes of his other servants, and exalts his repute among the people, who honour and revere him because of the appearance in him of the marks of greatness.

326 THE SERVANT OF THE PARDONING

completely pardons a crime and conceals it from the Servant of the Vanquisher. Thus he is always forgiving. Truly the Servant of the Pardoning abounds in forgiveness.

327 THE SERVANT OF THE THANKFUL

is constantly thankful to his Lord, because he never sees a blessing which does not emanate from him. Even though it may come in the form of tribulation and adversity, he can still perceive the blessing within it. As the Caliph 'Ali said: 'Praise be to him whose mercy to his friends increases even in the midst of his most intense retribution, and whose vengeance upon his enemies becomes ever harsher amidst the abundance of his mercy.'

328 THE SERVANT OF THE MOST HIGH

His worth has surpassed that of his fellows, and his aim has risen aloft in his quest for excellence. He has risen far above the ambitions of his brethren and has attained every high rank and every sublime perfection.

329 THE SERVANT OF THE GREAT

has become great through the grandeur of Truth, and has been magnified by its greatness, perfection and superiority over creation.

330 THE SERVANT OF THE PRESERVER

God has preserved him from every evil in his deeds, his words, his states, his thoughts and both his inward and his outward behaviour. He has illuminated him with the Name of the Preserver, until this quality of protection flows from him to those around him. Thus it was said of Abi Sulaiman Darani that no evil thought came to his mind for thirty years – nor to the mind of any companion of his, so long as they were together.

331 THE SERVANT OF THE NOURISHER

God has given him an insight into the need of the needy – how much, and when – and has enabled him to deal with it in accordance with his knowledge, without addition or deduction and without being either ahead of time or behind.

332 THE SERVANT OF THE RECKONER

God has made him carefully calculating concerning himself – even down to each breath he takes – and has enabled him, and whoever is of a like mind, to maintain this.

33 THE SERVANT OF THE SUBLIME

God has exalted him with his own glory, so that he is held in awe by all who see him. The sublimity of his rank arouses reverence for him in their hearts.

34 THE SERVANT OF THE GENEROUS

God has called on him to bear witness to the name of the Generous, so he has been irradiated with generosity and has accordingly verified the reality of worship. For generosity requires a knowledge of its own scope, without overstepping its limits. Such a person knows that man has no possessions, and that nothing belongs to him except that which is liberally bestowed by God Most High, such is his generosity to his servants. Thus the generosity of the Lord is especially apportioned to whomsoever he chooses.

Likewise he will not see a fault committed by someone without covering it up in his generosity; and no one will do him any harm without being forgiven by him for it, and without being repaid for it with the noblest of dispositions and the most beautiful of deeds.

It is related of the Caliph 'Umar that when he heard God's words: '... what blinded thee to thy generous Lord?'* – he replied, 'Thy very generosity, O my Lord.' The sage, Sheikh Ibn Arabi said that this was of proven instructional value.

To sum up, such a person will not attach any significance to the faults of God's servants, when weighed against the generosity of God Most High, nor will he see any limit to the blessings pouring forth from that generosity. Thus he becomes the noblest of people, since his actions are the result of the generosity of his Lord, with which he has been illuminated and towards which he has been striving.

35 THE SERVANT OF THE LIBERAL

is the manifestation of the Name of the Liberal and the channel of God's liberality towards his servants, such that no one in creation is more liberal than he. And indeed, why should this not be so? – seeing that he gives so generously of himself to his beloved that his Heart is attached to nothing else.

36 THE SERVANT OF THE VIGILANT

sees that his Guardian is closer to him than his own Self, as he observes the annihilation of the latter and its passage into the

illumination of the Name of the Vigilant. Thus he will not go beyond any of God's limits, and no one is more assiduously attentive to these than he is. When his friends are in his presence, he watches over them with the vigilance of God Most High.

337 THE SERVANT OF THE RESPONSIVE
has responded to the call of truth, and obeyed God on hearing the words: '... answer God's summoner.'* So God has answered his call by illuminating him with the Name of the Responsive. Thus he answers all the prayers of God's servants, since he is part of the collective answer that God has given. For God has answered him in these words:

> 'And when my servants question thee concerning me, I am near to answer the call of the caller when he calls to me; so let them respond to me.'*

Such a person can see their call as his own, by virtue of the nearness and unification necessary for faith to be experienced – as shown in the words:

> '... and let them believe in me.'*

338 THE SERVANT OF THE ALL-EMBRACING
can encompass everything, the length and breadth of it, and nothing can encompass him, due to the broad scope of his comprehension at all levels. He never sees a deserving individual without bestowing on him some of his grace.

339 THE SERVANT OF THE JUDICIOUS
God has enlightened him concerning the occasions for wisdom in his affairs, and has enabled him to say and do the right thing. He never sees any gap without filling it, or any imperfection without correcting it.

340 THE SERVANT OF THE LOVING
His love of God and all his saints has been perfected; so God loves him and spreads the love of him throughout his creation. Thus everyone loves him, except the ignorant and the dull-witted. The Prophet said: 'If God loves a servant of his, he calls Gabriel to him and says, "I love such and such a person, so you love him, too." And

so Gabriel loves him, and makes a proclamation in heaven, saying: "God loves this person, so you, too, must love him." And the denizens of heaven love him and prepare a favourable reception for him on earth.'

41 THE SERVANT OF THE ILLUSTRIOUS

God has glorified him among men because of the perfection of his character and qualities, and because he has verified the virtues of God. Thus the people glorify him for his grace and the beauty of his nature.

42 THE SERVANT OF THE REVIVER

God has revived his Heart with true life, after he has voluntarily died to the characteristics of the Self – its lusts and longings – and made himself a manifestation of the Name of the Reviver. Thus he revives through knowledge those who are dead through ignorance, and arouses them to search for Truth.

43 THE SERVANT OF THE WITNESS

sees the Truth bearing witness to everything; so he witnesses it in himself and in the rest of God's creation.

44 THE SERVANT OF THE TRUTH

Truth has illuminated him, thus safeguarding him from falsehood in his actions, his words and his states. Thus he sees the Truth in everything, because it is that which is constant, necessary, self-subsistent. That which is called 'correct' is invariably false and transitory; whereas he sees the forms of Truth as Truth, and those of falsehood as falsehood.

45 THE SERVANT OF THE GUARDIAN

sees Truth in the forms of the causes affecting all the actions which people who are veiled from the Truth ascribe to those causes. Thus he disregards the causes and assigns these things to the One who assumes and accepts responsibility for them.

46 THE SERVANT OF THE POWERFUL

has been given strength by the power of God to vanquish Satan and his cohorts – the forces at work in his own Self, such as anger, lust

and greed. After which he has been given the power to conquer his enemies among the *jinn* and devils of mankind; so that nothing in God's creation can resist him without being vanquished; and none may show hostility towards him without being overcome.

347 THE SERVANT OF THE FIRM
is solid in his religion and unaffected by those who want to lead him astray. He is not the sort who can be tripped up and diverted from the Truth, such is his forcefulness; for he is firmer than every firm thing. Thus the Servant of the Powerful is the one who affects everything, while the Servant of the Firm is not affected by anything.

348 THE SERVANT OF THE PATRON
God has taken him into his care from among the righteous and the believers. The Most High says: '. . . and he takes into his protection the righteous.'* – and: 'God is the protector of those who have faith.'* Thus such a person protects, through God's patronage, his near ones among the believers and the righteous.

349 THE SERVANT OF THE PRAISEWORTHY
Truth has irradiated him with its laudable qualities. Thus people praise him, while he himself praises none but God.

350 THE SERVANT OF THE QUANTIFIER
has verified this Name in its manifestation to him, and Truth has illuminated him with it, so that he knows the number of all that has existed and will exist; and he has a comprehensive and quantifiable knowledge of everything.

351 THE SERVANT OF THE INITIATOR
God has given him an insight into the very beginning, so that he witnesses the beginning of creation and the command. Thus he initiates, with God's permission, such good deeds as are his to initiate.

352 THE SERVANT OF THE RESTORER
God has enlightened him concerning the return of creation and all things in it to him; so, with God's permission, he returns what ought

to be returned to him. He experiences his future life and his return to it, which is the finest happiness there is.

53 THE SERVANT OF THE QUICKENER
Truth has illuminated him in the Name of the Quickener. Thus God enlivens his Heart for him and empowers him – like Jesus – to revive the dead.

54 THE SERVANT OF THE MORTIFIER
God has caused him to die to his own Self – his greed, his anger and his lust. So his heart has become enlivened and his mind illuminated by the life and light of Truth, until he affects others by mortifying the power of the Self through the determination impressed on him by God. Such is the quality with which God has illuminated him.

55 THE SERVANT OF THE LIVING
Truth has irradiated him with its eternal life; so he lives within God's everlasting life.

56 THE SERVANT OF THE ETERNAL
witnesses the consummation of things through Truth; so that he is illuminated by God's everlastingness and takes charge of the interests of humanity, staying true to God and constantly observing the commands which God gives to his people via his Eternity, assisting them in their undertakings, with their subsistence, their welfare, their very lives.

57 THE SERVANT OF THE FINDER
God has singled him out for existence in the very Union of Oneness. Thus he found the One, existing through the existence of the Existence of Oneness, and was able to dispense with everything else; because whoever wins this has won everything – losing nothing, wanting nothing.

58 THE SERVANT OF THE GLORIOUS
God has honoured him with his qualities and given him what he is ready for – and what he is capable of bearing – of his splendour and honour. He is like the Servant of the Illustrious.

359 THE SERVANT OF THE ONE
God has imparted to him the Presence of the One and revealed the oneness of the totality of his Names, so that he grasps what can be grasped and understands what can be understood by contemplating the facets of God's Beautiful Names.

360 THE SERVANT OF THE UNIQUE
stands alone in time – the Master of Duration. To him belongs the title of Major Pole-star, and attainment to the Primordial Oneness.

361 THE SERVANT OF THE EVERLASTING
is the outward manifestation of the Everlasting, and can withstand the impact of misfortune and channel the benefit of good works on God's behalf to eliminate suffering. Such a person is the locus of God's perception of the world as he rules over it.

362 THE SERVANT OF THE MASTERFUL
has been irradiated with the Name of the Masterful and has witnessed the mastery of God over all destinies. Thus he takes the form of the divine hand, which, when it strikes, nothing can stop. He witnesses God's influence on everything and the permanent connection of the support of existence with things which are non-existent – despite the fact that they are essentially non-existent. He also sees himself as essentially non-existent, even though he is influenced by God's mastery over all things.

363 THE SERVANT OF THE POTENT
is like the foregoing, except that this individual witnesses the inception of the process of coming into existence, and experiences this state.

364 THE SERVANT OF THE PROMOTER
God has given him preference and made him one of the people of the first rank. And so, being illuminated with this Name, he affords advancement to anyone who is entitled to be offered the Name, together with every appropriate action.

365 THE SERVANT OF THE RESTRAINER
God has enabled him to impede any excessive person who rebelliously oversteps God's bounds. Thus by virtue of this Name he restrains every rapacious tyrant, and returns him to his limits, and

deters him from tyranny and oppression. The same applies to any actions which God may have sparked off in certain people, and which it may be necessary to restrain.

66 THE SERVANT OF THE FIRST

has witnessed the primacy of Truth over everything and its Eternity-without-beginning. Thus he becomes the first to verify this Name before all the others in the various developmental stages – each vying with the other in devotion and the race towards good works – and before all those who came to a standstill with creation. All this by virtue of his verification of Eternity-without-beginning. For phenomena are the hallmark of the created universe.

67 THE SERVANT OF THE LAST

has witnessed the hereafter of God and its permanence after the annihilation of creation; and he has verified the meaning behind God's words: 'All things on earth perish: only his face abides, most majestic and bountiful.'* For the aspect of permanence has arisen in him; so he endures in his permanence – safe now from annihilation, by dint of having undergone it. This would seem to be a characteristic of some of God's saints, or even most of them.

68 THE SERVANT OF THE OUTWARD

has emerged through acts of devotion and charity until God reveals to him his literal Name, the Outward, by which he is known. So this person assumes the characteristics of outwardness, calling on the people to adorn themselves with visible perfections. He tends to prefer anthropomorphism to pure abstraction, as was the case of the calling of Moses. That is why he promised the people paradise and physical pleasures, and glorified the Torah for its large size and its gold lettering.

69 THE SERVANT OF THE INWARD

has gone deeply into the transactions of the Heart, and is sincerely faithful to God. So God has sanctified his Secret Faculty and irradiated him with the Name of the Inward, until his spirituality becomes dominant and he surveys the inner mysteries and reports about the things of the invisible world, calling people to mystical perfections. Such a person tends to prefer pure abstraction to

anthropomorphism, as was the case with the calling of Jesus – the calling to the heavenly, spiritual things of the invisible world, as well as to poverty and retirement from society.

370 THE SERVANT OF THE RULER

God has made him the ruler of the people by manifesting in the form of the Name of the Ruler. Thus he rules himself and others in the divine administration, and executes God's justice among his people, calling them to the good, commanding them to do what is lawful and shun what is not. So God has honoured him and made him the first of the Seven whom he keeps in the shadow of his throne. Such a person is the just sovereign, the shadow of God on God's earth. His is the weightiest balance of all, because the good deeds and charitable acts of the people are put into his scale without their own reward being reduced in any way. For it is through him that God establishes his religion in them and carries them towards good works; so he is God's hand and helper, and God is his supporter and protector.

371 THE SERVANT OF THE SUPREME

The Supreme is the one who attains a superior degree of consciousness to the rest; and his servant is someone who is the outward manifestation of this – someone who does not stop at any perfection or level of sublimity he may have reached. Rather he strives for higher perfection through his aspiration to rise to even greater heights. For from his higher level he has witnessed true, absolute, holy sublimity, without any restriction. So he never ceases his quest for the sublime in all its perfection. Do you not see how the most excellent and highest rank of people was addressed in these words of God: '... and say, O my Lord, increase me in knowledge!'*

372 THE SERVANT OF THE PIOUS

has become imbued with all the various kinds of piety – in reality as well as in appearance – so that there is no type of piety which he does not show, and no form of bounty which he does not bestow.

> True piety is this:
> To believe in God and the Last Day,
> The angels, the Book and the Prophets,
> To give of one's substance, however cherished,
> To kinsmen and orphans, the needy, the traveller, beggars,

And to ransom the slave,
To perform the prayer, to pay the alms.
And they who fulfil their covenant
When they have engaged in a covenant,
And endure with fortitude
Misfortune, hardship and peril,
These are they who are true in their faith,
These are the truly godfearing.*

73 THE SERVANT OF THE RELENTING
has returned to God, constantly turning away from himself and away from everything other than Truth – until he witnesses true Unity and accepts the repentance of all who have turned to God in contrition for their sin.

74 THE SERVANT OF THE AVENGER
God has appointed him to carry out the punishments prescribed for his servants, within the framework of Holy Law, without showing pity or mercy. As God said:

'And in the matter of God's religion let no tenderness for them seize you.'*

75 THE SERVANT OF THE PARDONER
His forgiveness of the people is great and his punishments are few. Indeed no one ever does him any harm without being forgiven by him for it. The Prophet said: 'God is forgiving and loves forgiveness.' He also related the following:

There was once a wealthy man, before your time, whose only virtue was that he used to command his servants to show forbearance to anyone in need. God said: 'Forbearance belongs more by rights to us than it does to him: therefore let him be forgiven.'

76 THE SERVANT OF THE BENIGN
God has caused him to manifest divine benevolence and mercy; so he is the most gracious of God's creatures towards mankind – except concerning the punishments decreed by Holy Law. For he sees what the legal punishment is, and what it is that obliges him to impose it for the crime which through God's decree has come under his

jurisdiction. His judgement is a mercy from God upon the wrong-doer, even though externally it may appear like vengeance. This is something which is unknown except intuitively among the elite. Thus what is outwardly the administration of a punishment is inwardly the very essence of compassion.

377 THE SERVANT OF THE LORD OF THE KINGDOM

has witnessed the dominion of God over his Kingdom; so he sees himself as belonging purely to God, along with all his other possessions. Thus he becomes confirmed in his service to God, and not at all concerned with his own property, or anything of the sort. God therefore rewards him by making him a manifestation of the Lord of the Kingdom, since nothing has the power to distract him from his Lord. He has become free from the slavery of existence, owning everything through God, not himself; for he is God's servant in the true sense.

378 THE SERVANT OF THE MOST MAJESTIC AND NOBLE

God has made him majestic and noble because he has acquired his characteristics and verified the reality of his Names. And as his names are sanctified, glorified, purified and illuminated, the same befalls their outward manifestations and forms. None of his enemies can see him without being filled with dread of him and submitting to him because of the majesty of his rank; and likewise there are none near to him who do not honour him, since God has done so. Such a person treats the friends of God with reverence and holds God's enemies in contempt.

379 THE SERVANT OF THE EVEN-HANDED

is the soundest of people in terms of his fairness. He takes what is rightfully his and gives it to others without their being aware of it. This is because he deals justly, according to the justice of God, with which he has been illuminated; so he accords everyone his rights and removes every injustice that he may come across. He sits on a throne of light, lowering those who ought to be lowered and raising up those who ought to be raised. As the Prophet said, 'The even-handed stand on platforms of light.'

80 THE SERVANT OF THE UNIVERSAL

God has combined all his Names in him and made him a manifestation of his universality; so he gathers together in the divine totality everything of himself and others that has been scattered and dispersed.

81 THE SERVANT OF THE INDEPENDENT

God has made him independent of all created beings, and given him all that he needs without his having to ask, except implicitly in the language of potential.* For such a person has realised the poverty of his own essence and his utter need for God throughout the whole range of his endeavours.

82 THE SERVANT OF THE BENEFACTOR

After perfecting his independence, God has made him the benefactor of mankind, facilitating their needs and removing their shortcomings. This is achieved by virtue of his own high aim, which God has supported from his own capacity by illuminating the Name of the Benefactor in him.

83 THE SERVANT OF THE PREVENTER

God has protected and restrained him from anything that might cause his corruption, even though he may himself desire and like it, considering it a means to his welfare. Such things as wealth, reputation, health, etc. God has made him experience the meaning of his words:

> 'Yet it may happen that you will hate a thing which is better for you; and it may happen that you will love a thing that is worse for you.'*

Anyone who has verified the reality of this Name prevents his friends from doing what is harmful and corrupting for them; and it is through him that God prevents corruption, whatever its source, even though people may reckon that what is forbidden is the advantageous and prudent thing to do.

84 THE SERVANT OF THE HARMFUL AND THE BENEFICIAL

God has made him witness that he does whatever he wants to do, and has revealed to him the unity of actions; so that he does not see any harm or benefit, any good or evil, that does not come from him. If he

verified both these Names and became a manifestation of them both, then, through his Lord, he might become both beneficial and harmful to the people. However God has conferred on some of his servants only one of the two, making some a manifestation of the Harmful – like Satan and his followers, and others a manifestation of the Beneficial – like Khidr, and those who have an affinity with him.

385 THE SERVANT OF THE LIGHT

has been irradiated with the light, so he experiences the meaning of the exalted words: 'God is the Light of the heavens and the earth.'* Light is the visible, by which everything becomes apparent in being and knowledge, for he is the light of the worlds, by which we are guided aright. As the Prophet said: 'O my Lord, let there be light in my heart!'

386 THE SERVANT OF THE GUIDE

is the manifestation of this Name. God has made him a guide to his creation, speaking eloquently and sincerely of the Truth, and communicating what has been commanded and revealed to him – as did the Prophet, both directly and through hereditary transmission.

387 THE SERVANT OF THE CREATIVE

has witnessed the creativity of God Most High in his essence, his qualities, and his actions; and God has made him a manifestation of this Name, so that he is able to create things which others would be incapable of achieving.

388 THE SERVANT OF THE ENDURING

God has made him witness his everlastingness, and caused him to endure when all else has been annihilated. He worships him with the pure adoration which is inherent in his specific individuation. For he is both worshipper and worshipped, general and particular, specific and real; since neither form nor trace of him remains when the face of the Enduring becomes manifest. As God says in the holy Tradition, 'Whomsoever I have slain, his blood price is charged to me; and for anyone whose blood price is charged to me – I am that blood price.'

389 THE SERVANT OF THE INHERITOR

is the personification of this Name, which numbers among the

necessary attributes of the Servant of the Enduring. For if he endures through the immortality of Truth, after the annihilation of his own Self, it follows that he must inherit what Truth bequeaths of everything after it has been annihilated, in terms of knowledge and possessions. Thus he inherits the knowledge, wisdom and guidance of the Prophets, for they have merged with the totality.

90 THE SERVANT OF THE MATURE
God brings him to maturity by irradiating him with this Name; as he said of Abraham, 'We gave Abraham aforetime his rectitude.'* So he begins to guide humanity towards God and towards their welfare in this world and the next – both their livelihood and their ultimate destination.

91 THE SERVANT OF THE PATIENT
is steadfast in his affairs by virtue of the illumination within him of this Name. Such a person is in no haste to blame or punish or avert misfortunes; and he is patient in his struggles and whatever acts of obedience God requires of him, and whatever trials and tribulations he may inflict on him.

92 THE ADMONITION
The means by which a lesson is learnt concerning good and evil in the outwardly visible states of people, and what happens to them in the world, and the way in which information about them is communicated to the hereafter and the abode of retribution. It also makes clear the state of the admonisher and the inner conditions of things and their secrets; so that the consequences of events become apparent to one, and the wisdom of the hidden faculty, and what one's aim ought to be.

The Prophet said: 'I was commanded to keep my speech for commemoration, my silence for thought, and my glance for admonition.'

Included with this is the transition from seeing wisdom in the external aspects of creation to the vision of the sage, and from the externalities of existence to its inwardness, until the Truth and its qualities are seen in everything.

393 THE EAGLE

For Sufis this sometimes expresses the Primal Intellect, while at other times it expresses nature in its totality. This is because they refer to the Rational Soul as a 'dove', which the Primal Intellect snatches up, like an eagle, from the depths of the lower, physical world, to the sublime world and sacred outer reaches of space. Alternatively it may be snatched and captured by nature, and fall down with it to the lower depths. That is why both have been called the Eagle: the difference between them lies in the context.

394 THE CAUSE

An expression for the continuing preservation of the individual in work, state or stage, or his continuance in form or attribute.

395 CLOUDS

According to us, this is the Presence of Oneness, because no one knows it except God, for he is behind the veil of majesty. It has also been said that it is the Presence of the One, which is the origin of the Names and the Qualities; because the fine clouds are a thin screen between heaven and earth, whose presence forms a barrier between the heaven of oneness and the earth of the plurality of creation.

The Prophetic tradition is not very helpful here: when the Prophet was asked, 'Where was our Lord before he created creation?' he replied, 'In heavy clouds'.

The above-mentioned Presence is destined for the Primary Individuation, because it is the abode of multiplicity and the appearance of the Names and their interrelationships. Everything that becomes individuated is by that token created, and constitutes the Primal Intellect. The Prophet said: 'The first thing created by God was intellect.' Therefore there was nothing before he created the first creation: only afterwards. There is further evidence for this in that the advocates of this teaching call this presence the Presence of Contingency. The presence of the union between the principles governing necessity and contingency and human reality – all of this comes under the heading of created things. Admittedly, Truth illuminates this presence with the attributes of creation: all of which logically requires that it did not exist before creation was created.

An alternative possibility is that by creation the questioner meant the creation of the material world. In this case the 'clouds' become the Divine Presence, which is known as the Universal Intermediate

LETTER 'AIN

World, and this is helpful in answering the question of where the Lord was, since the Divine Presence is the Source of Lordship.

396 SPIRITUAL PILLARS
These are the things which support the heavens, as is indicated by the exalted words: 'God is he who raised up the heavens without pillars you can see.'* This implies that there are unseen pillars; and these are the soul, heart and self of the universe; and they are also the reality of the Perfected Man. The latter is known only to God, for as he has said: 'My friends are beneath my domes – none knows them but myself.'

397 THE 'ANQA' BIRD
A metaphor for Primordial Matter, because, like the '*Anqa*' bird, it cannot be seen and does not exist except figuratively; so it is an intellectual concept denoting the absolute Primordial Matter which is common to all physical bodies. The Major Element.*

398 THE MAJOR ELEMENT
This is the '*Anqa*' bird.*

399 THE WORLDS OF APPAREL
These are all the levels downward from the Presence of Oneness. For the Most Sacred Essence lowers itself through its individuation within these levels, and takes on the characteristic garb of the Names as well as their spiritual and allegorical qualities, and becomes clothed in them – right down to the sensory level.

400 THE ESTABLISHED ESSENCE
This is the reality of a thing in a scholarly context. It has no existence of its own, being merely established in the knowledge of God. Its rank is secondary to that of real existence.*

401 THE ESSENCE OF THINGS
Sublime Truth.

402 THE EYE OF GOD AND THE EYE OF THE WORLD
This is the perfected human being, who has verified the reality of the Greater Intermediate World.* For God casts his eyes on the world

and confers on it the mercy of existence, as in the words of the Tradition:

'But for you, I would not have created the heavens.'

Alternatively it refers to the human being who has verified the Name of the Seer, since all of the things which he sees in the world he sees by virtue of this Name.

403 THE ESSENCE OF LIFE

This is the inward aspect of the Name of the Living, and whoever has verified its reality has drunk of the water of the essence of life. Whosoever has drunk this will never die, because he has his life by virtue of the life of Truth. Every living thing in the world has its life through this man's life, in that his life has its being in the life of Truth.

404 THE RECURRING FEAST

Whatever it is that returns to the Heart from an illumination – or any sort of mystical experience of illumination.*

LETTER FĀ'

405 LOOSENING
The opposite of Binding, seen in terms of the elaboration of absolute matter into its specific forms.* Alternatively, it is the manifestation of everything that is inward in the Presence of the One, such as the interrelationships of the Names; and it is the emergence into view of whatever essential matters lie concealed in the Essence of Oneness, such as the universal realities subsequent to their particularization in the outside world.

406 OPENINGS
All that is opened up to the individual by God, after having been closed to him: outward and inward blessings, such as livelihood, service, knowledge, wisdom, revelation, and so on.

407 IMMINENT VICTORY
Whatever has unfolded for the individual from the Stage of the Heart and the appearance of its qualities and perfections while he traverses the Stations of the Self. This is what is alluded to in the sacred words, '. . . help from God and imminent victory.'*

408 MANIFEST VICTORY
Whatever has unfolded for the individual from the Stage of Sainthood and the irradiations of the Divine Names, which clarify the attributes and perfections of the Heart. This is indicated in God's words: 'Surely we have given thee a manifest victory, that God may forgive thee thy former and thy latter sins,' – sins meaning the characteristics of the Self and the Heart.*

409 ABSOLUTE VICTORY
The highest triumph, and the most perfect: it is whatever has unfolded for the individual from the illumination of the Essence of Oneness and immersion in utter Union, through the annihilation of all the forms of creation. This is alluded to in the words: 'When comes the help of God, and victory...'*

410 COOLING OFF
The abating of the ardour of the quest, which is necessary before a start can be made.

411 THE FIRST SEPARATION
The veiling of Truth by creation, and the continuance of the forms of creation in their present state.

412 THE SECOND SEPARATION
Witnessing creation being sustained by Truth, and seeing unity in multiplicity and multiplicity in unity, without the subject being veiled by either of them.

413 THE PROOF
The detailed knowledge that distinguishes between Truth and falsehood. The Qur'an is the inspired compendium of knowledge which unites all realities.

414 THE SEPARATION OF UNION
The proliferation of the One, manifesting at the levels which are the manifestation of the features of the Essence of Oneness; which features, in fact, are simply subjective and unverified assumptions – except when the One Truth displays itself in their forms.

415 THE SEPARATION OF THE QUALITIES
The manifestation of the Essence of Oneness and its qualities in the Presence of the One.

416 THE DIFFERENCE BETWEEN THE EMULATOR AND THE VERIFIER
The Emulator is someone who acquires moral excellence and praiseworthy qualities in a forced and affected manner. But since he shuns vice and blame, he does have traces of the Divine Names. The

Verifier, on the other hand, is someone whom God has made the embodiment of his names and qualities. He has irradiated him with them, thus obliterating the habitual patterns of his character and personal attributes.

417 THE DIFFERENCE BETWEEN PERFECTION AND HONOUR

Perfection is an expression of the attainment in the human being to the divine assembly and the cosmic realities. Thus whoever has greater fortune with the divine Names and the universal realities, and manifests them more completely, and in whom the divine assembly, with all its qualities and names, is predominant – will be more perfect; whereas anyone whose fortune in these things is less will be inferior and further from the rank of the divine deputyship.

As for Honour, this is an expression of the level of the intermediate links between a thing and its creator. Thus whenever the links between Truth and creation are fewer, and the properties of necessity prevail over those of contingency, then that thing is more honourable. On the other hand, whenever the links between creation and Truth Most High are more numerous, then that thing is baser. That is why the Primal Intellect and the angels close to God are more honourable than the Perfected Man, whilst he is more perfect than they are.

418 THE SPLIT

The division between Truth and creation, through individuation and its consequences.

419 THUSNESS

The message of Truth, as opposed to the World of Ideas.*

LETTER ṢĀD

420 THE MASTER OF DURATION AND THE MASTER OF MOMENT AND STATE
has verified the reality of the first assembly of the Intermediate World, and is apprised of the realities of things outside the control of time; things, that is, outside the control of his past and future actions – except for those in the Eternal Present, which is the vehicle of his states, his qualities and his deeds. For this reason he handles time by a process of folding and unfolding, and he handles space by a process of contraction and expansion. He is someone who has verified alike the realities and natures of the many and the few, the long and the short, the great and the small. For unity, diversity and quantity are all merely accidental phenomena; and while he operates with them in his imagination, and likewise in his intellect, his behaviour is validated and becomes comprehensible through contemplation and direct revelation. Thus the verifier of Truth, as he deals with the realities is active in a mode which goes far beyond the limits of sensory perception, imagination and intellect; and he controls and modifies accidental phenomena.

421 THE FAIR OF FACE
has verified the Name of the Generous, and its manifestations – as did the Prophet of God. Jābir once said. 'No one ever asked the Prophet for anything and had him say no.'* If anyone asked him to mediate with God on his behalf, he would never refuse the request. As Ali, the Commander of the Faithful pointed out, 'If you need anything of God, start by invoking blessings on the Prophet; then ask for what you need: God is far too generous, when two things are asked of him, to grant one and reject the other.'

The person who verified the inheritance of the Prophet's liberality

was Ash'ath, one of the hidden ones. Of him the Prophet said: 'There's many an Ash'ath, driven away from door after door, who, if he were to entreat God, would not be refused.'

Such a person is called 'fair of face', because of the tradition of the Prophet which says: 'Seek what you need from the fair of face.'

422 THE EASTERLY BREEZE
This refers to the merciful zephyrs that come from the eastern, spiritual direction and are a stimulus to good.*

423 THE SINCERE FRIEND
A person who has taken sincerity to the utmost. He has perfected his belief in everything issuing from the Prophet of God – knowledge, sayings and deeds – through his inner purity and his closeness to the inner nature of the Prophet, such is his high degree of affinity with him. It is for this reason that in God's book there is no distinction in rank between the two, as is shown in the words

> 'They are with those whom God has blessed: prophets, sincere friends, martyrs and righteous men.'*

The Prophet said: 'Abu Bakr and I are like two race horses: if he had run faster than me, I would have believed in him; but I was the faster, so he believed in me.'

424 THE AUTHENTICITY OF LIGHT
This is revelation without any subsequent veiling. It has been compared with lightning that produces rain, so it is called true, while lightning that is not followed by rain is called false. The state of the seeker in whom illumination is followed by veiling is one of confusion. However, if revelation has brought him to the Stage of Unity, this is called the True Light, since there is no veiling or concealment afterwards.

425 RUST
Whatever has been precipitated on the Heart, as for example the murky darkness of the characteristics of the Self and the forms of existence. These obscure one's capacity for the realities and the irradiations of the lights. This is assuming that the condition has not yet crystallised. If crystallisation has reached the limit of exclusion

and total concealment, then it is called Possession, which is described below.*

426 THE THUNDERCLAP
The annihilation in Truth through the illumination of the Essence.

427 THE ELITE
Those who have verified purity, as opposed to the cloudiness of unreality.

428 THE IMAGE OF TRUTH
This is Muhammad, by virtue of his verification of the reality of oneness and the one. It may also be expressed by the letter Ṣād, as was indicated by Ibn Abbas.* When he was asked about the meaning of that letter, he said: 'A mountain at Mecca where the throne of the Merciful was situated.'

429 THE IMAGE OF GOD
The Perfected Man, who has verified the realities of the Divine Names.

430 THE CELLS OF REMEMBRANCE
The divine states and the abodes of spirituality which safeguard the commemorator from being separated from the One he is commemorating and which concentrate his aspiration entirely on him.

431 SAFEGUARDING THE WILL
This is when the Self ceases to see anything take place which is not the will of God. It means experiencing everything that happens as being the will of Sublime Truth.

LETTER QAF

432 THE FIRST TENDENCY
The Source of Sources. It is also the Primary Individuation.

433 THE TENDENCY TOWARDS MANIFESTATION
This is the initial love indicated in God's words: '... and I loved to be known.'*

434 THE TWO BOW-LENGTHS
This is the stage of the relatedness of the Names in terms of the contrast between the Names in the divine command known as the circle of existence. For example, initiating and repeating, descending and ascending, active and receptive. It is the union with Truth, whilst retaining distinction and dualism. This has been described as Connectedness. There is no higher stage than this, except the Stage of 'Even Nearer' which is oneness in the very midst of the Union of the Essence – described in God's words,

'... or even nearer.'*

There, in place of a high degree of subjective distinction and duality, there is pure annihilation and the total effacement of all forms.

435 SETTING OUT FOR GOD
This means to awaken from the sleep of heedlessness, to arise from idle slumber and start out on the journey to God.

436 ARISING WITHIN GOD
This is uprightness in the Permanence which follows Annihilation and the traversing of all the Stations. It is the journey from God to God within God, by divesting oneself of the forms in their totality.

437 CONTRACTION

takes hold of the Heart, as has been mentioned in connection with those things which oppress it, such as rejection, loneliness, etc. This has been mentioned in passing as the counterpart of Expansiveness.* Contraction mostly occurs after Expansiveness, as a consequence of the bad conduct of the seeker while he is in the latter state. The difference between this pair and that of fear and hope is that the latter are associated with anticipated desire and repulsion in the Stage of the Self. Contraction and Expansiveness, however, are linked to the present moment and not to the future.

438 THE FOOT

This is the precedence by virtue of which Truth holds eternal sway over the devotee. It especially applies to the means by which Truth fulfils and completes the preparations for the final gift to him.

In the words of the Prophet, 'Hell keeps on saying, "Are there any more?", until the Almighty brings his foot down on it, and it calls out, "O my back, my back!"' However, what is alluded to here by the word *Foot* is the fact that the foot is the last part of any form; thus it is the last of the Names to which Truth exposes the devotee; and if the latter becomes attached to it and verifies its reality, he will be perfected.

439 THE SURE FOOTING

This is the beautiful precedence and the ample gift that was commanded by Truth Most High for his upright and faithful servants. In his own exalted words: '... and give thou good tidings to the believers that they have a sure footing with their Lord.'* The word 'sure' here means the best of all.

440 NEARNESS

An expression for the fulfilment of a pledge, previously made in the earliest time, between Truth and the individual, as is shown in his exalted words: '"Am I not your Lord?" They said, "Yes, indeed!"'* The term may also refer to the Stage of Two Bow-lengths.*

441 THE SHELL

This refers to any outer knowledge which protects inner knowledge, which is the kernel, from corruption – as in the case of Holy Law

protecting the Sufi Path, and the Path protecting Reality. If someone does not guard his state and his path by means of Holy Law, then it will become corrupted and his path will lead him into confusion, causing him to wander and stumble, a prey to suggestion. Likewise, anyone who does not fervently seek by means of the Path to arrive at Reality, and who has not safeguarded the latter by means of the former, will find that his reality has been corrupted; and this will lead him to heresy and atheism.

442 **THE POLE-STAR**
The locus of God's sight throughout the world and throughout all time. He is in the mould of the angel Isrāfīl.*

443 **THE MAJOR POLE-STAR**
This is the rank of the Pole of Poles – the esoteric aspect of the prophecy of Muhammad, which is the exclusive property of his heirs. This is due to the Prophet's unique brand of perfection: no one may become the Seal of the Saints and the Pole of Poles, except by virtue of the inner aspect of the Seal of Prophethood.

444 **THE HEART**
An incorporeal, luminous substance located midway between the Spirit and the Self. It is the means by which humanity verifies reality, and sages call it the Rational Soul. Its inner aspect is the spirit, while its vehicle and external aspect is the animal soul, which mediates between heart and body. Thus in the Qur'an it is likened to a crystal and a shining star. In God's words:

> The likeness of his light is as a niche
> Wherein is a lamp
> The lamp in a glass,
> The glass as it were a glittering star
> Kindled from a blessed tree,
> An olive that is neither of the east nor of the west.*

The tree is the Self, the niche is the body, which is the centre of existence, and the levels of revelation are the likeness in the world of the Preserved Tablet.*

445 RESTRAINTS

Anything which restrains a human being from the requirements of nature, the Self and desire, and which keeps him away from these things. They also refer to the help given by the Names and the assistance given by God to the People of Providence on the journey towards God.

446 RESURRECTION

Resurrection into eternal life after death may be divided into three types. The first is the resurrection, following physical death, into a life within either the higher or the lower Intermediate Worlds, depending on the state of the dead person during his life on earth.* For as the Prophet said:

> 'As you live, so shall you die; and as you die, so shall you be resurrected.'

This is the Minor Resurrection, as is indicated in the words of the Prophet: 'When someone dies, his resurrection has already taken place.'

The second is the resurrection, after voluntary death, into the eternal life of the Heart in the Holy World. As it has been said: 'He who dies a voluntary death will live out his natural life.'* This is the Intermediate Resurrection, referred to in God's words:

> Can he who was dead, to whom we gave life,
> And a light whereby to walk amongst men,
> Be like him who is in the depths of darkness,
> From which he can never come out?'*

The third is the resurrection, after annihilation in God, into the life of reality, whilst enduring within Truth. This is the Major Resurrection, which is indicated in God's words: 'Then, when the great catastrophe comes...'*

LETTER RĀ'

447 THE SHEPHERD
This is someone who has verified the wisdom of the science of administration – someone capable of managing the organisation which is necessary for the welfare of the world.

448 POSSESSION
The veil that screens the Heart from the Holy World when it is taken over by sensual states and the darkness of the body, in such a way that the light of divinity becomes totally obscured.

449 THE LORD
A name for the Truth, seen from the standpoint of the relationship of the Essence to really existing things, whether they are spirits or physical bodies. The relationship between the Essence and the Established Essences is the starting point of various Divine Names such as the Capable and the Aspirant; and its connection with the physical world is the origin of the Names of Lordship such as the Provider and the Protector.

   The Name of the Lord, therefore, is a special one, which logically implies the existence of a subordinate who will affirm it, and that of God implies the establishment and individuation of that subordinate. Everything that becomes visible in the universe is a form of the Name of the Lord, which is nurtured by Truth, who takes hold of and does what he does with it; while it turns for its needs to Truth, and he is the one who provides it with whatever is asked of him.

450 THE LORD OF LORDS
This is Truth, seen from the viewpoint of the Greatest Name and the Primary Individuation, which is the starting point of all the Names,

and is the ultimate goal. To him are directed all desires, and he is the focus of all seekers. It is to this that his exalted words refer: '... and that the final end is unto thy Lord.'* The Prophet is the embodiment of the Primary Individuation; so the lordship that is his particular province is the Major Lordship.

451 CLASSES OF THE NAMES
There are three of these: Essential, Qualitative and Functional. When the name is applied to the Essence from the standpoint of derivation and individuation, then the standpoint is either a purely relative, inconsequential matter, like the Independent, the First, or the Last; or else it is not relative, like the Most Holy, or the Salvation. This class is entitled the Names of the Essence.

Alternatively, it has an existential meaning, which is viewed by the mind without it exceeding the Essence, or going beyond the scope of the mind, for that would be absurd. Either it does not depend on the understanding of others, like the Living, or the Necessary, or else it is dependent on the understanding of others without their existence, like the Knowing, or the Capable. These are called the Qualitative Names.

Finally it may depend upon the existence of other things, like the Creator, or the Maintainer; and these are called the Functional Names, because they are the source of actions.

452 BINDING
The unified totality of substance known as the major binding of the absolute element prior to the creation of the heavens and the earth. Loosening took place after their individuation within creation.*

This term may also be applied to the relationships of the Presence of the One, taking into consideration its non-manifestation. Indeed it may be applied to anything inward and invisible, like the realities concealed in the Essence of Oneness, before its elaboration in the Presence of the One – like the tree latent in the date stone.

453 THE COMPASSIONATE
A name for Truth, seen from the standpoint of the Names which are in the Divine Presence, and from which existence, and the perfections appertaining to it, flow out in abundance into all potentialities.

454 THE MERCIFUL
A name for Truth, seen in terms of the flood of spiritual perfections – such as wisdom and unity – which pour down upon the people of faith.

455 GRATEFUL COMPASSION
Compassion which is the consequence of past blessings in the work, and it embraces everything.

456 OBLIGATORY COMPASSION
The compassion promised to the devout and the charitable. In the words of God:

> '... and I shall prescribe it for those who are godfearing.'*

and:

> ' – surely the mercy of God is nigh to those who do good.'*

This is contained within the term Grateful Compassion, because the promise of it to the worker is the purest kindness.

457 THE MANTLE
This is the manifestation in an individual of the qualities of Truth.

458 RUIN
This is when an individual declares the attributes of Truth to be false. God says: 'I shall turn from my signs those who wax proud on earth unjustly.'* It is derived from the word meaning to perish, and hence means destruction. God Most High said: 'Grandeur is my cloak and Majesty my loincloth; and if anyone disputes with me for either of them, I will shatter him.'

459 FORM
This is creation and its attributes, because forms are traces, and for everything other than God, its traces are a result of its actions. This is what the writer meant who said, 'Form is a description taking place in Eternity-without-end of what took place in Eternity-without-beginning.' For created things and all their attributes exist by the decree of God.

A GLOSSARY OF SUFI TECHNICAL TERMS

460 THE FORMS OF COGNITION AND THEIR MARKS
These are the five senses of the human being. They are forms of the Divine Names, such as the Knower, the Hearer, the Seer, which have manifested themselves in the veils of the bodily frame – idly waiting at the threshold of resolution, midway between Truth and Creation. Thus, if anyone discovers that his own Self and all its characteristics are merely traces of the Truth, its qualities and the forms of its Names and its images – such a person has discovered the Truth.

461 FRIVOLITY
Coming to a standstill at the pleasures of the Self and the demands of its nature.

462 DELICACY
This is spiritual subtlety. It may also be applied to the subtle medium that connects two things together, like assistance arriving from the Truth to the devotee, in which case it is called the delicacy of descent – or else like the means by which the devotee approaches Truth, through knowledge, deeds, correct morality, and the attainment of elevated Stages; and in this case it is called the delicacy of ascent or elevation.

Alternatively, delicacy may be applied to the science of the Way and the science of conduct, and everything conducive to the subtle refinement of the Secret Faculty in the individual and the eradication of the coarseness of the Self.

463 THE SPIRIT
In popular usage, this is the incorporeal human subtlety. In the parlance of physicians it is the subtle vapour produced in the heart which is susceptible to the life energy, sense perception and movement. This they call the Self. Those in between, who are able to understand the universal and the particular, call it the Heart. The sages, however, do not make a distinction between the Heart and the primary Spirit, and they refer to it as the Rational Soul.

464 THE GREATEST SPIRIT, THE OLDEST, THE FIRST AND THE LAST
The Primal Intellect.

LETTER RĀ'

465 THE SPIRIT OF INSPIRATION
The one who communicates to the Heart the knowledge of hidden things. It refers to the angel Gabriel, and may also be applied to the Qur'an, as is indicated by God's words:

> 'Exalter of ranks is he, possessor of the throne, casting the spirit of his bidding upon whomever he will of his servants.'*

466 TESTIMONY
The influence which presents itself to the Heart as a result of contemplation. It is that which attests for him that he has genuinely been favoured in his contemplative vision – either with intuitive knowledge, which he did not possess until then, or else with Ecstasy, the Mystical State, Illumination, or the Vision of God.

467 THE GATHERING OF DIVISION
The unifying of distinctions through the ascent from the Presence of the One to the Presence of Oneness. Its opposite is the Division of Gathering, which is the descent from Oneness to the One, the State of Permanence after Annihilation in the summons to perfection.

468 ROVING
This is an expression of movement. The watermill is called 'wayward' because of the frequent gyrations of the millstone. People also say the water 'strayed' from the river if it floods its banks, due to excess of water and the narrowness of the river. In traditional Sufi parlance, however, it refers to the movements caused by the Secret Faculties of ecstatics, when their rapture is so powerful that it overflows the vessel of their preparedness.

469 THE EVEN NUMBER
This is creation. The oath '... by the even and the odd,' is sworn because the Divine Names become verified through creation, so that whatever does not combine the even number of the Presence of the One with the odd number of the Presence of Oneness will not manifest the Divine Names.*

470 THE VISION OF GOD
The sight of Truth by Truth.

471 THE VISION OF THE PARTICULAR IN THE UNIVERSAL
Contemplating multiplicity in the Essence of Oneness.

472 THE VISION OF THE UNIVERSAL IN THE PARTICULAR
Contemplating Oneness in multiplicity.

473 THE EVIDENCE OF TRUTH
These are the realities of the worlds, for they bear witness to the Creator.

474 THE EVIDENCE OF UNITY
These are the individuations of things, because everything has its own individuation of Oneness, which makes it distinct from other things. As it has been said, 'In everything he has a sign showing that he is one.'

475 THE EVIDENCE OF THE NAMES
The diversity of various beings in terms of states, characteristics and functions. Thus, for example, the Prosperous bears witness to the Provider, the Living to the Quickener, the Dead to the Fatal, etc.

476 MATTERS
Actions.

477 ESSENTIAL MATTERS
The viewpoint that the emblems of the essences and the realities are in the Essence of Oneness: just as the tree, its branches, leaves, flowers and fruit – are all in the seed. It is these which become manifest in the Presence of Oneness, and which become differentiated through the written word.*

478 THE MASTER
The Perfected Man in the science of Holy Law, the science of the Path, and the science of Reality. In all of these he has attained the utmost degree of perfection, through his knowledge of the evils of

the various selves, their maladies and ailments – and through his knowledge of how to treat them, and his ability to cure them and undertake their guidance – providing the Self is willing and amenable to being so guided.

LETTER TĀ'

479 TĀ'
This letter stands for the Essence, seen from the viewpoint of specific individuations and multiplicity.

480 FAMILIARISATION
This is illumination in external sensory perception, familiarising the novice seeker with purification and refinement. It is called Practical Illumination, because it takes the form of images of ways and means.

481 ILLUMINATION
The lights of the invisible world, manifesting in the Heart.*

482 PRIMARY ILLUMINATION
This is the Essential Illumination, and the illumination of the Essence by and for itself.

It refers to the Presence of Oneness, which has neither properties nor form, since the Essence is the pure existence of Truth, whose unity is precisely itself. For anything apart from existence, seen in terms of existence, is nothing other than absolute non-existence – which is pure nothingness. So, having its own unity, it has no need of any particular unity or specific individuality to distinguish it from anything else, since there is nothing there in the first place from which to differentiate itself. Thus its unity is, precisely, its essence.

This unity is the source both of Oneness and the One, because it is identical with the Essence, in the sense that it is completely unconditional. In other words, the absolute, which by its nature includes the condition that nothing is included with it, is in fact Oneness; whilst that which carries the condition that something must be included with it is the One. The realities of the Essence of Oneness

are like the tree latent in the seed, which is the most hidden of hidden things.

83 SECONDARY ILLUMINATION
This is the means by which emerge the Established Essences of the Potentialities, which are the concern of the Essence of God Most High himself, and that is the Primary Individuation, with its universal quality and capacity. For the Essences are the first information concerning this, and the individuality which is the vehicle of visionary illumination. In this illumination, Truth descends from the Presence of Oneness to the Presence of the One by means of the relationship of the Names.

84 VISIONARY ILLUMINATION
The manifestation of the presence that is known by the Name of 'The Light'. It is also the manifestation of the Truth in the forms of God's Names in the worlds which are its forms. And that manifestation is the Breath of the Merciful, by which everything is brought into being.

85 VERIFICATION
The vision of Truth in the forms of its Names, which are the worlds and the Essences, in such a way that the verifier is neither veiled by the Truth from creation, nor by creation from the Truth.

86 SUFISM
The acquisition of the Divine Qualities.*

87 CHANGE
This refers to the veiling of the properties of an exalted mystical state or stage by the effects of a lowly state or stage – and to the gradual disappearance of this condition. The final result is the change, in the stage of the comprehensive irradiation of the illuminations of the Divine Names, in the state of Permanence after Annihilation.

Ibn Arabi said: 'According to us, this is the most perfect of the Stages; whilst to most others it is an incomplete stage.' This is because what he meant by Change is Separation after Union, in which the multiplicity of the separation does not veil the oneness of union: and that is the Stage of Oneness of Separation after Union,

and the revelation of the real meaning of God's words: 'Every day he is upon some labour.'* There is no doubt that this is the highest of the Stages, and according to the Sufis it is the highest degree of authority.

As for the change which is the last of the changes, it is at the beginning of Separation after Union, when the creator becomes veiled, through the manifestation of the effects of multiplicity, from the properties of Unity.

LETTER KHĀ'

IDEA
Any kind of message which occurs to the Heart; alternatively something which arrives without any conscious effort on the part of the individual. Such messages may be divided into four types:

Divine Idea – the first of the ideas, called by Sahl 'the first cause' and 'the piercing of the mind'. It is known as the force or influence, and is something which does not plunge impulsively into things.

Angelic Idea – the prompting to whatever has been recommended or decreed, in short, to everything that is righteous. It is known as inspiration.

Selfish Idea – everything which concerns the pleasures of the Self. It is known as impulse.

Satanic Idea – whatever prompts the contradiction of the Truth. God Most High says: 'Satan threatens you with poverty and bids you unto indecency.'* And the Prophet said: 'The call of Satan is the denial of Truth and the threat of evil.' This is known as temptation.

According to the yardstick of Holy Law, it is expressed thus: whatever shows nearness to Truth belongs to the former two groups, and whatever shows an aversion to Truth or a contradiction of Holy Law belongs to the latter two. It is like a secret conversation, in which anything tending to contradict the Self forms part of the first groups, while anything tending towards desire and the convenience of the Self forms part of the latter ones. For the truthful and the pure of heart, in the presence of Truth, it is easy to tell the difference between the two tendencies – through the resources and assistance of God.

THE SEAL
Someone who has crossed all of the Stages and reached the extremity

of perfection; and it is in this sense that the seal proliferates and multiplies.

490 THE SEAL OF PROPHECY
The person through whom God has set a seal on the prophethood. There is only one such person, namely our Prophet Muhammad.

491 THE SEAL OF THE SAINTS
The person through whom the welfare of this world and the next is attained to perfection. When he dies, the whole order of the universe is disturbed. He is the Rightly Guided One, the *Mahdi*, the one who is promised at the end of time.

492 THE PATCHED ROBE OF SUFISM
This is what the disciple puts on from the hand of his master, who enters his will and enables him to gain forgiveness. There are a number of reasons for this. Firstly, by wearing the garment of intent, he is inwardly enveloped in the Master's qualities, just as outwardly he is clothed in his mantle, which is the garment of comfort, both inwardly and outwardly. God Most High said:

> 'Children of Adam! We have bestowed a garment on you to cover your shame, and for adornment: but the garment of righteousness – that is the best.'*

A second reason is to receive the Master's blessing, in that he clothes the pupil with his own blessed hands. Another reason is to acquire the particular mystical state dominating the Master at the moment of investiture, in which he sees with penetrating vision, illuminated by the Sacred Light, what it is that the disciple needs in order to raise the obstructing veils and adjust himself in preparation. For if the Master comes to know the state of the one who repents in his hands, then he knows by the light of Truth what he needs. So he brings this down from God, until his heart is imbued with it, and it emanates from his inwardness to the inwardness of his pupil. Yet another purpose is the link forged by the robe between the student and the Master, so that there will always remain a contact of hearts and an affection between them, constantly reminding the former to follow the path, the customs, the character and the states of the latter. Thus the Master is a true father to him. As the Prophet said,

'Fathers are of three kinds: the father who gave you birth, the father who taught you, and the father who brought you up.'

3 KHIDR, THE GREEN ONE
Khidr stands for Expansiveness and Elias for Contraction.* As for the question whether Khidr is a human individual who has been alive since the time of Moses, or a spiritual being, who assumes the form of whoever is guided by him, this is something which I have not verified. However, it would seem that the concept of Khidr is assimilated in the form of one of his dominant attributes, which then disappears and becomes the spirit of that person. Alternatively, it is the Holy Spirit.

4 COMPULSION
This is a call summoning the devotee to his Lord in such a way that he is unable to resist its bidding.

5 SINCERE FRIENDSHIP
The verification by the devotee of the qualities of Truth. He becomes so permeated with the Truth that he will not relinquish any of its qualities. Such an individual thus becomes a mirror of the Truth.

6 SECLUSION
This is the secret dialogue with Truth, in which one does not see anything other than that. This is the reality and meaning of seclusion. As for the form it takes: it is a fervent plea for this condition, while secluding oneself for God and cutting oneself off from others.

7 THE RENUNCIATION OF HABITS
This is the verification of the reality of service in accordance with the command of Truth, so that nothing prompts one to heed the call of one's own nature and habits.

8 RENEWED CREATION
This is the connection of the support of existence, through the Breath of the Merciful, with every contingent thing. This is due to the essential non-existence of the latter, when viewed apart from its sustainer, or the abundance of existence incessantly pouring into it, so that at every instant it becomes a new creation. This is because of

variations, with the passage of time, in the relationship between creation and itself, and the persistence of its own essential non-existence.

LETTER DHĀL

99 THE TREASURES OF GOD
The tribe of God's friends, through whom he staves off tribulation from his servants, just as treasure is used to stave off poverty.

100 TASTING
This refers to the first steps of the vision of Truth, during the successive flashes which are minor traces of the illumination known as Lightning. If this is increased and reaches the intermediate stage of the vision, it is called Drinking; while if it reaches the conclusion, it is called Quenching. All of this depends on keeping the Secret Faculty pure from the glance of others.

101 THE MAN OF REASON
Someone who sees creation externally and Truth internally, so that for him Truth is the mirror of creation. For the mirror is obscured by the external image appearing in it and veiling the absolute with the limited.

102 THE MAN OF INSIGHT
Someone who sees Truth externally and creation internally, so that for him creation is the mirror of Truth. This is due to the appearance for him of Truth and the disappearance in it of creation – like the disappearance of the mirror because of the image.

103 THE MAN OF REASON AND INSIGHT
Someone who sees Truth in creation and creation in Truth, without either of them being veiled by the other; rather he sees one existence in its reality – as Truth from one point of view, and as creation from another. Thus he is not veiled by multiplicity from witnessing the

face of the One and Only in its Essence. Nor does he have any difficulty contemplating the multiplicity of the manifestations of the Oneness of the Essence, by which he is illuminated. Similarly, he is not veiled by the Oneness of the face of Truth from witnessing the multiplicity of created things; neither does he have any trouble witnessing the Oneness of the Essence revealing itself in the manifestation of multiplicity. The perfected Master, Ibn Arabi, referred to the foregoing three ranks in these words:

> So in creation lies the essence of Truth
> If you are a man of insight;
> And in Truth lies the essence of creation
> If you are a man of reason;
> But if you were a man of insight and of reason,
> Then you could not help but see:
> The essence and the form of a thing are one.

LETTER ḌĀD

04 THE SPECIAL ONES
There are special people among the people of God, whom he holds back because they are so precious to him. As the Prophet said:

> 'Among God's creation there are the special ones, whom he clothes in brilliant light and causes to live and die in prosperity.'

05 SPLENDOUR
Seeing things with the eye of Truth – the Essence of Truth.

LETTER ẒĀ'

506 THE EXTERNAL ASPECT OF CONTINGENT PHENOMENA
This is the manifestation of Truth in the forms of its essences and qualities. It is what has been called secondary existence. It may also be referred to as the outward aspect of existence.

507 THE SHADOW
This is the secondary existence that is apparent in the individuation and properties of the contingent essences. The latter are non-existent entities that only become apparent by virtue of the Name of the Light, which is the external existence that has been attributed to them and which veils the darkness of their non-existence. Thus the external light reflected from their forms becomes a shadow; since the appearance of a shadow is due to the presence of light. God Most High says:

> 'Hast thou not regarded thy Lord, how he has stretched out the shadows?'*

In other words: how he extended secondary existence for the contingencies. So darkness, in contrast to this kind of light, is non-existence, and every darkness is an expression of the absence of any light coming from something which by its nature ought to be lit up. That is why godlessness is called darkness: due to the absence of the light of belief in the heart of a human being, who ought by his nature to be enlightened. God Most High says:

> 'God is the protector of the believers; he brings them forth from the shadows into the light.'*

98 THE FIRST SHADOW
This is the Primal Intellect, because it is the first essence that appeared in God's light and received the form of multiplicity which is the concern of the Oneness of the Essence.

99 THE SHADOW OF GOD
This is the Perfected Man, who has verified the reality of the Presence of the One.

LETTER GHAĪN

510 THE CROW
This stands for the universal body, because it is at the utmost distance from the Sacred World and the Presence of Oneness, and because it is devoid of consciousness and luminosity. It is given this name because the crow is the symbol of remoteness and darkness.

511 THE FILM AND THE VEIL
Whatever covers the mirror of the Heart with rust and dulls the eye of insight, spreading over the face of its mirror.

512 WEALTH
Complete dominion. For the wealth of the Essence is none other than Truth, since to this belongs the essence of everything. The wealthy among the devotees is someone who through Truth has become independent of everything else. For if he is successful with the existence of Truth, he will succeed with everything. Not only that: he pays no heed to transient existence, but simply gains his desire and rejoices in the contemplation of his Beloved.

513 THE HELPER
This refers to the Pole-star, at a time when he is being sought as a refuge. He is not called this except at such a time.*

514 THE MYSTERY OF THE ESSENTIAL IDENTITY
This is the Essence of Truth, from the standpoint of non-individuation.

515 THE HIDDEN MYSTERY AND THE GUARDED MYSTERY
This is the secret of the Essence and its innermost nature, which is

known to none apart from itself. That is why it is guarded from others, hidden from their minds as well as their sight.

516 THE ERROR WHICH FALLS SHORT OF POSSESSION*

This is the Rust which is mentioned above. For rust is a thin veil that is made visible through purification and eliminated through the light of illumination resulting from an enduring faith. As for Possession, this is a thick veil that forms an obstacle between the Heart and the belief in Truth. The error consists in being distracted from the vision of Truth, and being veiled from it, despite the correctness of one's conviction.

NOTES ON THE TRANSLATION

Numbers refer to entries in the Glossary.

References to the Qur'an are given in the format Q N1.N2, *where* N1 *is the chapter or* sura *number, and* N2 *is the verse or* aya *number.*

Introduction
    conventional scientific research: in Qashani's day this referred exclusively to Islamic theology and jurisprudence.
    second part: unfortunately we only have the first part of Qashani's work at our disposal – the *Glossary of Sufi Technical Terms*.
1 In Sufi thought a distinction is made between Eternity-without-end (*abad*) and Eternity-without-beginning (*azal*). Cf. entry 25.
4 Cf. entry 82.
5 Dr Kamal Ja'far merges this with the previous entry, so that it reads: 'When Oneness is considered, all other considerations are dropped.' Cf. entry 81.
7 Q.23.10.
8 *evolution*: the Arabic for 'state' (*Hal*) derives from a root meaning to evolve or be transformed. Hence the word-association in Qashani's definition, which has to be underlined, since the force of the English term is – static. This is a recurring problem when translating between languages as diverse as English and Arabic.
9 *devotee*: this word ('*abd*. servant or slave) is scattered profusely throughout the text. Like its Persian counterpart (*banda*) it frequently means no more than 'a person', 'an individual', 'one' (especially in the genteel usage meaning 'I'). One has consequently felt free to render it in a variety of ways.
    . . . *as if you saw him*: a reference to the Prophet Muhammad's injunction, 'Worship God as if you saw him'.
15 The '*technical term*' itself seems to have fallen by the wayside.
16 *The Heights*: This is the title of Sura 7 of the Qur'an.

And on the heights...: Q.7.46. There are several interpretations of this passage (See Yusuf Ali, op. cit. note 1025). The Heights (or battlements, or ramparts) are seen by some as a kind of purgatory, whose denizens, while not yet in paradise itself, are nonetheless able from their relatively elevated spiritual vantage point to survey both heaven and earth and discern which of the approaching travellers are destined to be 'Companions of the Garden'.

17 *Steingass* (see Bibliography) has: 'Figures emblematic of the names of God'.
18 *Pole-star*: see entry 442.
20 *presence*: the Arabic concept (*ḥaḍra*), used frequently throughout the text, is altogether richer, with undertones of majesty and dominion.
21 It is unfortunately not possible to feel confident that we have unravelled the ambiguity of this entry. The Arabic letters *mlk* may be read variously as 'property', 'dominion', 'kings', or 'angel', according to which diacritical points are added. None of the manuscripts agree.
24 Traditionally the 'Mother of the Book' refers either to the first Sura of the Qur'an, or else to the eternal archetype, from which the physical Qur'an is said to derive.
31 *individuation*: this concept (*ta'yīn*), which is used liberally throughout the book, has given us much to think about. We have variously rendered it as 'specification', 'individuation', 'instantiation', 'instance', 'elaboration', etc. The notion seems close to that of the emergence from the (Platonic) World of Ideas into the World of Appearances, subject to space, time and number.
39 Literally 'interval' (*barzakh*): this is traditionally thought to lie between death and resurrection.
41 Dr Kamal's version merges the next two entries into one.
Contraction cf. 437.
Hidden Centre (*khafa'*): a reference to one of the 'subtleties', or higher functions of the mind. Cf. Shah: *The Sufis, The Perfumed Scorpion*; also Shah Waliullah: *The Sacred Knowledge*.
58 *Creation* (*khalq*) also implies the creatures within it – especially people, humanity. In Sufi thought the term is frequently balanced and contrasted with Truth.
67 Q.42.13.
68 Cf. 422.
71 Traditionally the third person masculine pronoun (*hu*) refers to God.
78 Cf. 45
79 *Primordial matter* (*hayuli*): cf. the Aristotelian term *hyle*.
81 (also 82) Cf. entries 4 and 5.
86 Cf. 469.
90 Q.2.115.

92 *Preserved Tablet*: Q.85.22. This refers either to the Mother of the Book (see note on entry 24) or, more generally, a record held in Eternity of the transactions of mankind.
Clear book: Q.6.59.
99 Q.7.172.
strength and power: an extremely common exclamation in the Muslim world is, 'There is no power and no strength save in God.'
101 The text uses two closely related terms for 'time': *waqt* is rendered as '*moment of time*', and *zaman* (entry 110) as '*duration of time*'.
105 Q.7.196.
108 Q.24.35.
115 Q.2.33.
117 ... *such screening entities*: not found in Sprenger.
118 Ibn-Arabi, *Manazil al Insaniya (Stations of Humanity)*. The quotation is garbled in the Sprenger edition, so we have followed Dr Kamal Ja'far.
127 Q.2.269.
143 Q.38.75. Note that some of the names given in this entry are not described elsewhere in the text.
145 *Clear Book*: Q 6.59.
Preserved Tablet: Q.85.22.
Cf. entry 92.
148 Q.16.40. Cf. Q.3.47 and Q.36.82.
152 Q.6.76. This famous verse continues '... and (Abraham) said, "This is my Lord." But when it set, he said, "I do not love those that set."'
154 *Alchemy of Happiness*: this is also the title of a brilliant work by al-Ghazzali.
160 Presumably 'former Stage' refers to the *Kernel* (159) and 'the latter' to the *Kernel of Kernels*.
161 Q.6.9. The context is given in the opening words of the previous verse: 'They (the unbelievers) say: "Why is not an angel sent down to him?"' The nub of the argument is that for humanity to be able to perceive an angel, the latter would have to come in the guise of a human being; and then, as Yusuf Ali points out in his commentary, '... they would say: "We wanted to see an angel, and we have only seen a man!"' The Arabic root of the headword for this entry (*LBS*), which figures prominently in the quotation from the Qur'an, has an interesting spectrum of meanings: to clothe, cloak, obscure, confuse.
166 Cf. entries 92 and 145.
167 '*Umar*: second Caliph of Islam.
168 *common sense*: the Arabic retains what the English has lost – the notion of a sense which unifies the other five outward senses.

169 *The Night of Power* ('... better than a thousand months!' – Q.97.3) is traditionally located in the holy month of Ramadan. Some specify it as the night of the 27th (the night of the 'descent' of the Qur'an); whilst others say that the precise date in unknown and thus only the alert will benefit from it.
175 This entry is missing from Sprenger's edition.
179 *Even Nearer*: a reference to Q.53.9, where it is said (presumably of the Archangel Gabriel) that he '... was at a distance of two bow-lengths, or even nearer'. See entries for 278 and 434.
181 Cf. 434.
187 *theoretical knowledge*: theology and jurisprudence.
189 *but God threw*: Q.8.17. At the battle of Badr, in which the Muslim forces were greatly outnumbered, the Prophet Muhammad threw a handful of dust at the enemy, which, as Yusuf Ali comments, was 'symbolical of their rushing blindly to their fate', and it '... had a great psychological effect'.
Three men conspire...: Q.58.7.
They are unbelievers...: Q.5.76. An allusion to the Nicene doctrine of the Trinity.
191 *Audience (muhadara)*: Steingass glosses that as 'a degree of mystic contemplation of the Deity'. It is also the standard Arabic for 'lecture'.
196 *five Manifestations*: see entry 179.
200 *Secret Faculty (sirr)*: see Shah, *The Sufis*, p. 295–299; also Shah Waliullah of Delhi, *The Sacred Knowledge*, Chapter 5.
206 Q.57.22. The complete verse runs: 'No misfortune can happen on earth, or in your souls, but it is recorded in a decree.'
207 Steingass glosses 'victory' (*fath*) as 'Divine Grace bestowed on those advanced in Sacred knowledge'.
215 Q.2.33.
217 *Contingent Essences (al-A'yan al-Mumkinat)*: this phrase is listed by Steingass as 'the most excellent of creatures'.
218 *Basic Root*: this is also a standard term for the triliteral (occasionally quadriliteral) radical consonants, from which the vast majority of Arabic words are formed.
223 Q.54.55.
232 Q.20.135.
234 *prostration*: i.e. to Adam.
235 *Plato*: the inference to be made from this remark is that a life given over to the senses is not 'natural' for humanity.
... Now turn in repentance...: Q.2.54.
He who was dead...: Q.6.122.

238 *May I fare as well with you . . .*: the poet's 'enemies' were instrumental in his self-realisation.
244 Q.24.35 (the Light Verse). The word 'self' (*nafs*) in Arabic and arabised languages has vastly more reverberations than it does in English; so it has often seemed necessary throughout the text to emphasise it by such devices as 'his own self', rather than simply letting it be weakly assimilated as the mere reflexive pronoun 'himself'.
245 Q.12.53.
246 Q.75.2.
247 Q.89.27.
255 Q.68.1.
258 Q.10.2.
266 Q.53.14: '. . . *the Lote tree, beyond which none may pass.*' An image of the last stunted vestiges of vegetation and shade before the desert proper begins. A metaphor for the Intermediary World (see 39 & 40) between death and resurrection.
267 Q.16.40. Cf. Q.3.47 and Q.36.82.
276 The full Tradition runs: 'I have a time with God when neither any prophet sent by God nor any angel set near to God is able to encompass me.'
278 *Journeys*: Cf. 250–3.
Even nearer: Cf. entries 179 and 434.
282 *Blackness of face*: a metaphor for extreme poverty.
284 Steingass glosses this as 'the highest heaven'.
290 *Very hateful . . .*: Q.61.3.
Will you bid others . . .: Q.2.44.
292 The following 99 entries, which describe the characteristics of Servants of God, may help to explain the popularity among the Muslims of proper names of the format '*Abd al-* (+ one of the 'ninety-nine' names of God).
There are in fact more than ninety-nine in common use, so we may take the term to mean 'quite a large number'. Many of the definitions throughout the Glossary involve the extensive use of cognate words, a feature which is virtually impossible to sustain in translation. This is especially true of the entries on the Servants of God. For example, the short section 356 contains no fewer than eight words based around the root *QWM*.
293 Q.72.19.
305 Q.67.3.
334 Q.82.6.
337 Q.2.186.
348 *. . . and he takes . . .*: Q.7.196.
God is the protector . . .: Q.2.257.
367 Q.55.26.

371 Q.20.114.
372 Q.2.177.
374 Q.24.2.
381 *implicitly in the language of potential*: i.e. his deeds and his being are themselves the only prayer he needs to utter.
383 Q.2.216.
385 Q.24.35.
390 Q.21.51.
396 Q.13.2.
397 Steingass glosses that as follows: '... known as to name but unknown as to body; hence anything scarce, rare, wonderful, difficult or impossible to be got.'
398 Without an entry like this, no dictionary would be complete.
400 Cf. entry 17.
402 Note that the Arabic for 'eye' (*'ain*), which is used with great frequency throughout Qashani's text, can also mean 'essence'. Other meanings are: well, spring, best part, individual, self, important person, cash, property, and the name of a letter in the alphabet. In short, it is not an easy word to translate.
Greater Interval: cf. 40.
404 Standard Arabic for a holy festival.
405 Cf. 452.
407 Q.61.13.
408 Q.48.1.
409 Q.110.1.
419 *thusness (fahuanīya)*; Derived from *fa huwa*, which Steingass gives as 'indeed, but it is'.
421 *Jābir*, an early Sufi, often known in western writings as Geber the Alchemist.
422 Cf. 68.
423 Q.4.69.
425 Cf. 448.
428 Letter *Ṣād* being the initial letter of the word *Ṣadiq* – true, genuine.
433 Cf. 249.
434 Q.53.9. Cf. entry 179.
437 Cf. entry 41.
439 Q.10.2.
440 Q.7.172. Cf. 434.
442 *Isrāfīl*, the angel of death, who is to blow the trump of doom.
444 Q.24.35 (the Light Verse).
Preserved Tablet: Q.85.22.

125

446 *voluntary death*: Cf. the Prophet Muhammad's famous admonition: 'Die before you die'. The implication is 'dying to the world'.
Can he who was dead...: Q.6.122.
...the great catastrophe... Q.79.34.
450 Q.54.42.
452 Cf. 405.
456 *...and I shall prescribe...*: Q.7.156.
surely the mercy of God...: Q.7.56.
458 Q.7.146.
465 Q.40.15.
469 Q.89.2. Cf. entry 86.
477 *the written word*: Manuscripts vary, between *qalam*, and pen – and *'ilm*, science. In either case the inference is similar: that the Established Essences are secondary phenomena.
481 For a discussion of illumination (*tajalli*) see Shah, *The Sufis*, pp 297–9.
486 Here is yet another interesting definition of Sufism. It helps to explain Qashani's extreme preoccupation with the Names of God, as reflections of the Divine Qualities. It is suggested that by contemplating the reflections the qualities themselves may be acquired.
487 Q.65.29.
488 Q.2.268.
492 Q.7.26.
493 *Khidr*: a legendary figure who discovered and drank the water of life. He symbolises a guiding spirit which is present and active in every age. The mysterious personage, described in the Qur'an as 'one of our servants', who gives Moses some object lessons in higher knowledge, is generally taken to be Khidr. (Q.18.62–82) Sometimes also he is equated with Elias – and even St. George, the patron saint of England.
507 *Hast thou not regarded...*: Q.25.4.5
God is the Protector...: Q.2.257.
513 'Helper' is a somewhat lame rendering of the Arabic *gauth*. 'Redeemer' might be better, except that this word has been given an exclusive, once-and-for-all connotation in Nicene Christianity – whereas the implication is that there is an exemplar of the *gauth* in every age. The standard Arabic meaning is: (a call for) help.
516 This title is a mnemonic expression (*al-ghain dun al-rain*). Cf. entries 425 and 448.

BIBLIOGRAPHY

Abdullah Yusuf Ali (translator): *The Holy Quran*, Lahore, 1938.
Arberry, A. J. (translator): *The Koran Interpreted*, Oxford University Press, 1964.
Kamal-ad-din Mohammad Ibrahim Ja'far (editor): *Istilaḥāt al-Ṣūfīya*, Cairo, 1981.
Shah, Idries: *The Sufis*, W. H. Allen, London, 1964;
     A Perfumed Scorpion, Octagon Press, London, 1978.
Sprenger, Aloys (editor): Abdu-r-Razzaq's *Dictionary of the Technical Terms of the Sufis*, edited in the Arabic original, Calcutta, London, Paris, Leipzig Bonn, 1845.
Steingass, F.: *A Comprehensive Persian-English Dictionary (including the Arabic words and phrases to be met with in Persian Literature)*, Routledge & Kegan Paul, 1963.
Shah Waliullah of Delhi: *The Sacred Knowledge* (Jalbani & Pendlebury, translators), Octagon Press, London, 1982.

NOTE ON THE TRANSLATOR

Nabil F. Safwat was born in Baghdad, Iraq and educated there, in the United States and Britain. Since 1977 he has worked for the State Department of Antiquities and Heritage, and has been Assistant to the Iraqi National Committee for the Development and Conservation of the Qal'a of Kirkuk. He has qualifications in early Christian and Islamic History, Art and Architecture. He is interested in the nature of Sufi thought and in the visual and literary approaches open to that kind of study. He has translated into English a biography of Rabi'a al-'Adawiyya. He has also written on al-Hariri's *Maqamat*, Rashid al-Din's *Jami' al-Tawarikh*, and produced a number of other scholarly works.

Dr Safwat is currently lecturing in the History of Islamic Art at the School of Oriental and African Studies, University of London.

INDEX

Notes:

1. Numbers refer to sections in the Glossary (not pages).
2. A zero section number refers to the Introduction.
3. Italicized section numbers refer to section headings.
4. Throughout the Glossary the following words occur so frequently that it would serve little purpose to include each instance in the index: *God, Truth, Essence, Names, Heart, Self.*
5. In keeping with the Glossary, the Names of God are grouped under the heading '*Servant*' (e.g: *Servant of the Almighty*).

Abi Sulaiman Darani 330
Abjad 0
Abode of the Greatest Name 202
Abolition of Viewpoints 279
Abraham 36, 390
Absolute Victory 409
Abu Bakr 423
Abu Muhammad Ruwaym 175
Abu Said ibn Abi al-Khair 209
Abu Talib al Makki 170
Abundance of the Heart 277
Accusing Self 246
Adam 115, 215, 234
Admonition 392
Adoration of the Heart 264
Agitation 28
Alchemy 153
Alchemy of Happiness 154
Alchemy of the Elect 156
Alchemy of the Masses 155
Alīf 1
Ali 153, 327, 421
Allah 14
Ambition 73, 74, 75
Angelic Idea 488
Angelic World 193, 196
Animal Soul 244
Annihilation 96, 106, 120, 177, 208, 264, 436

in God 174, 282, 446
in Truth 49, 426
Anqa' Bird 397, 398
Arising within God 436
Ash'ath 421
Attacks 78
Attracted *178*
Attraction 50, 88
Audience 191
Authentic Existence 222
Authentic Undertaking *104*
Authentic Word 147
Authenticity of Light 424

Bā' 32
Balance *239*
Basic Root 218
Basis of Deep Knowledge 203
Beauty 56, 182
  of Truth 234
Behind the Outer Covering 93
Beloved 99, 238, 242, 512
  Companion 233
Bestower 220
Be! 31, 148, 267
Binding 405, 452
Black Death 238
Blackness of Face in the Two Abodes 282

A GLOSSARY OF SUFI TECHNICAL TERMS

Body 52
Breast 165
Breath 242
Breath of the Merciful 3, 195, 222, 232, *243*, 281, 484, 498
Burning 120
Burning bush of Moses 213

Cause 394, 488
Cells of Remembrance 430
Change 487
Charity 9
Cherubim 234
Chiefs 248
Clarification 54
Clarity 53
Classes of the Names 451
Clear Book 92, *145*, 166
Clouds 395
Collective Presence 231
Combination 57
Commanding Self 245
Commemoration 201
Common people 99, 129, *289*, 291
Compassion 455, 456
Compulsion 494
Concrete Word 147
Conduct 462
Connection 3
Connubial Bond 249
Consumed 204
Contemplation 466
Contemplative vision 212, 466
Contingencies 283
Contingency 211, 233, 277, 281, 417
Contingent Essences 217
Contraction 41, 45, 114, *437*, 493
Conversation *193*
Cooling off *410*
Corpulence 37, 44
Correspondence between Qualities and Realities 210
Correspondence between the Presences and Creation 211

Covenant 99, 100, 121, 122
Cow 44
Craving 76
Creation 41, 58, 59, 367, 395
Crow 510
Crushing 265

Dawning of Inner Minds 209
Dawnings of the Sun of Reality 208
Dawnings of Victory 207
Day of Assembly *144*
Death 235, 236, 237, 238, 446
Deep knowledge 67, 96, 203, 287
Deity 273
Delicacy 462
Demonstration to Mankind 115
Desire 10
Destiny 206, 219
Discernment 43
Disdainful Ambition 74
Disguise *161*
Dispersal 57
Divine Idea 488
Divine Names 31, 66
Divine Nature *158*
Divine Oneness 146
Divine Presence 9, 14, 25, 56, 196, 199, 395, 453
Division of Gathering 467
Door of Doors 33
Drinking 500
Duration of Time 110
Dust 72

Eagle 393
Easterly Breeze 68, *422*
Eastern 244, *422*
Ecstasy 466
Effacement *141*, 190
Egoism 26
Elect 291
Elect among the Elect 291
Elias 493

130

INDEX

Elite *427*
Eloquence *162*
Emerald *109*
Emulator *416*
End of the First Journey *250*
End of the Fourth Journey *253*
End of the Second Journey *251*
End of the Third Journey *252*
End Results *174*
Enlarger of Aspirations *228*
Enraptured *234*
Enumerating the Names *7*, *96*
Equity *229*
Eradication *190*
Error which falls short of Possession *516*
Essence of life *403*
Essence of Oneness *123*, *149*, *172*, *179*, *196*, *271*, *405*, *409*, *414*, *415*, *452*, *471*, *477*, *482*
Essence of Things *401*
Essence of Truth *87*, *89*, *240*, *505*, *514*
Essence of Union *278*
Essence of Unity *1*, *253*
Essences *86*, *93*, *117*, *189*, *243*, *274*, *281*, *477*, *485*, *506*
Essential Attribute of Creation *95*
Essential Attribute of Truth *94*
Essential Illumination *482*
Essential Matters *477*
Essential Names *11*, *13*, *201*
Essential Relationship *233*
Essential Word *147*
Established Essence *400*
Established Essences *17*, *66*, *205*, *273*, *449*, *483*
Establishment *106*
Eternal Present *25*, *102*, *110*, *420*
Eternal Time *102*
Eternity *272*, *273*, *274*, *356*
  without beginning *1*, *25*, *98*, *366*, *459*
  without end *25*, *98*, *459*
Even Nearer *179*, *278*, *434*
Even Number *86*, *469*

Evening Talk *200*
Event *84*
Evidence of the Names *475*
Evidence of Truth *473*
Evidence of Unity *474*
Evolution *8*
Exalted Position *223*
Existence *2*, *3*, *27*, *32*, *87*, *89*, *189*, *197*, *283*, *482*, *498*
Existence of Oneness *357*
Expanse *65*
Expansion *45*
Expansiveness *41*, *114*, *437*, *493*
Explicit Wisdom *128*
External Aspect of Contingent Phenomena *506*
External Obliteration *186*
Eye of God *402*
Eye of the World *402*

Face of Truth *90*
Facing *192*
Fair of Face *421*
Familiarisation *480*
Far-reaching Ambition *73*
Film *511*
Final Lote Tree *266*
First cause *488*
First Key *218*
First Separation *411*
First Shadow *508*
First Teacher *215*
First Tendency *432*
First Way *230*
Fission *151*
Five Senses *460*
Floating *260*
Foot *438*
Foremost Names *31*
Forgiveness *375*
Form *459*
Forms of Cognition and their Marks *460*
Foundation of Sufism *175*

Fountainhead of Liberality 232
Fraud 224
Freedom 119
Friend of God 105, 378
Frivolity 461
Fulfilment of the Covenant 99
Functional Names 451

Gabriel 340, 465
Gathering of Division 467
Genuine Love 184, 235
Gift 254
Glass 108
Glimmer 34
Goal of all Servants 91
Grateful Compassion 455
Great Reproach 290
Greater Intermediate World 266, 402
Greater Interval 40
Greatest Name 14, 124, 293, 450
Greatest Spirit 464
Green Death 237
Guarded Mystery 515

Hā' 70
Habits 100
Halt 103
He 71
Heart 444
Heavenly Kingdom 179, 226
Heights 16
Helper 23, 513
Hereafter 367, 392
He-ness 55
Hidden Centre 41
Hidden Mystery 515
Hidden Treasure 149, 249
Holy Law 67, 128, 150, 239, 289, 314, 374, 376, 441, 478, 488
Holy Spirit 493
Holy War 235
Holy World 446, 448
Honour 417

Honourable Ones 64
House of Glory 49
House of Wisdom 46
Human Subtlety 165

Iblis 143
Ibn Abbas 428
Ibn Arabi 0, 170, 334, 487, 503
Idea 488
Illumination 120, 157, 171, 404, 424, 466, 480, 481, 483, 500
Image of God 429
Image of Truth 428
Imminent Victory 407
Impulse 488
Incoming Thought 83
Information, Knowledge and Reunion 111
Inner Knowledge 251
Inner Name 248
Insight 212
Inspiration 488
Intermediate Resurrection 446
Intermediate World 39, 179, 277, 420, 446
Intuitive Impulses 45, 78
Invisible World 84, 242, 263, 282, 285, 369, 481
Inward Name 283
Inward Obliteration 187
Inwardly Pure 135
Isolated Individuals 18
Isrāfil 442

Jabir 421
Ja'far Sadiq 96, 213, 235
Jesus 353, 369
Jewels of Science, Prophecy and Deep Knowledge 67
Jinn 346
Journeys 250, 251, 252, 253, 278

Keeping the Covenant 121
  of Conduct 100
  of Lordship and Service 122

INDEX

Kernel *159*
Kernel of Kernels *160*
Key to the Secret of Destiny *217*
Keys to the Invisible 13, *179*
Khidr 384, *493*
King 23, 296
King of the Kingdom *227*
Kingdom 23, 179, *225*

Labid 35
Last Night of the Moon *276*
Learned *288*
Letters *117*
Light *256*
Light of Lights 119, 141, *257*
Light Verse *108*
Lightning *38*, 120, *500*
Limitation 65
Loosening *405*, 452
Lord 8, 66, 99, 122, 274, 377, 384, *449*, 494
Lord of Lords *450*
Lordship 31, 122, 395, 449
Love 10, 184, 235, 249, 433
Lover 99, 242

Mahdi 491
Mainstays 30
Major Element 397, *398*
Major Lordship 450
Major Pole-star 360, *443*
Major Resurrection 179, 446
Man of Insight *502*
Man of Reason *501*
Man of Reason and Insight *503*
Manifest Victory *408*
Manifestation of the Active Names *180*
Mantle *457*
Master 139, *478*, 492
Master Names 13
Master of Duration 360, 420
Master of Moment and State 420
Matters *476*

Mediator of Grace and Assistance 85
Meeting of Desires *182*
Meeting of Opposites *183*
Meeting of the Two Seas 179, *181*
Minor Resurrection 446
Mirror of Being *197*
Mirror of Existence *198*
Mirror of the Two Presences *199*
Moment of Time *101*
Morning Star *152*
Moses 193, 368, *493*
Mother of the Book 24
Movement 96
Muhammad 0, 124, 129, 220, 428, 443, 490
  (See also Prophet)
Multiplicity 97, 188, 233, 249, 250, 253, 395, 412, 471, 472, 479, 487, 503, 508
Mystery of the Essential Identity *514*
Mystical State 75, 101, *114*, 224, 466, 487, 492
Mystical time 25

Name *12*
Names of Lordship 31, 449
Names of the Essence *451*
Nearness 8, 64, 106, 174, 254, *440*
Nearness of the Lord 33, 38
Necessity 211, 233, 277, 281, 417
  and Contingency 66, 395
  and Possibility 143, 181, 199
Niche *108*
Night of Power *169*
Noble *241*
Noble-minded Ambition 75
Nullity 35
Nūn *255*

Obligatory Compassion *456*
Obliteration 190
  of Service 189
  of True Union *188*

Obscure Issue *205*
Odd Number *86*
Oil *113*
Olive Tree *112*, 244
One 3, *4*, 63, 82, 196, 345, 357, 414, 467, 482, 503
One God 243
One Who Holds 170
One Who is Confirmed in Truth *176*
One Who is Confirmed in Truth and Creation *177*
Oneness 5, 29, 81, 86, 93, 96, 172, 230, 249, 467, 472, 474, 482, 503
   of the Essence 151, 204, 218, 249, 279, 503, 508
   of Union and Separation 174, 253
Openings *406*
Original *172*
Outward Name 256
Outwardly Pure *134*

Paradise of Actions 60
Paradise of Deeds 7, 60
Paradise of Inheritance 7, *61*
Paradise of Morality 61
Paradise of Qualities 62
Paradise of the Essence 63
Paradise of the Heart 62
Paradise of the Self 60
Paradise of the Spirit 63
Patched Garment 237
Patched Robe of Sufism 237, *492*
Path 73, 88, 96, 239, 276, 291, 441, 478
   of Blame 22
   of Conduct 44
Paths of Total Praise *201*
Perfect Man 48, 85, 115, 170, 196, 199, 202, 239, 277, 396, 417, 429, 478, 509
Perfection 417
Permanence 177, 436
   after Annihilation 174, 278, 367, 467, 487

Piercing of the Mind 488
Place 223
Plato 235
Point of Departure *213*
Pole of Poles 443
Pole-star 18, 23, 194, 293, *442*, 513
Possession 425, *448*, 516
Possibilities 17
Potentialities 483
Practical Illumination 480
Precedent *258*
Presence of Contingency 395
Presence of Existence 87, 123, 231
Presence of Oneness 6, 7, 20, 189, 203, 243, 255, 278, 395, 399, 467, 469, 477, 482, 483, 510
Presence of the Divinity 20, 91
Presence of the One 6, 7, 11, 40, 232, 249, 278, 359, 395, 405, 415, 452, 467, 469, 483, 509
Presence of Union 87, 123, 231
Preserved Tablet 92, 145, 444
Primal Intellect 24, 69, 393, 395, 417, 464, 508
Primary Illumination 271, *482*
Primary Individuation 31, 124, 395, 432, 450, 483
Primary Names 13
Primordial Matter 72, 79, 260, 397
Primordial Oneness 360
Proof *413*
Prophecy *240*
Prophet (Muhammad) 9, 16, 25, 35, 61, 68, 69, 129, 131, 206, 213, 220, 228, 235, 267, 276, 293, 340, 379, 385, 386, 395, 421, 423, 438, 443, 446, 450, 488, 490, 492, 504
Prophetic mission 240
Protected *185*
Pure *133*, 134, 135, 136, 137

Qualitative names 451
Qualities 4, 8, 9, 12, 16, 62, 240, 278, 284, 395, 486

Quenching 500
Qur'an 0, 16, 213, 228, 244, 258, 293, 413, 444, 465

Ram 44
Rapture 468
Rational Soul 165, 235, 244, 393, 444, 463
Rays 168
Realities 17
Realities of the Names 125
Reality 9, 10, 26, 89, 126, 127, 129, 150, 239, 441, 478
  of Muhammad 124
  of Realities 123
Record Sheet 92
Recurring Feast 404
Red Death 235
Red Ruby 142
Relaxed One 206
Release from Sorrow and Anxiety 219
Renewed Creation 498
Renunciation of Habits 497
Repentance 33, 373
Reprover 107
Request of the Two Presences 281
Rest 96
Restraints 445
Resurrection 446
Retreat 194
Reunion 96, 98
  of Reunion 98
  of Separation 97
Revelation 34, 39
Rightly Guided One 491
Ringing Bell 51
Rising Stars 132
Robes of Honour 254
Roving 468
Ruin 458
Rust 425, 511, 516

Sacred Essence 53
Sacred House 47
Sacred Light 43, 112, 159, 160, 239, 312, 492
Sacred Power 43
Sacred Water 171, 178
Sacred World 510
Sacrosanct House 48
Safeguarding the Will 431
Sahl 273, 488
Sainthood 21, 106
Saints 367
Satan 346, 384
Satanic Idea 488
Screens 262
Seal 489
Seal of Prophecy 490
Seal of Prophethood 443
Seal of the Saints 443, 491
Seclusion 496
Second Separation 412
Second Shadow 283
Secondary Existence 506, 507
Secondary Illumination 483
Secondary Names 31
Secret 267
Secret Faculty 200, 369, 462, 468, 500
Secret Name 209
Secret of a State 269
  of Deity 273
  of Destiny 272
  of Knowledge 268
  of Reality 270
  of the Illuminations 271
  of the Secret of Deity 274
Secrets of the Traces 275
Secretly and Overtly Pure 137
Secretly Pure 136
Self 244, 245, 246, 247
Selfhood 27
Selfish Idea 488
Separation 96
Separation after Union 29, 59, 278, 487
Separation of the Qualities 415

Separation of Union 97, *414*
Serene Self *247*
Servant of –
  God *293*
  the Active 143
  the Adept *323*
  the All-embracing *338*
  the Almighty *302*
  the Aspirant *449*
  the Avenger *374*
  the Beautiful 143
  the Benefactor *292, 382*
  the Beneficial 143, 384
  the Beneficiary 143
  the Benign *376*
  the Capable 12, 31, 449, 451
  the Clement *324*
  the Compassionate *294*, 453
  the Constrainer *313*
  the Creative *387*
  the Creator 31, 156, *304*, 451
  the Dead *475*
  the Enduring *388, 389*
  the Eternal *356*
  the Even-handed *379*
  the Everlasting *361*
  the Exalter *316*
  the Expansive *314*
  the Faithful *299*
  the Fashioner *306*
  the Fatal *475*
  the Fearful 143
  the Finder 31, *357*
  the Firm *347*
  the First *366*, 451
  the Forgiving 246, *307*
  the Friend 143
  the Generous 309, *334*, *421*
  the Gentle 143, *322*
  the Glorious 201, *325*, 358
  the Great *329*
  the Guardian *345*
  the Guide *386*
  the Harmed 143

Servant of –
  the Harmful 143, 384
  the Haughty *303*
  the Hearer 31, *319*, 460
  the Holy 12, 201, *297*
  the Hopeful 143
  the Humbler *315*, *316*
  the Humiliator *318*
  the Illustrious *341*, 358
  the Independent *381*, 451
  the Inheritor *389*
  the Initiator *351*
  the Inward *369*
  the Judge *320*
  the Judicious *339*
  the Just 31, *321*
  the King *296*
  the Knower 12, 13, 31, *312*, 451, 460
  the Last *367*, 451
  the Liberal 31, *335*
  the Light 205, *385*, 484, 507
  the Living 31, 249, *355*, 403, 451, 475
  the Lord 449
  the Lord of the Kingdom *377*
  the Loving *340*
  the Maintainer 451
  the Maker *305*
  the Masterful *362*
  the Mature *390*
  the Merciful 0, 243, 246, *295*, 305, 454
  the Mighty 292, *301*
  the Mortifier *354*
  the Most High 201, *328*
  the Most Holy 451
  the Most Majestic and Noble *378*
  the Munificent *309*
  the Necessary 451
  the Nourisher *331*
  the One *359*
  the Opener *311*
  the Outward *368*
  the Pardoner *375*
  the Pardoning *326*
  the Patient *391*

INDEX

Servant of –
  the Patron *348*
  the Pious *372*
  the Potent *363*
  the Powerful *346*, *347*
  the Praiseworthy *349*
  the Preserver *330*
  the Preventer *383*
  the Promoter *364*
  the Prosperous *475*
  the Protector *300*, *449*
  the Provider *31*, *292*, *310*, *449*, *475*
  the Quantifier *350*
  the Quickener *353*, *475*
  the Receptive *143*
  the Reckoner *332*
  the Relenting *373*
  the Responsive *337*
  the Restorer *352*
  the Restrainer *365*
  the Reviver *342*
  the Ruler *370*
  the Salvation *12*, *201*, *298*, *451*
  the Seer *31*, *319*, *402*, *460*
  the Speaker *31*
  the Strengthener *317*
  the Sublime *143*, *333*
  the Supreme *371*
  the Thankful *327*
  the Timid *143*
  the Truth *201*, *344*
  the Unique *360*
  the Universal *380*
  the Vanquisher *143*, *308*, *326*
  the Vigilant *336*
  the Willing *31*
  the Witness *343*
Servants of God *292*
Service *9*, *497*
Sesame Seed *280*
Setting of the Sun *216*
Setting out for God *435*
Seven *370*
Severance of Union *29*

Shadow *283*, *507*, *508*
Shadow of God *370*, *509*
Shafi'i *237*
Shahabuddin Suhrawardi *213*
Shaybani *56*, *182*, *262*
Shell *441*
Shepherd *447*
Sign *157*
Signs *167*
Signs Identifying the Qualities *214*
Sincere Friend *423*
Sincere Friendship *495*
Sins *408*
Son of Time *101*
Source of Lordship *395*
Source of Sources *432*
Source of Time *25*
Source of Union *144*, *169*, *179*, *252*
Special Ones *504*
Spirit *52*, *68*, *108*, *158*, *165*, *216*, *444*, *463*
Spirit of Inspiration *465*
Spiritual Medicine *138*
Spiritual Physician *139*
Spiritual Pillars *396*
Splendour *55*, *56*, *505*
Split *418*
Stage *37*, *50*, *75*, *103*, *114*, *140*, *221*, *462*, *487*, *489*
Stage of Divine Descent *222*
  of Oneness of Separation after Union *487*
  of Oneness of Union *239*
  of Sainthood *408*
  of Separation *239*
  of Testimony *9*
  of the Heart *19*, *41*, *278*, *407*
  of the Oneness of Union and Separation *291*
  of the Self *437*
  of the Soul *278*
  of the Spirit *9*, *20*
  of Union *98*
  of Unity *424*

of Uprightness 253
Starting Points 174
States 8
Station of Abasement 232
Station of Drawing Near 232
Stations 221, 436
Stations of the Self 278, 407
Sublime Letters 118
Substitutes 36
Subtlety 164, 165, 462, 463
Sufi 0, 12, 89, 101, 235, 393, 441, 468
Sufis 79, 89, 165, 487
Sufism 175, 486
Suggestions 77
Supreme Horizon 20, 278
Sure Footing 439
Sustained Existence 195

Tā' 479
Tablet 166
Tacit Wisdom 129
Taste 205
Tasting 500
Teacher of the Angels 215
Tendency towards Manifestation 433
Testimony 466
Thing Greatly Hated 290
Thrones of Unity 11
Thunderclap 426
Thusness 419
Tongue of Truth 163
Torah 368
Totality 146
Tradition 85, 96, 161, 174, 213, 235, 276, 277, 297, 319, 388, 402
Treasures of God 499
True Light 424
Trusted Ones 22
Truth and Creation 85, 137, 177, 229, 253, 417, 418, 460, 501, 502, 503
Truth of Certitude 126
Truth of Truths 179
Two Aspects of Desire 66

Two Aspects of Providence 88
Two Bow-lengths 179, 181, 278, 434, 440
Two Hands 143
Two Imams 23

Ultimate Knowledge 232
Umar 167, 334
Unconditional and Conditional 89
Ungrateful 150
Unification 89, 96
Union 2, 49, 58, 94, 151, 409
Union of Oneness 98, 126, 231, 357
Union of the Essence 434
Union of Union 59
Unity 65, 93, 96, 97, 172, 188, 230, 249, 250, 251, 412, 482, 487
Unity of Truth 233
Unity of Union 6
Unity with Multiplicity 249
Universal Death 235
Universal Intermediate World 395
Universal Interval 40
Universal Manifestations 179
Universal Ranks 196
Universal Soul 92, 109, 152, 166
Universal Wisdom 131
Unknown Wisdom 130
Utter Separateness 231
Utterly Concealed 218

Veil 116, 261, 263, 511
Veils 263
Verification 485
Verifier 416
Victory 207, 407, 408, 409
Visible Horizon 19, 278
Visible World 286
Vision of God 466, 470
Vision of the Particular in the Universal 471
Vision of the Universal in the Particular 472
Visionary Illumination 484

INDEX

Voluntary Death 446

Wāw 80
Way 111, 128, *140*, 150, 221, 230, 462
Wayfarer *259*
Wealth *512*
West Wind *68*
Western 244
White Death *236*
White Pearl *69*, 142
Wisdom *127*

Wise *287*
Word *147*
Word of the Presence *148*
World *283*
World of Command 285
World of Creation 286
World of Ideas 39, 167, 179, 196, 419
World of Power 179, 196, *284*
World of the Heavenly Kingdom 285
World of the Kingdom 286
Worlds of Apparel *399*
Worship 186, *291*

كتاب

اِصطلاحات الصّوفيّة

تصنيف

كمال الدّين ابى الغنائم عبد الرّزاق
بن جمال الدّين الكاشى السّمرقندى
متوفّى ٧٣٠ هجرية

كتاب
اصطلاحات الصوفية تصنيف
كمال الدين ابى الغنايم عبد الرزاق
بن جمال الدين الكاشى
السمرقندي

بسم الله الرحمن الرحيم

الحمد لله الذي نجّانا من مباحث العلوم الرسمية بالمنّ والافضال * وافنانا بروح المعاينة من مكابدة النقل والاستدلال * وانقذنا مما لا طائل تحته من كثرة القيل والقال * وعصمنا من المناظرة والمعارضة والخلاف والجدال * فانها مثار الشبه ومظانّ الريب والشك والضلال والإضلال * فسبحان من كشف عن بصائرنا حجب الاغيار والاشكال والإشكال * والصلوٰة على

باب الالف

من هدانا في ظلمة استار الجلال ٭ الى نور الجمال ٭ محمد المصطفى و على آله و صحبه خير صحب و آل ٭ و بعد ٭ فاني لما فرغتُ من تسويد شرح كتاب منازل السائرين وكان الكلام فيه وفي شرح فصوص الحكم وتاويلات القرآن الحكيم مبنيا على اصطلاحات الصوفية ولم يتعارفها اكثر اهل العلوم المنقولة والمعقولة ولم يشتهر بينهم ذلك سألوني ان اشرحها لهم وقد اشرت في ذلك الشرح الى ان الاصول المذكورة في الكتاب من مقامات القوم يتفرع الى الف مقام ولوّحتُ الى كيفية تفريعها وما بينتُ كيفية تفاريعها بتنويعها ولم افصّل فروعها ودرجاتها ولم اصرح بصنوفها و تعريفها صدّيتُ للاسعاف بسؤلهم وزدت على ذلك ترويحا لقبولهم بيان ما اُجمل من

تعريفها ج
من ضج
تعريفاتها ج
لاسعاف سوالهم ج

باب الالف (۴)

ذلك وتفصيل ما أجمل هنالك فكسّرت هذه الرسالة على قسمين قسم في بيان المصطلحات ما عدا المقامات فانها مذكورة في متن الكتاب مشروحة في جميع الابواب وقسم في بيان التفاريع المذكورة باسرها والاشارة الى ترتيبها وحصرها ٭ اما القسم الاول فمبوّب تبويبا مبنيا على ترتيب حروف ابجد تسهيلا لمن يتفحص عنها ويتطلّب واحدا واحدا منها ٭ واما القسم الثاني فمرتّب على ترتيب الكتاب مبيّن في كل قسم لتفاريع كل باب باب ٭ القسم الاول ثمانية وعشرون بابا

٭ باب الالف ٭

(۱) الالف ٭ اشارة يشار به الى الذات الاحديّة اى الحق من حيث هو اول الاشياء في ازل الآزال

ابي جاد ـع

باب الالف (٥)

(٢) الاتحاد ٭ هو شهود وجود الحق الواحد الوجود مع المطلق الذي الكل به موجود بالحق فيتحد به الكل من حيث كون كل شيء موجودا به معدوما بنفسه لا من حيث ان له وجودا خاصا اتحد به فانه محال

(٣) الاتصال ٭ هو ملاحظة العبد عينه متصلا بالوجود الاحدى بقطع النظر من تقيّد وجوده بعينه واسقاط اضافته اليه فيرى اتصال مدد الوجود ونَفَس الرحمن اليه على الدوام بلا انقطاع حتى يبقى موجودا به ج

(٤) الاحد ٭ هو اسم الذات باعتبار انتفاء تعدّد الصفات والاسماء والنسب والتعينات عنه عنها ج

(٥) الاحديّة ٭ اعتبارها مع اسقاط الجميع

(٦) احديّة الجمع ٭ اعتبارها من حيث هي هي بلا اسقاطها ولا اثباتها بحيث يندرج فيها نسب الحضرة الواحديّة والاحديّة مج

باب الالف (٦)

(٧) احصاء الاسماء الآلهية ∗ هو التحقق بها في الحضرة الواحدية بالفناء من الرسوم الخلقية والبقاء ببقاء الحضرة الاحدية واما احصاؤها بالتخلق بها فهو يوجب دخول جنة الوراثة بصحة المتابعة وهي المشار اليها بقوله تعالى اولئك هم الوارثون الذين يرثون الفردوس هم فيها خالدون ∗ واما احصاؤها بتيقن معانيها والعمل بفحاويها فانه يستلزم دخول جنة الافعال بصحة التوكل في مقام المجازاة

(٨) الاحوال ∗ هى المواهب الفائضة على العبد من ربه اما واردة عليه ميراثا للعمل الصالح المزكى للنفس المصفى للقلب واما نازلة من الحق تعالى امتنانا محضا و انما سميت الاحوال احوالا لتحوّل العبد بها من الرسوم الخلقية و دركات البعد الى الصفات الحقية ودرجات القرب و ذلك هو

نازلة صح

صح
فج مع لتحول ج

(٧) باب الالف

معنى الترقى

(٩) الاحسان ٭ هو التحقق بالعبودية على مشاهدة الحضرة الربوبية بنور البصيرة اى رؤية الحق موصوفا بصفاته بعين صفته فهو يراه يقينا ولايراه حقيقة و لهذا قال كانك تراه لانه يراه وراء حجب صفاته بعين صفاته فلا يرى الحق بالحقيقة لانه تعالى هو الرائي وصفه بوصفه وهو دون مقام المشاهدة فى مقام الروح

(١٠) الارادة ٭ جمرة من نار المحبة فى القلب مقتضية لاجابة دواعى الحقيقة

(١١) ارائك التوحيد ٭ هى الاسماء الذاتية لكونها مظاهر الذات اولا فى الحضرة الواحدية

(١٢) الاسم ٭ باصطلاحهم ليس هو اللفظ بل هو ذات المسمى باعتبار صفة وجودية

صفاته ج

ولانه ج

فلايرى الحقيقة ج

الذات ج

باب الألف (۸)

كالعليم والقديم أو عدمية كالقدوس والسلام

(۱۳) الاسماء الذاتية * هي التي لا يتوقف وجودها على وجود الغير وان توقفت على اعتباره وتعقله كالعليم وتسمى الاسماء الازلية ومفاتيح الغيب وائمة الاسماء *

(۱٤) الاسم الاعظم * هو الاسم الجامع لجميع الاسماء وقيل هو الله لانه اسم للذات الموصوفة بجميع الصفات اي المسماة بجميع الاسماء ولهذا يطلقون الحضرة الالهية على حضرة الذات مع جميع الاسماء و عندنا هو اسم الذات الالهية من حيث هي هي اي المطلقة العارفة عليها مع جميعها او بعضها اولا مع واحد منها لقوله تعالى قل هو الله احد

الذات — ع

(۱٥) الاعطلام * هو الوله الغالب على القلب وهو قريب من الهيمان

(١٦) الاعراف * هو المطلع وهو مقام شهود الحق في كل شيء متحليا بصفاته التي ذلك الشيء مظهرها وهو مقام الاشراف على الاطراف قال الله تعالى وعلى الاعراف رجال يعرفون كلا بسيماهم * و قال النبي صلى الله عليه وسلم ان لكل آية ظهرا و بطنا و حدا و مطلعا *

(١٧) الاعيان الثابتة * هي حقائق الممكنات في علم الحق تعالى *

(١٨) الافراد * هم الرجال الخارجون عن نظر القطب *

(١٩) الافق المبين * هو نهاية مقام القلب

(٢٠) الافق الاعلى * هو نهاية مقام الروح وهي الحضرة الواحدية والحضرة الالوهية

(٢١) الالهية * كل اسم الهي مضاف الى ملك جسماني او روحاني *

(٢٢) الامناء * هم الملامتية وهم الذين

باب الالف (١٠)

لم يظهروا مما في بواطنهم اثرا على ظواهرهم وتلامذتهم ينقلبون في مقامات اهل الفتوة *

(٢٣) الامان * هما الشخصان اللذان احدهما عن يمين الغوث اي القطب و نظرة في الملكوت و الآخر عن يساره و نظرة في الملك وهو اعلى من صاحبه وهو الذي يخلف القطب *

(٢٤) أُمّ الكتاب * هو العقل الاول *

(٢٥) الآن الدايم * هو امتداد الحضرة الآلهية الذي يندرج به الازل (في الابد) وكلاهما في الوقت الحاضر لظهور ما في الازل) على احايين الابد و كون كل حين منها مجمع الازل و الابد فيتحد به الازل والابد والوقت الحاضر فلذلك يقال له باطن الزمان و اصل الزمان و سرمد لان الآنات الزمانية نقوش عليه

باب الالف (١١)

وتغيرات يظهر بها احكامه و صوره وهو
ثابت على حاله دائما سرمدا وقد يضاف
الى الحضرة العندية لقوله عليه السلام
ليس عند ربك صباح ولا مساء *

(٢٦) الانية * الحقيقة التي يضاف اليها
كل شيء من العبد كقوله نفسي و روحي
و قلبي و يدي *

(٢٧) الاية * تحقق الوجود العيني من
حيث رتبة الذاتية *

(٢٨) الانزعاج * تحرك القلب الى الله
تعالى بتأثير الوعظ والسماع فيه *

(٢٩) انصداع الجمع * هو الفرق بعد الجمع
بظهور الكثرة في الوحدة واعتبارها فيها

(٣٠) الاوتاد * هم الرجال الاربعة الذين
على منازل الجهات الاربع من العالم
اى الشرق والغرب والشمال والجنوب
بهم يحفظ الله تعالى تلك الجهات لكونهم

(١٢) باب الالف

محال نظره تعالى *

(٣١) امّ الاسماء * هى الاسماء السبعة الاولى المسماة بالاسماء الآلهية وهي الحي والعالم والمريد والقادر والسميع والبصير والمتكلم وهي اصول الاسماء كلها وبعضهم اوردوا مكان السميع والبصير الجواد والمقسط وعندى انهما من الاسماء الثانية لاحتياج الجود والعدل الى العلم والارادة والقدرة بل الى الجميع لتوقفهما على رؤية استعداد المحل الذي يفيض عليه الجواد الفيض بالقسط و على سماع دعاء السائل بلسان الاستعداد وعلى اجابة دعائه بكلمة كُنْ. على الوجه الذى يقتضيه استعداد السائل من الاعيان الثانية فهي كالموجد و الخالق والرازق التي هى من اسماء الربوبية وجعلوا الحي امام الائمة لتقدمه على العالم بالذات لان الحيوة

الاولى	الحق
اورد	ع
الثانية	ج
لتوقفها	ج
ج
الثابتة	ج

باب الباء

شرط العلم والشرط متقدّم على المشروط طبعا وعندي ان العالم بذلك اولى لان الامامة امر نسبي يقتضي ماموما وكونه اشرف من المأموم والعلم يقتضي بعد الذي قام به معلوما والحيوة لايقتضي غير الحي فهي عين الذات غير مقتضية للنسبة واما كون العلم اشرف منها فظاهر ولهذا قالوا ان العالم هو اول ما يتعين به الذات دون الحي لانه في كونه غير مقتضى النسبة كالموجود والواجب ولا يلزم من التقدم بالطبع الامامة الا ترى ان المزاج المعتدل للبدن شرط الحيوة ولا شك ان الحيوة متقدمة عليه بالشرف

باب الباء

(٣٢) الباء * يشار به الى اول الموجودات الممكنة وهي المرتبة الثانية من الوجود

(٣٣) باب الابواب * هو التوبة لانها اول

مقدم ج

كون الامام ج

فهو ج

العلم ج
الذات منها ج
للنسبة ج
بالذات ج

باب الباء

باب ج بها ج — ما يدخل به العبد حضرات القرب من جناب الرب

لائحة ترد ج — (٣٤) اللائحة ٭ هى لائح يرد من الجناب الاقدس وينطفى سريعا وهى من اوائل الكشف ومباديه

الحق تعالى ج — (٣٥) الباطل ٭ ما سوى الحق وهو العدم
للحق ج — اذ لا وجود فى الحقيقة الا الحق لقوله عليه الصلوة والسلام اصدق بيت قالته العرب قول لبيد ٭ ألَا كل شىء ما خلا الله باطل ٭

من موضع ع — (٣٦) البدلاء ٭ هم سبعة رجال يسائر احدهم من موضعه ويترك فيه جسدا على صورته بحيث لا يعرف احد انه فقد وذلك معنى البدل لا غير وهم على قلب ابراهيم عليه السلام

(٣٧) البَدَنة ٭ كناية من النفس الآخذة فى السير القاطعة لمنازل السائرين مراحل السالكين

باب الباء

(٣٨) البرق ✱ أول ما يبدو للعبد من اللامع النوري نيدعوه الى الدخول في حضرة القرب من الرب للسير في الله

(٣٩) البرزخ ✱ هو الحائل بين الشيئين و يعبر به عن عالم المثال الحاجز بين الاجسام الكثيفة و عالم الارواح المجردة اعنى الدنيا والآخرة ومنه الكشف الصورى

اعنى ضع ‏/ الاجساد ج

(٤٠) البرزخ الجامع ✱ هو الحضرة الواحدية والتعين الاول الذى هو اصل البرازخ كلها و لهذا يسمى البرزخ الاول والاعظم والاكبر

(٤١) البسط ✱ في مقام القلب بمثابة الرجا في مقام النفس وهو وارد يقتضيه اشارة الى قبول و لطف و رحمة و انس و يقابله القبض كالخوف في مقابلة الرجاء في مقام النفس

يقتضى ج

(٤٢) البسط ✱ في مقام الخفاء هو ان يبسط

الخفي ج

الله العبد مع الخلق طاهرا و بقبضه اليه الله تعالى باطنا رحمة للخلق فهو يسع الاشياء ولا يسعه شيء و يؤثر في كل شيء ولا يؤثر فيه شيء

(٤٣) البصيرة * هي قوة للقلب منورة بنور القدس يرى بها حقائق الاشياء و بواطنها بمثابة البصر للنفس الذي يرى به صور الاشياء و ظواهرها وهي القوة التي تسميها الحكماء العاقلة النظرية و اما اذا تنورت بنور القدس و انكشف حجابها بهداية الحق فيسميها الحكيم القوة القدسية

(٤٤) البقرة * كناية عن النفس اذا استعدت للرياضة وبدت فيها صلاحية قمع الهوى الذي هو حيوتها كما يكنى عنها بالكبش قبل ذلك و بالبدنة بعد الاخذ في السلوك *

(٤٥) البوادة * جمع بادهة وهي ما يفجأ

(١٧)

باب الجيم

القلب من الغيب فيوجب بسطا او قبضا * عن

(٤٦) بيت الحكمة * هو القلب الغالب عليه الإخلاص *

(٤٧) بيت المقدس * هو القلب الطاهر من التعلق بالغير *

(٤٨) بيت الحرام * قلب الانسان الكامل الذي حُرِم على غير الحق * المحرم ع

(٤٩) بيت العزة * هو القلب الواصل الى مقام الجمع حال الفناء في الحق *

* باب الجيم *

(٥٠) الجذبة * هي تقريب العبد بمقتضى العناية الالهية المهيئة له كلَّ ما يحتاج اليه في طيّ المنازل الى الحق بلا كلفة وسعى منه * منازل الحق ع

(٥١) الجرس * اجمال الخطاب بضرب

باب الجيم

(٥٢) الجسد ۞ هو ما ظهر من الارواح و تمثل في جسم ناري او نوري ۞

(٥٣) المجلاء ۞ هو ظهور الذات المتقدسة لذاته في ذاته ۞

(٥٤) الاستجلاء ۞ ظهورها (يعني الذات) لذاته في تعيناته

(٥٥) الجلال ۞ هو احتجاب الحق تعالى عنا بعزّته ان نعرفه بحقيقته وهُوِيّته كما يعرف هو ذاته فانّ ذاته سبحانه لا يراها احد على ما هي عليه الا هوَّ ۞

(٥٦) الجمال ۞ هو تجليه بوجهه لذاته فلجماله المطلق جلال هو قهاريته للكل عند تجليه بوجهه فلم يبق أحد حتى يراه وهو علوّ الجمال وله دنوّ يدنو به منّا وهو ظهوره في الكل كما قال الشيباني

۞ جمالك في كل الحقايق سائر ۞
۞ و ليس له الآ جلالك ساتر ۞

باب الجيم

ولهذا الجمال جلال (هو احتجابه بتعينات الاكوان فلكل جمال جلال) و وراء كل جلال جمال ولما كان في الجلال و نعوته معنى الاحتجاب والعزة لزمه العلو والقهر من الحضرة الآلهية و الخضوع والهيبة منا ولما كان في الجمال و نعوته معنى الدنو والسفور لزمه اللطف والرحمة والعطف من الحضرة الآلهية و الانس منا *

(٥٧) الجمعية * اجتماع الهم في التوجه الى الله والاشتغال به عما سواه و بازائها التفرقة وهى توزع الخاطر للاشتغال بالخلق *

(٥٨) الجمع * شهود الحق بلا خلق *

(٥٩) جمع الجمع * شهود الخلق قائما بالحق و يسمى الفرق بعد الجمع *

(٦٠) جنة الافعال * هى الجنة الصورية

باب الميم (٢٠)

الهنيئة ج — من جنس المطاعم اللذيذة والمشارب الهنيئة
البهيئة ج — والمناكح البهية ثوابا للاعمال الصالحة و تسمى جنة الاعمال وجنة النفس

(٦١) جنة الوراثة * هي جنة الاخلاق الحاصلة بحسن متابعة النبي صلى الله عليه و سلم

(٦٢) جنة الصفات * هي الجنة المعنوية من تجليات الصفات والاسماء الالهية وهي جنة القلب *

(٦٣) جنة الذات * هي من مشاهدة
الجمال الاحدي ع جمال الاحدية وهي جنة الروح

(٦٤) الجنائب * هم السائرون الى الله
من ج — في منازل النفوس حاملين لزاد التقوى والطاعة ما لم يصلوا الى مناهل القلب و مقامات القرب حتى يكون سيرهم في الله

(٦٥) جهتا الفيض والسعة * هما اعتباران

(٢١) باب الجيم

للذات اما بحسب تنزيهها من كل ما   تنزيهها ع
يفهم و يعقل وهو اعتبار الوحدة الحقيقية
التي لا اتساع معها للغير لا وجودا ولا
تعقلا و هو الضيق كقولهم لا يعرف الله
الا الله و اما بحسب ظهورها في جميع
المراتب باعتبار الاسماء والصفات المقتضية
للمظاهر الغير المتناهية و هي السعة كما   الظاهر ج مع ع
قيل   (شعر)

* لا تقل دارها بشرقي نجد *   بر ج
* كل نجد للعامرية دار *
* ولها منزل على كل ماء *
* و على كل دمنة آثار *

(٦٦) جهتا الطلب * هما جهتا الوجوبية   جهة ج
والامكانية وهما طلب الاسماء الربوبية
ظهورها بالاعيان الثابتة وطلب الاعيان   الاعيان ج
ظهورها بالاسماء و ظهور الرب في شوٓنه   شونه ج
اجابة للسائلين و حضرتهما حضرة التعيين   السوالين ع

الاول

(٦٧) جواهر المعلوم والانباء والمعارف * هي الحقايق التي لا تتبدل ولا تتغير باختلاف الشرايع والامم والازمنة كما قال الله تعالى شرع لكم من الدين ما وصى به نوحا والذي اوحينا اليك وما وصينا به ابراهيم وموسى وعيسى ان اقيموا الدين ولا تتفرقوا فيه

* باب الدال *

(٦٨) الدبور * صولة داعية هوى النفس و استيلاؤها شبّهت بريح الدبور التي تأتي من جهة المغرب لانتشائها من جهة الطبيعة الجسمانية التي هي مغرب النور ويقابلها القبول وهي ريح الصبا التي تأتي من جهة المشرق وهي صولة داعية الروح واستيلاؤها ولهذا قال عليه الصلوة والسلام نُصرتُ بالصبا و أُهلكت

باب الهاء (٢٣)

مار بالدبور

(٦٩) الدرة البيضاء * هي العقل الاول لقوله عليه الصلوة والسلام اول ما خلق الله درة بيضاء الحديث * واول ما خلق الله العقل *

* باب الهاء *

(٧٠) الهاء * هي اعتبار الذات بحسب الحضور والوجود

(٧١) الهُو * اعتبارها بحسب الغيبة والفقد *

الظهور ع
باعتبار ج

(٧٢) الهباء * هو المادة التي فتح الله فيها صور العالم وهو العنقاء المسماة بالهيولى *

مرة ع

(٧٣) همّ الإفاقة * هي اول درجات الهمة وهي الباعثة على طلب الباقي و ترك الفاني *

(٧٤) همّ الانفة * هي الدرجة الثانية وهي التي تورث صاحبها الانفة من

باب البهاء (٢٨)

طلب الاجر على العمل حتى يأنف قلبه ان يشتغل بتوقع ما وعده الله من الثواب على العمل فلا يفرغ من التوجه الى مشاهدة الحق بل يعبد الله على الاحسان فلا يفرغ (من التوجه الى الحق) طلبا للقرب منه الى طلب ما سواه *

(٧٥) همم ارباب الهمم العالية * هي الدرجة الثالثة وهى التي لا تتعلق الا بالحق ولا تلتفت الى غيره فهي اعلى الهمم حيث لا ترضى بالاحوال والمقامات ولا بالوقوف مع الاسماء والصفات ولا تقصد الا عين الذات *

(٧٦) الهوى * هو ميل النفس الى مقتضيات الطبع والاعراض من الجهة

―――――

* الهمة توجه القلب وقصده بجميع قواه الروحانية الى جانب الحق لحصول كمال له او لغيره منها من كتاب التعريفات

العلوية بالتوجه إلى الجهة السفلية *

(٧٧) الهواجس * هى الخواطر النفسانية *

(٧٨) الهواجم * ما يرد على القلب بقوة الوقت من غير تعمّل من العبد و هى البواده المذكورة

(٧٩) الهيولى * عندهم اسم للشيء بنسبته الى ما يظهر فيه من الصور فكل باطن يظهر فيه صورة يسمونه هيولى

* باب الواو *

(٨٠) الواو * هو الوجه المطلق في الكل

(٨١) الواحدية * اعتبار الذات من حيث انتشاء الاسماء منها و واحديتها بها مع وحدانيتها تكثرها بالصفات

(٨٢) الواحد * اسم الذات بهذا الاعتبار

(٨٣) الوارد * كل ما يرد على القلب من المعانى من غير تعمّل من العبد

(٨٤) الواقعة * ما يرد على القلب من عالم

باب الواو (٢٦)

الغيب بأي طريق كان

(٨٥) واسطة الفيض و واسطة المدد ۞ هو الانسان الكامل الذي هو الواسطة بين الحق و الخلق بمناسبته للطرفين كما قال الله لولاك لما خلقت الافلاك

الرابطة ع

فع

(٨٦) الوتر ۞ هو الذات باعتبار سقوط جميع الاعتبارات فان الاحدية لا نسبة لها الى شيء ولا نسبة لشيء اليها ان لا شيء في تلك الحضرة اصلا بخلاف الشفع الذي باعتباره تعينت الاعيان و حقايق الاسماء

العبارات ج

(٨٧) الوجود ۞ وجد ان الحق ذاته بذاته و لهذا تسمى حضرة الجمع حضرة الوجود

بحضرة الجمع
وحضرة الوجود ج

(٨٨) وحبها العناية ۞ هما الجذبة و السلوك اللذان هما جهتا الهداية

(٨٩) وجها الاطلاق والتقييد ۞ هما جهتا اعتبار الذات بحسب سقوط جميع الاعتبارات وبحسب اثباتها فان ذات الحق

باب الواو

هو الوجود من حيث هو وجود فان اعتبرتَه كذلك فهو المطلق اى الحقيقة التى مع كل شيء لا بمقارنة فان ما غير الوجود البَحْت هو العدم المحض فكيف يقارنه ما هو به وجود و بدونه معدوم و غير كل شيء لا بمزايلة فان ما عداه هي الاعيان المعدومة و هى غير الوجود البحت فان فارقها لم يكن شيا فالكل به موجود وهو بذاته موجود فان قيدتَه بالتجرّد اى بقيد ان لا يكون معه شى فهو الاحد الذي كان ولم يكن معه شى ولهذا قال المحقّقون هو الآن كما كان وان قيدته بقيد ان لا يكون معه شى فهو عين المقيّد الذي هو به موجود و بدونه معدوم وقد تجلى في صورته فاضيف اليه الوجود فاذا اسقطت الاضافة فهو معدوم فى ذاته وهذا معنى قولهم التوحيد اسقاط الاضافات وقد

باب الواو (٢٨)

صدق من قال ان الوجود عين حقيقة الواجب وغير حقيقة كل ممكن لانه زائد على كل ماهية وعين ان لا نشك ان سوادية السواد وانسانية الانسان مثلا شي غير وجوده وهو بدون الوجود معدوم *

(٩٠) وجه الحق * هو ما به الشيء حقا ان لاحقيقة لشيء الا به تعالى وهو المشار اليه بقوله تعالى فاينما تولّوا فثمّ وجه الله وهو عين الحق المقيم لجميع الاشياء فمن رأى قيومية الحق للاشياء فهو الذي يرى وجه الحق في كل شي

(٩١) وجهة جميع العابدين * هى الحضرة الالوهية *

(٩٢) الوَرقاء * هى النفس الكلية التى هى قلب العالم وهو اللوح المحفوظ والكتاب المبين *

(٩٣) وراء اللبس * هو الحق في الحضرة

باب الواو

الاحدية قبل الواحدية ؛ فانه فى الحضرة الثانية وما بعدها يتلبس بمعانى الاسماء و حقايق الاعيان ثم بالصور الروحانية ثم بالصور المثالية ثم بالحسية ؛

(٩٤) الوصف الذاتى للحق * هو احدية الجمع والوجوب الذاتى والغنى عن العالمين

(٩٥) الوصف الذاتى للخلق * هو الامكان الذاتى والفقر الذاتى

(٩٦) الوصل * هو الوحدة الحقيقية الواصلة بين البطون و الظهور وقد يعبّر به عن سبق الرحمة بالمحبة المشار اليها فى قوله فاحببت ان اعرَفَ فخلقت الخلق وقد يعبّر به عن قيّومية الحق للاشياء فانها تصل الكثرة بعضها ببعض حتى تتحد بالفصل من تنزّه من حَدَثَنها ؛ قال الامام المعصوم ؛ ابو عبد الله جعفر بن محمد الصادق رضى الله عنهما من عرف الفصل

باب الواو

القرآن ع | من الوصل والحركة من السكون فقد بلغ مبلغ القرار في التوحيد ويروى في المعرفة و المراد بالحركة السلوك و بالسكون القرار في

الاحدية ج | عين احدية الذات وقد يعبّر بالوصل عن فناء العبد باوصافه في اوصاف الحق وهو

عنه ج | التحقق باسمائه تعالى المعبّر عنها باحصاء الاسماء كما قال عليه الصلوة والسلام من احصاها دخل الجنة *

فع | (٩٧) وعلى الفصل * شعب الصدع وجمع الفرق وهو ظهور الوحدة في الكثرة فان الوحدة واصلة لفصولها باتحاد الكثرة بها و جمعها لشتاتها كما ان فصل الوصل هو ظهور الكثرة في الوحدة فان الكثرة فاصلة لوصل الوحدة مكثرةً لها با لتعيّنات الموجبة لتنوع ظهور الوحدة في القوابل المختلفة (اختلاف اشكال الوجه الواحد في المرايا

فج | المختلفة) *

باب الواو

(٩٨) وصل الوصل * هو العود بعد الذهاب والعروج بعد النزول فان كل احد منا نزل من اعلى المراتب وهو عين الجمع الاحدية التى هى الوصل المطلق في الازل الى ادنى المهاوي وهو عالم العناصر المتضادة فمنّا من اقام في غاية الحضيض حتى هبط اسفل السافلين ومنا من رجع وعاد الى مقام الجمع بالسلوك الى الله و في الله بالاتصاف بصفاته والفناء في ذاته حتى حصل على الوصل الحقيقي في الابد كما كان في الازل *

(٩٩) الوفاء بالعهد * هو الخروج عن عهدة ما قيل عند الاقرار بالربوبية بقول بلى حيث قال الله تعالى الست بربكم قالوا بلى وهو للعامة العبادة رغبة في الوعد ورهبة من الوعيد وللخاصة العبودية على الوقوف مع الامر لنفس الامر وقوفا عند ما حدّ

باب الواو

ولا ج

غرضاً ج العبودة تـ ع
التبري ج

يندمل ج
فج الاوقات ج

لك ع
الوقت ج

ووفاءً بما اخذ على العبد بلا رغبةٍ ولا رهبةٍ ولا فرضٍ ولخاصة الخاصة العبودية على التبرُّع من الحول والقوة وللمحب صون قلبه عن الاتساع لغير المحبوب ومن لوازم الوفاء بعهد العبودية ان ترى كل نقص يبدو منك راجعاً اليك ولا ترى كمالاً لغير ربك

(١٠٠) الوفاء بحفظ عهد التصرف * ان لا تذهب هلعاً من عبوديتك و عجزك في اوقات ما يمنحك من التصرفات وخرق العادات (١٠١) الوقت * ما حضرك في الحال فان كان من تصريف الحق فعليك الرضاء و الاستسلام حتى تكون بحكم الوقت لا يخطر ببالك غيره وان كان مما يتعلق بكسبك فالزم ما اهمك فيه لا يتعلّق بالك بالماضي والمستقبل فان تدارك الماضي تضييع للوقت (وكذا الفكر فيما يستقبل فانه مَتى فانه لا تبلغه وقد فاتك

باب الواو

الوقت) ولهذا قيل الصوفي ابن الوقت *

(١٠٢) الوقت الدائم * هو الآن الدائم

(١٠٣) الوقفة * هي التوقف بين المقامين سواء ما بقى عليه من حقوق الاول والتهيىُّ لما يرتقى اليه بآداب الثاني *

نح باقي ج
والتهيؤ ج

(١٠٤) الوقوف الصادق * هو الوقوف مع مراد الحق *

(١٠٥) الولى * من تولى الحق وُ امرَه و حفظه من العصيان ولم يخلّه و نفسه بالخذلان حتى يبلّغه فى الكمال مبلغ الرجال قال الله تعالى وهو يتولّى الصالحين *

نح

(١٠٦) الولاية * هي قيام العبد بالحق عند الفناء عن نفسه و ذلك بتولى الحق اياه حتى يبلّغه غاية مقام القرب والتمكين

غايته ج

باب الزاء

باب الزاء

(۱۰۷) * الزاجر * واعظ الله في قلب المؤمن وهو الفؤز المقذوف فيه الداعي له الى الحق *

(۱۰۸) * الزجاجة * المشار اليها في آية النور هي القلب والمصباح هو الروح والشجرة التي يتّقد منها الزجاجة المشبّهة بالكوكب الدري هي النفس والمشكاة البدن *

(۱۰۹) * الزمرّد * هي النفس الكلية *

(۱۱۰) * الزمان * المضاف الى الحضرة العندية هو الآن الدائم المذكور في باب الالف *

(۱۱۱) * زواهر الانباء، وزواهر العلوم وزواهر الوُصلة * هي علوم الطريقة لكونها اشرف العلوم و انورها وكون الوصلة الى الحق متوقفة عليها *

(۱۱۲) * الزيتونة * هي النفس المستعدّة للاشتعال بنور القدس بقوة الفكر *

باب الحاء (٣٥)

(١١٣) الزيت * نور استعدادها الاصلي والله الموفق *

* باب الحاء *

(١١٤) الحال * ما يرد على القلب لمحض الموهبة من غير تعمّل واجتلاب كحزن او خوف او بسط او قبض او شوق او ذوق و تزول بظهوره صفات النفس سواء يعقبه المثل اولا فاذا دام وصار ملكاً سمى مقاما [بمحض ج] [مَلَكَة ط]

(١١٥) حجة الحق على الخلق * هو الانسان الكامل كآدم عليه السلام حيث كان حجة على الملائكة في قوله تعالى * ياآدم انبئهم باسمائهم الى قوله وُما كنتم تكتمون [مج]

(١١٦) الحجاب * انطباع الصور الكونية في القلب المانعة لقبول تجلى الحقائق [مج]

(١١٧) الحروف * هى الحقائق البسيطة من الاعيان * [مج]

(١١٨) والحروف العاليات * هى الشؤن [الشيون. ج الشيئان]

(٣٦)

الذاتية الكامنة في غيب الغيوب كالشجرة في النواة و اليها اشار الشيخ بقوله ؏ كنا حروفا عاليات لم يُقَل ؏ متعلقات في ذرى اعلى القُلَل ؏ انما انت فيه ونحن انت وانت هو ؏ والكل في هو هو فسل ؏ ممن وصل ٭

(١١٩) الحرية ٭ هي الانطلاق من رق الاغيار وهي على مراتب حرية العامة عن رق الشهوات وحرية الخاصة عن رق المرادات لفناء ارادتهم في ارادة الحق وحرية خاصة الخاصة عن رق الرسوم والآثار لانمحاقهم في تجلي نور الانوار ٭

(١٢٠) المحق ٭ هو واسط التجليات الجاذبة الى الفناء التي اوايلها حرق و اواخرها الطمس في الذات ٭

(١٢١) حفظ العهد ٭ هو الوقوف عند ما جدَّ الله تعالى لعباده فلا يفقد حيث ما

باب السماء (٣٧)

امر ولا يوجد حيث ما نهى *

(١٢٢) حفظ عهد الربوبية والعبودية * هو ان لا ينسب كمالا الا الى الرب ولا نقصا الا الى العبد * [نقصانا ج]

(١٢٣) حقيقة الحقائق * هي الذات الاحدية الجامعة لجميع الحقائق و تسمى حضرة الجمع و حضرة الوجود *

(١٢٤) الحقيقة المحمدية * هي الذات مع التعين الاول فله الاسماء الحسنى كلها و هو الاسم الاعظم *

(١٢٥) حقائق الاسماء * هي تعينات الذات و نسبها لانها صفات تتميز بها الاسماء بعضها من بعض *

(١٢٦) حق اليقين * هو شهود الحق حقيقة في مقام عين جمع الاحدية * [الجمع ع]

(١٢٧) الحكمة * هي العلم بحقائق الاشياء و اوصافها و خواصها و احكامها على ما

باب الحكمة (٣٨)

نظام انضباط ج / هي عليه و ارتباط الاسباب بالمسببات و اسرار انضباط نظام الموجودات والعمل
يوتي ج / بمقتضاه و من يؤت الحكمة فقد اوتي خيرا كثيرا *

(١٢٨) الحكمة المنطوق بها * هي علوم الشريعة والطريقة *

(١٢٩) الحكمة المسكوت عنها * هي اسرار الحقيقة التي لا يفهمها علماء الرسوم والعوام على ما ينبغي فتضرهم او تهلكهم كما روي ان رسول الله صلى الله عليه وسلم
سك صح / كان يجتاز في بعض سكك المدينة ومعه اصحابه فتنسمت عليه امرأة ان يدخلوا منزلها فدخلوا فيها فراوا نارا مضطرمة و اولاد المرأة يلعبون حولها فقالت يا نبي الله الله ارحم بعبادة ام انا باولادي فقال بل
مر صح / الله ارحم فانه ارحم الراحمين فقالت اترانى يا رسول الله احب ان القى ولدي في

الذى هو النفس الناطقة الى مركزها فتموت عن الحيوة الحقيقية العلمية التى له بالجهل فاذا ماتت النفس عن هواها بقمعه انصرف القلب بالطبع والمحبة الاصلية الى عالمه عالم القدس والنور والحيوة الذاتية التى لا تقبل الموت اصلا والى هذا الموت اشار افلاطون بقوله مُت بالارادة تحى بالطبيعة قال الامام المعصوم جعفر بن محمد الصادق عليهما السلام الموت هو التوبة قال الله تعالى فتوبوا الى بارئكم فاقتلوا انفسكم فمن تاب فقد قتل نفسه ولهذا اذا صنّفوا الموت اصنافا خصّوا مخالفة النفس بالموت الاحمر ولما رجع رسول الله صلى الله عليه وسلم من جهاد الكفار قال رجعنا من الجهاد الاصغر الى الجهاد الاكبر قالوا يا رسول الله وما الجهاد الاكبر قال مخالفة النفس و في حديث آخر المجاهد

(٧٢)

من جاهد نفسه فمن مات عن هواه۔ فقد حيي بهداه من الضلالة و بمعرفته من الجهالة قال الله تعالى فمن كان ميتا فاحييناه يعنى ميتا بالجهل فاحييناه بالعلم و قد سمّوا ايضًا هذا الموت بالموت الجامع لجميع انواع الموتات *

(٢٣٦) الموت الابيض * الجوع لانه ينوّر الباطن و يبيض وجه القلب فاذا لم يشبع السالك بل لا يزال جائعا مات بالموت الابيض فحينئذ يحيى فطنته لان البطنة تميت الفطنة (فمن ماتت بطنته حييت فطنته) *

(٢٣٧) الموت الاحمر * لبس المرقع من الخرق الملقاة التي لا قيمة لها فاذا قنع من اللباس الجميل بذلك و اقتصر على ما يستر العورة و يصح فيه الصلوة فقد مات الموت الاخضر لاخضرار عيشه بالقناعه

(٧٣)

ونضارة وجهه بنضرة الجمال الذاتي الذي حيى به و استغنى عن التجمل العارضي كما قيل * شعر * اذا المرأ لم يدنس من اللوم عرضه * فكل رداء يرتديه جميل * ولّما روىٔ الشافعي رضي الله عنه في ثوب خلق لا قيمة له فعابه بعض الجهال بذلك قال * شعر * لئن كان ثوبي فوق قيمتها الفلس * فلى فيه نفس دون قيمتها الانس * فثوبك شمس تحت انوارها الدجى * وثوبي ليل تحت ظلمته الشمس *

(٢٣٨) الموت الاسود * هو احتمال اذىٔ الخلق لانه اذا لم يجد في نفسه حرجا من اذاهم ولم يتألّم نفسه بل يلتذّ به لكونه يراه في محبوبه كما قيل * شعر * (وقف الهوى بي حيث انت فليس لي بتأخر عنه ولا متقدّم) * اجد الملامة في هواك لذيذة * حبّا لذكرك فليلُمنى اللّوم *

اشبهت اعدائي فصرت احبهم ۞ إذا كان حظى منك حظى منهم ۞ و اهنتني فاهنت نفسي صاغرا ۞ نا مَن يهون عليك فمَن يُكرَّم ۞ (فقد مات بالموت الاسوٕ) وهو الفناء في الله لشهوٕه الاذى منه برؤية فناء الافعال في فعل محبوبه بل برؤية نفسه و انفسهم فانيين في المحبوب وحينئذ يحيي بوجود الحق من اسدائ حضرة الجود المطلق ۞

(٢٣٩) الميزان ۞ ما به يتوصل الانسان الى معرفة الآراء الصائبة والاقوال السديدة والافعال الجميلة و تمييزها من اضدادها و هو العدالة التي هي ظل الوحدٕة الحقيقية المشتملة على علم الشريعة والطريقة والحقيقة لانها لم يتحقق بها صاحبها الا عند تحققه بمقام احدية الجمع والفرق فان ميزان اهل الظاهر هو الشرع و ميزان اهل الباطن هو

العقل المنوَّر بنور القدس و ميزان اهل الخصوص هو علم الطريقة و ميزان خاصة الخاصة هو العدل الآلهى الذي لا يتحقق به الا الانسان الكامل *

* باب النون *

النبوّة * هو الاخبار عن الحقائق الآلهية اى من معرفة ذات الحق و اسمائه و صفاته و احكامه و هى على قسمين نبوة التعريف و نبوة التشريع والاولى هى الانباء عن معرفة الذات والصفات والاسماء والثانية جميع ذلك مع تبليغ الاحكام والتاديب بالاخلاق والتعليم بالحكمة والقيام بالسياسة وتختص هذه بالرسالة *

(٢٤١) النجباء * هم الاربعون القائمون باصلاح امور الناس و حمل اثقالهم المتصرفون في حقوق الخلق لاغير *

(٢٤٢) النَّفَس * ترويح القلوب بلطائف

الغيوب و هو للمحب الانس بالمحبوب *
(٢٤٣) النَّفَس الرحمانى * هو الوجود الاضافى
الوُحدانى بحقيقته المتكثر بصورة المعانى — بصور المعانى ج
التى هى الاعيان واحوالها فى الحضرة
الواحدية سمى به تشبيها بنفس الانسان
المختلف بصور الحروف مع كونه هواء
ساذجاً فى نفسه و نظرًا الى الغاية التى — ساذجا ج
هى ترويح الاسماء الداخلة تحت حيطة
الاسم الرحمن من كُربها و هو تكوّن — كمون ج
الاشياء فيها و كونها بالقوة كترويح الانسان
بالتنفس *

(٢٤٤) النَّفْس * هو الجوهر البخارى اللطيف
الحامل لقوة الحيوة والحس والحركة الارادية
و سمّاها الحكيم الروح الحيوانية و هى — النفس ج
الواسطة بين القلب الذى هو النفس
الناطقة و بين البدن المشار اليها فى القران — البه ج
بالشجرة الزيتونة الموصوفة بكونها مباركة

لا شرقية ولا غربية لازدياد رتبة الانسان و بركته بها ولكونها ليست من شرق عالم الارواح المجرّدة ولا من غرب عالم الاجساد الكثيفة *

(٢٤٥) النفس الامّارة * هى التى تميل الى الطبيعة البدنية وتآمر باللذات والشهوات الحسية و تجذب القلب الى الجهة السفلية فهى مأوى الشر ومنبع الاخلاق الذميمة والافعال السيّئة قال الله تعالى ان النفس لامّارة بالسوء *

(٢٤٦) النفس اللوّامة * هى التى تنوّرت بنور القلب تنوّرا قدر ما تنبهت به من سِنَة الغفلة فتيقظت و بدأت باصلاح حالها مترددة بين جهتى الربوبية والخلقية فكلما صدرت منها سيّئة بحكم جبلّتها الظلمانية و سنخها تداركها نور التنبيه الالهى فاخذت تلوم نفسها وتنوب عنها مستغفرة راجعة الى

(٧٨)

نوع ج باب الغفار الرحيم ولهذا نوّهها الله بذكرها بالإقسام بها في قوله تعالى لا اقسم بالنفس اللوامة ¤

(٢٤٧) النفس المطمئنة ¤ هي التي تم تنوّرها
صفاته ج بنور القلب حتى انخلعت من صفاتها الذميمة و تخلّقت بالاخلاق الحميدة و توجهت الى جهة القلب بالكلية متابعة له في الترقي الى جناب عالم القدس
خبائث متنزهة من جانب الرجس مواظبة على
ماكنه ج الطاعات ماسكنة الى حضرة رفيع الدرجات حتى خاطبها ربها بقوله يا ايتها النفس المطمئنة ارجعي الى ربك راضية مرضية فادخلي في عبادي وادخلي جنتي
نهج للتجرد

(٢٤٨) النقبا، ¤ هم الذين تحققوا بالاسم
واستخرجوا ج الباطن فاشرفوا على بواطن الناس فاستخرجوا
انكشاف ج خفايا الضمائر لانكشاف الستائر لهم

من وجوه السرائر وهم ثلثمائة

(٢٤٩) النكاح السارى فى جميع الزرارى * هو التوجه المجسَّى المشار اليه فى قوله تعالى كنت كنزا مخفيا (فاحببت ان أعرف فان قوله كنت كنزا) يشير الى سبق الخفاء والغيبة والاطلاق على الظهور والنعز سبقا ازليا ذاتيا وقوله فاحببت ان أعرف. يشير الى ميل اصلي وحب ذاتي وهو الوصلة بين الخفاء والظهور المشار اليه بان اعرف فتلك الوصلة هى اصل النكاح الساري في جميع الذرارى فان الوحدة المقتضية لحب ظهور شئون الاحدية تسرى فى جميع مراتب التعينات المترتبة (من العقل الاول الى آخر المراتب) وتفاصيل كلياتها بحيث لا يخلو منها شيء وهى الحافظة لشمل الكثرة في جميع الصور من الشتات والتفرقة فاقتران تلك الوحدة بالكثرة هو وصلة النكاح اولا فى مرتبة

الحمى ج نع

نع

من ج التعين ج

نع

نع

بشتمل ج

الحضرة الواحدية باحدية الذات في صور التعينات و باحدية جمع الاسماء ثم باحدية الوجود الاضافى في جميع المراتب والاكوان بحسبها حتى في حصول النتيجة في حدود القياس والتعليم والتعلم والغذاء والمغتذى والذكر والانثى فهذا الحبُ المقتضى للمحبية والمحبوبية بل العلم المقتضى للعالمية والمعلومية هو اول سريان الوحدة في الكثرة و ظهور التثليث الموجب للايجاد بالتاثير والفاعلية والمفعولية و ذلك هو النكاح السارى في جميع الذرارى ٭

(٢٥٠) نهاية السفر الاول ٭ هي رفع حجب الكثرة عن وجه الوحدة ٭

(٢٥١) نهاية السفر الثانى ٭ هو رفع حجاب الوحدة عن وجوه الكثرة العلمية الباطنية ٭

(٢٥٢) نهاية السفر الثالث ٭ هو زوال التقيد بالضدين الظاهر والباطن بالحصول

في احدية عين الجمع *

(٢٥٣) نهاية السفر الرابع * عند الرجوع من الحق الى الخلق في مقام الاستقامة هو احدية الجمع والفرق بشهود اندراج الحق في الخلق و اضمحلال الخلق في الحق حتى يرى العين الواحدة في صور الكثرة الصور الكثيرة في عين الوحدة

(٢٥٤) النوالة * كل ما ينيله الحقُ اهلَ القرب من خِلَع الرضاء و قد تطلق على كل خِلعةٍ يخلعها الله على احدٍ و قد يخص بالافراد *

(٢٥٥) نون * في قوله تعالى ن والقلم هو العلم الاجمالي في الحضرة الاحدية والقلم حضرة التفصيل *

(٢٥٦) النور * اسم من اسماء الله تعالى وهو تجليه باسمه الظاهر اعني الوجود الظاهر في صور الاكوان كلها وقد يطلق

على كل ما يكشف المستور من العلوم الذاتية والواردات الالهية التى تطرد الكون من القلب *

(٢٥٧) نور الانوار * هو الحق تعالى *

* باب السين *

(٢٥٨) السابقة * هى العناية الازلية المشار اليها فى التنزيل بقوله وبشر الذين آمنوا ان لهم قدم صدق عند ربهم *

(٢٥٩) السالك * هو السائر الى الله المتوسط بين المريد والمنتهى ما دام فى السير

(٢٦٠) السبحة * هى الهباء المسماة بالهيولى لكونها غير واضحة ولا موجودة الا بالصور لا بنفسها *

(٢٦١) الستر * كل ما يحجبك عما يعنيك كغطاء الكون والوقوف مع العادات والاعمال

(٢٦٢) الستائر * صور الاكوان لانها مظاهر الاسماء الالهية يُعرف من خلقها

(٨٣)

كما قال الشيبانى ٭ تجليتُ للأكوان خلفَ ستورِها ٭ فنمتُ بما ضمّت عليه الستائر ٭ | الأكوان ج | مستورتمت ج

(٢٦٣) الستور ٭ تخصّ بالهياكل البدنية الانسانية المرخاة بين عالم الغيب والشهادة والحق والخلق ٭

(٢٦٤) سجود القلب ٭ هو فناؤه فى الحق عند شهوده اياه بحيث لا يشغله ولا يصرفه عنه استعمال الجوارح ٭ | الفناء ج | غير مشهودة ج | عند ش

(٢٦٥) السَخَن ٭ ذهاب تركيب العبد تحت القهر ٭

(٢٦٦) سرّة المنتهى ٭ هى البرزخية الكبرى التى ينتهى اليها مسير الكلّ و اعمالهم وعلومهم و هى نهاية المراتب الاسمائية التى لا تعلوها رتبة ٭ | الكونية ش | مسير الكل ج | علومهم ج

(٢٦٧) السرّ ٭ هو ما يخصّ بكلّ شيء من الحق عند التوجه الايجاديّ اليه المشار اليه بقوله انما امرنا لشيء اذا اردناه | كل ج اسم ش | فج | قولنا ج

(۸۴۰)

يقول ع ان نقول له كن فيكون ولهذا قيل لايعرف الحق الا الحق ولا يطلب الحق الا الحق

ع (ولا يحب الحق الا الحق ج) لان ذلك السر هو الطالب للحق والمحب له والعارف به كما قال النبي صلى الله عليه وسلم عرفتُ ربي بربي *

العالم ع ج (۲٦۸) سر العلم * هو حقيقة سرّ العالم به لان العلم عين الحق فى الحقيقة غيره بالاعتبار *

(۲٦۹) سر المحال * ما يعرف من مراد الله فيها *

يغني ع (۲۷۰) سر الحقيقة * ما لا يغشي من حقيقته ش حقيقة الحق في كل شيء *

المتجلي ع (۲۷۱) سر التجليات * هو شهود كل شيء احدية ج في كل شيء و ذلك بانكشاف التجلي الاول للقلب فيشهد الاحدية الجمعية بين الاسماء كلها لاتصاف كل اسم لجميع

(٨٥)

الاسماء لاتحادها بالذات الاحدية وامتيازها بالتعينات التى تظهر فى الاكوان التي هي صورها فيشهد كلُّ شيء في كل شيء

(٢٧٢) سر القدر ٭ ما علمَّه الله من كل عين فى الازل ممّا انطبع فيها من احوالها التى تظهر عليها عند وجودها فلا يحكم على شيء الا بما علمَّه من عينه فى حال ثبوتها ٭

علم ج
فح طبع الله ج
بعلمه ج
فى الازل ح

(٢٧٣) سر الربوبية ٭ هو توقفها على المربوب لكونها نسبة لا بدّ لها من المنتسبين واحد المنتسبين هو المربوب وليس الآ الاعيان الثابتة في العدم والموقوف على المعدوم معدوم ولهذا قال سهل للربوبية سرّ لو ظهر لبطلت الربوبية وذلك لبطلان ما يتوقف عليه

سرًا ج العبودية ش

(٢٧٤) سرّ سرّ الربوبية ٭ هو ظهور الرب بصور الاعيان فهى. من حيث مظهريتها

الحقيقة فالحق للرب القائم بذاته الظاهر بتعيّناته قائمة به موجودة بوجوده فهى عبيد مربوبون من هذه الحيثية والحق رب لها فما حصلت الربوبية فى الحقيقة الا بالحق والاعيان معدومة بحالها فى الازل فلسر الربوبية سر به ظهرت ولم تبطل *

(٢٧٥) سرائر الآثار * هى الاسماء الآلهية التى هى بواطن الاكوان *

(٢٧٦) السرار * انمحاق السالك فى الحق عند الوصول التام واليه الاشارة بقوله صلعم لى مع الله وقت الحديث وقوله تعالى اوليائى تحت قبابى لايعرفهم غيرى *

الوصل ج
نع
نع

(٢٧٧) سة القلب * هى تحقق الانسان الكامل بحقيقة البرزخية الجامعة للامكان والوجوب فان قلب الانسان الكامل هو هذا البرزخ ولهذا قال ما وسعنى ارضى

قال ج نع

ولا سمائى ولكن وَسِعَنى قلب عبدي المؤمن *

(٢٧٨) السَفَر * هو توجّه القلب الى الحق والاسفار اربعة الاول هو السير الى الله من منازل النفس الى الوصول الى الافق المبين وهو نهاية مقام القلب و مبتدأ التجليات الاسمائية الثانى هو السير فى الله بالاتصاف بصفاته والتحقق باسمائه الى الافق الاعلى وهو نهاية (مقام الروح و) الحضرة الواحدية والثالث هو الترقى الى عين الجمع والحضرة الاحدية و هو مقام قاب قوسين مّا بقيتْ الاثنينية فاذا ارتفعت فهو مقام او ادنى وهو نهاية الولاية والسَفَر الرابع هو السير بالله من الله للتكميل وهو مقام البقاء بعد الفناء والفرق بعد الجمع *

(٢٧٩) سقوط الاعتبارات * هو اعتبار

احدية الذات *

(۲۸۰) السميسر * معرفة تدق عن العبارة

(۲۸۱) سوال الحضرتين * هو السوال الصادر عن حضرة الوجوب بلسان الاسماء الالهية الطالبة في نفس الرحمن ظهورها بصور الاعيان وعن حضرة الامكان بلسان الاعيان ظهورها بالاسماء و امداد النفس على الاتصال اجابة سوالهما ابدا *

(۲۸۲) سواد الوجه في الدارين * هو الفناء في الله بالكلية بحيث لا وجود لصاحبه ظاهرا و باطنا دنيا وآخرة وهو الفقر الحقيقي والرجوع الى العدم الاصلي ولهذا قالوا اذا تم الفقر فهو الله (والله الهادي) *

* باب العين *

(۲۸۳) العالم * هو الظل الثاني وليس الّا وجود الحق الظاهر بصور الممكنات كلها فلظهوره بتعييناتها سمى باسم السوى

(٨٩)

والغير باعتبار اضافته الى الممكنات اذ لا وجود للممكن الا بمجرّد هذه النسبة والّا فالوجود مين الحق والممكنات ثابتة على عدميتها فى علم الحق وهو شوءٌ ونها الذاتية فالعالم صورة الحق والحق هويّة العالم و روحهُ وهذه التعينات فى الوجود الواحد احكامُ اسمه الظاهر الذى هو مجلي لاسمه الباطن ٭

شيءٌ ج شيئونه ج   اسمه ج

(٢٨٤) عالمُ الجبروت ٭ عالم الاسماء والصفات الالهية ٭

(١٨٥) عالم الامر وعالم الملكوت وعالم الغيب ٭ هو عالم الارواح والروحانيات لانّها وجدت بامر الحق بلا واسطة مادّة ومدّة ٭

(٢٨٦) عالم الخلق وعالم الملك وعالم الشهادة ٭ هو عالم الاجسام والجسمانيات وهو ما يوجد بعد الامر بمادّة ومدّة ٭

الاجسام ج

(٢٨٧) العارف ٭ من اشهده الله ذاتهُ و

(٩٠)

صفاته و اسمائه و افعاله فالمعرفة حال تجددت من شهوده *

(٢٨٨) العالِم * من اطلعه الله على ذلك لا عن شهود بل عن يقين *

(٢٨٩) العالِر * هم الذين اقتصر علمهم على الشريعة ويسمي علماؤهم علماء الرسوم

(٢٩٠) العار العظيم والمقت الكبير * هو نقض العهد اما بان يقول ما لا يفعل او يعهد ما لا يفي قال الله تعالى كبُر مقتا عند الله ان تقولوا ما لا تفعلون وقال ايضا اتأمرون الناس بالبر وتنسون انفسكم وانتم تتلون الكتاب افلا تعقلون و في تجهيلهم بقوله افلا تعقلون عار عظيم *

(٢٩١) العبادة * هي غاية التذلل وهي للعامة والعبودية للخاصة الذين صححوا النسبة الى الله بصدق القصد اليه في سلوك طريقه والعبودةُ لخاصة الخاصة الذين

(٩١)

شهدوا نفوسهم قائمة به فى عبوديته فهم يعبُدونه به في مقام احدية الفرق والجمع (٢٩٢) العِبَادُ ٭ هم ارباب التجليات الاسمائية اذا تحققوا بحقيقة اسم ما من اسمائه تعالى واتصفوا بالصفة التي هى حقيقة ذلك الاسم (نسبوا اليه بالعبودية لشهودهم ربوبية ذلك الاسم) وعبوديتهم للحق من حيث ربوبيبه لهم بكمال ذلك الاسم خاصة فقيل لاحدهم عبد الرزق و لآخر عبد العزيز وكذا عبد المنعم وغيره ٭ (٢٩٣) عبدالله ٭ هو العبد الذي تجلى له الحق بجميع اسمائه فلا يكون في عبادة ارفع مقاما واعلى شانا منه لتحققه باسمه الاعظم واتصافه بجميع صفاته ولهذا خص نبيّنا صلى الله عليه وسلم بهذا الاسم فى قوله وانّه لما قام عبد الله يدعوه فلم يكن هذا الاسم بالحقيقة الّا له وللاقطاب من

عبودته ج
ج
عبادلة ج

ج

للآخر ج

الاسماء ج
بالاسم ج

ورثته بتبعيّته وان اطلق على غيره مجازا
لاتّصاف كل اسم من اسمائه بجميعها الواحدية ج
بحكم واحديّة و احديّة جمع الاسماء *
(۲۹٤) عبد الرحمن * هو مظهر اسم الرحمن
فهو رحمة للعالمين جميعا بحيث لايخرج
احدٌ من رحمته بحسب قابليّة استعداده *
(۲۹٥) عبد الرحيم * هو مظهر اسم الرحيم يختص ج
و هو الذي يخصّ رحمته بمن اتقى و
اصلح و رضي الله عنه وينتقم ممن غضب
الله عليه *
(۲۹٦) عبد الملك * هو الذي يملك نفسه
وغيره بالتصرف فيه بما شاء الله و امره به
فهو اشدّ خلق الله على خليقته *
(۲۹۷) عبد القدّوس * هو الذي قدّس الله قدّسه ج
عن الاحتجاب فلا يسع قلبَه غيرُه وهوالذي حيرانه ج
وسّع قلبُه الحق كما قال تعالى لايسعني
ارضي ولاسمائي و يسعني قلبُ عبدي

المؤمن ومن وسع الحق قدّس عن الغير اذ لا يبقى عند تجلي الحق شيئ غيره فلا يسع القدوس الا القلب المقدس من الاكوان *

(٢٩٨) عبد السلام * هو الذى تجلى له الحق باسم السلام فسلمه من كل نقص وآفة وعيب

(٢٩٩) عبد المؤمن * هو الذى آمنه الله عن العقاب والبلاء وآمنَ الناس عن غيره ذواتهم و اموالهم واعراضهم *

(٣٠٠) عبد المهيمن * هو الذى يشاهد كونّ الحق رقيبا شهيدا على كل شيئ فهو يرقب نفسه وغيره بايفاء حق كل ذى حق عليه لكونه مظهر اسم المهيمن *

(٣٠١). عبد العزيز * هو الذي اعزّه الله بتجلي عزّته فلا يغلبه شيئ من ايدي الحدثان والاكوان وهو يغلب كل شيئ *

(٣٠٢) عبد الجبّار * هو الذى يجبر كسر كل

شيء ونقصه لان الحق جبر حاله وجعله | مستوليا ج
يتجلى هذا الاسم جابرا لحال كل شيء | مستهاما ش
مستعليا عليه * | يغني ج

(٣٠٣) عبد المتكبر * هو الذى فني تكبره
بتذلله للحق حتى قام كبرياء الله مقام كبره | عما ج
فيتكبر بالحق على ما سواء فلا يتذلل
لغير *

(٣٠٤) عبد الخالق * هو الذى يقدّر الاشياء
على وفق مراد الحق لتجليه له بوصف
الخلق والتقدير فلا يقدّر الا بتقديره تعالى*

(٣٠٥) عبد البارى * قريب من عبد الخالق
وهو الذى برأ عمله من التفاوت والاختلاف | من علة ش
فلا يفعل الا ما يناسب حضرة الاسم البارى | العلم ج
متعادلا متناسبا بريأ من التنافر كقوله | التنافي ج
تعالى ما ترى فى خلق الرحمن من
تفاوت لان البارى الذي تجلى له شعبة | فج
من شعب الاسماء التى هى تحت الاسم | فع

(٩٥)

الرحمن *

(٣٠٦) عبد المصوّر * هو الذي لا يتصوّر ولا يصوّر الا ما طابق الحق و وافق تصويره لان فعله يصدر عن مصوريته تعالى *

(٣٠٧) عبد الغفّار * هو الذي غفر جناية كل من يجنى عليه ويستر من غيره ما احب ان يُستر منه لان الله ستر ذنوبه وغفر له بتجلّى غفاريته فيعامل عباده بما عامله به *

(٣٠٨) عبد القهّار * هو الذي وفّقه الله بتائيده لقهر قوى نفسه فتتجلى له باسمه القهّار فيقهر كل من ناواه ويهزم كل من بارزه وعاداه ويوثّر في الاكوان ولا يتاثر منها *

(٣٠٩) عبد الوهّاب * من تجلى له الحق باسم الجواد فيَهَب ما ينبغى لمن ينبغى على الوجه الذي ينبغي بلا عوض ولا غرض ويمدّ اهل عنايته تعالى الامداد لانه واسطة

جوده ومظهره ۞

(٣١٠) عبد الرزاق ۞ هو الذي وسع الله رزقه فيوثر به على عباده ويبسطه لمن يشاء الله ان يبسط له لان الله جعل في قدمه السعة والبركة فلا ياتي له الا حيث تبارك فيه وبفيض الخيريّة ۞

عبد ج

فع

(٣١١) عبد الفتاح ۞ هو الذى اعطاه الله علم اسرار المفاتيح على اختلاف انواعها فيفتح به الخصومات والمغالق والمعضلات والمضايق ويرسل به فتوحات الرحمة وما امسك من النعمة ۞

ففتح ع

ارسل ع

(٣١٢) عبد العليم ۞ هو الذى علمه الله العلم الكشفى من لدنه بلا تعمل وتفكر بل مجرد الصفاء الفطريّ وتائيد النور القدسي ۞

بمجرد ج

(٣١٣) عبد القابض ۞ مَن قبضه الله اليه فجعله قابضاً لنفسه وغيره عما لا يليق

بهم ولا ينبغي ان يقبض عليهم فى حكمة الله وعدله وحاجزاً عن العباد ما ليس يصلح لهم وهم ينقبضون بقبضه وحجره

كلمة ج
علمه ج
بحجره ج

(٣١٤) عبد الباسط * من بسطه الله في خلقه فيرسل عليهم باذنه من نفسه وماله ما يفرحون به وينبسطون موافقا لامره لانه يبسط بتجلى اسمه الباسط فلا يكون مخالفاً لشرعه

(٣١٥) عبد الخافض * هو الذي يتذلل له في كل شيء ويخفض عن نفسه لرؤيته الحق فيه *

فج
كل ج

(٣١٦) عبد الرافع * هو الذى يترفع على كل شيء لنظره اليه بنظر السوء والغير ويرفع نفسه من رتبته لقيامه بالحق الذي هو رفيع الدرجات وقد يكون بالعكس لان الاول بمظهرية الاسم الخافض يخفض عن كل شيء لرؤيته عدما محضا ولا شيئا

مرتبته ج
فع

صرفا والثانى لتجلى اسمه الرافع له يرفع كل شيء لرؤيته الحق فيه وهذا عندي اولى لان العارف يطلب الرحمة ليتصف به فيصير رحيما لا مرحوما لان ذلك نصيب العامي من الرحمة *

(٢١٧) عبد المعزّ * من تجلى الحق له باسم المعزّ فيعزّ مَن اعزّه الله بعزته من اوليائه *

(٢١٨) عبد المذلّ * هو مظهر صفة الاذلال فيذل بمذلية الحق كلّ من اذله الله من اعدائه باسمه المذلّ الذى تجلى به له *

(٢١٩) عبد السميع وعبد البصر * من تجلى فيه بهذين الاسمين فاتصف بسمع الحق وبصره كما قال كنتُ سمعه الذي به يَسمع وبصره الذي به يُبصر فيسمع ويبصر الاشياء بسمع الحق وبصره *

(٢٢٠) عبد الحكم * هو الذى يحكم بحكم الله تعالى على عباده *

(٩٩)

(٣٢١) عبد العدل * هو الذى يعدل بين الناس بالعدل بالحق لانّه مظهر عدله تعالى وليس العدل هو التساوى كما يُظنّ من لا يعلم بل توفية حق كل ذى حق وتوفيرهُ عليه بحسب استحقاقه *

(٣٢٢) عبد اللطيف * من تلطّف بعباده لكونه بصيرًا بمواقع اللطف لطفُ ادراكهُ فيكون مطّلعا على البواطن و واسطةً للطف الحق بعباده وامداده وهم لا يشعرون به للطفه بتجلي الاسم اللطيف فيه وهو الذى لا يدركه الابصار *

(٣٢٣) عبد الخبير * هو الذى اطلعه الله علي علمه بالاشياء قبل كونها وبعده *

(٣٢٤) عبد الحليم * هو الذى لا يعاجل من يجنى عليه بالعقوبة ويَحلُم عنه ويتحمل اذيةَ من يوذيه وسفاهة السفهاء ويدفع السيئة بالتى هى احسن *

(٣٢٥) عبد العظيم * هو الذي تجلى له الحق بعظمته فيتذلل له غاية التذلل اداءً لحق عظمته فيعظمه الله في اعين عباده ويرفع ذكره بين الناس يبجلونه ويوقرونه لظهور آثار العظمة على ظاهره *

(٣٢٦) عبد الغفور * ابلغ في غفران الجناية وسترها من عبد الغفار فهو دائم الغفران وعبد الغفار كثير الغفران *

(٣٢٧) عبد الشكور * هو الدائم الشكر لربه لانه لا يرى (النعمة الّا منه ولا يرى منه الّا النعمة) وإنكانت في صورة البلاء والنقمة لانه يرى في باطنه النعمة كما قال علي رضى الله عنه سبحان من اشتدت نقمته لاعدائه في سعة رحمته واتسعت رحمته لاوليائه في شدة نقمته *

(٣٢٨) عبد العلي * من علا قدره عن اقرانه وارتفعت همته في طلب المعالي

عن همم اخوانه وحاز كل رتبة علية وبلغ كل فضيلة سنية *

(٣٢٩) عبد الكبير * من كبّر بكبرياء الحق وزاد بكبره في الفضل والكمال على الخلق *

(٣٣٠) عبد الحفيظ * هو الذي حفظه الله في افعاله واقواله واحواله وخواطره وظواهره وبواطنه من كل سوء فتجلى فيه باسم الحفيظ حتى سرى الحفظ منه في جلسائه كما يحكى عن ابي سليمان الداراني انه لم يخطر بباله خطرةُ سوءٍ ثلثين سنة ولا يبال جليسه ما دام جالسا معه *

(٣٣١) عبد المقيت * من اطلعه الله على حاجة المحتاج وقدرها ووقتها ووفقه بانجاحها على وفق عمله من غير زيادة ولا بقصان ولا تقدم على وقتها ولا تأخر عنه *

(٣٣٢) عبد الحسيب * من جعله الله حسيبا

لنفسه حتى في انفاسه ووفقه للقيام عليها وفطن كل من تابعه للحسبة ¤

(٣٣٣) عبد الجليل ¤ من اجلّه الله بجلاله حتى هابه كل من رآه بجلالة قدره ووقع في قلبه الهيبة منه ¤

(٣٣٤) عبد الكريم ¤ هو الذى اشهده الله وجهَ اسمِ الكريم فتجلّي بالكرم وتحقق بحقيقة العبودية بمقتضاه فان الكرم يقضي معرفة قدرها التعدّي عن طورها فيعرف ان لا مِلك للعبد فلا يجد شيأ ينسب اليه الا يجود به على عباده بكرمه تعالى فان كرم مولاه يختص بملكه من يشاء وكذا لا يرى ذنبا من احد الا وهو يستره بكرمه ولا يجني عليه احد الا ويعفو عنه (يستره بكرمه) ويقابله باكرم الخصال واجمل الفعال قيل ان عمر رضى الله عنه لما سمع قوله تعالى ما غرّك بربك

باب الطاء

النار فكيف يلقى الله عبيده فيها وهو
ارحم الراحمين قال الراوي فبكى رسول
الله صلى الله عليه وسلم وقال هكذا
اوحى الله الي *

(١٣٠) الحكمُ المجهول * عندنا هي ما خفى
علينا وجه الحكمة في ايجاده كايلام بعض
العباد و موت الاطفال والخلود في النار
فيجب الايمان به والرضاء بوقوعه و اعتقاد
كونه عدلا و حقا *

(١٣١) الحكمة الجامعة * معرفة الحق والعمل
به و معرفة الباطل والاجتناب عنه كما قال
عليه السلام اللهم ارنا الحق حقا و ارزقنا
اتّباعه و ارنا الباطل باطلا و ارزقنا اجتنابه
(انك مجيب الدعوات) *

* باب الطاء *

(١٣٢) الطوالع * اول ما يبدو من الطالع ج
تجليات الاسماء الالهية على باطن العبد تجليات ع

(٤٠) باب الطاء

فيحسن ج — فيحسن اخلاقه و صفاته بتنوير باطنه *

(١٣٣) الطاهر * مَن عصمه الله من المخالفات

(١٣٤) طاهر الظاهر * مَن عصمه الله من المعاصي *

(١٣٥) طاهر الباطن * من عصمه الله من

لوسواس ج — الوساوس والهواجس والتعلق بالاغيار *

(١٣٦) طاهر السر * من لا يذهل عن الله طرفة عين *

بتوفيقه ج — (١٣٧) طاهر السر والعلانية * من قام بتوفية حقوق الحق والخلق جميعا لسعيه برعاية الجانبين *

(١٣٧) الطب الروحاني * هو العلم بكمالات القلوب و افاتها و امراضها و ادوائها و

فع — بكيفية حفظ صحتها و اعتدالها و ازالة

فع — امراضها وردّ صحتها اليها *

(١٣٩) الطبيب الروحاني * هو الشيخ العارف بذلك القادر على الارشاد والتكميل

(١٤٠) الطريقة ٭ هى السيرة المختصة بالسالكين الى الله من قطع المنازل والترقى ج
والتوقى فى المقامات

(١٤١) الطمس ٭ هو ذهاب رسوم السيّار بالكلية فى صفات نور الانوار والله الهادي — نسخ

٭ باب الياء ٭

(١٤٢) الياقوت الحمراء ٭ هى النفس لامتزاج   النفس الكلية صح
نوريتها بظلمة التعلق بالجسم بخلاف   المفارق ج
العقل المفارق المعبّر عنه بالدرة البيضاء

(١٤٣) اليدان ٭ هما اسما الله المتقابلة
كالفاعلة والقابلة ولهذا وبّخ ابليس بقوله   ان لا صح
تعالى ما منعك ان تسجد لما خلقت   مجمع ج
بيدي ولما كانت الحضرة الاسمائية تجمع
حضرتي الوجوب والامكان قال بعضهم
ان اليدين هما حضرتا الوجوب والامكان
والحق ان التقابل اعم من ذلك فان الفاعل
قد يتقابل كالجميل والجليل واللطيف

(٨٢)

والقهّار والنافع والضارّ وكذا القابل كالانيس والهائب والراجي والخائف والمنتفع والمتضرر

(١٢٤) يوم الجمعة ٭ وقت اللقاء والوصول الى عين الجمع

٭ باب الكاف ٭

(١٢٥) الكتاب المبين ٭ هو اللوح المحفوظ المراد بقوله تعالى ولا رطب ولا يابس الّا في كتاب مبين ٭

(١٢٦) الكل ٭ هو اسم للحق تعالى باعتبار الحضرة الواحدية الآلهية الجامعة للاسماء كلها ولهذا يقال احد بالذات كل بالاسماء

(١٢٧) الكلمة ٭ هي عمّا يكنى بها عن كل واحدة من الماهيات والاعيان والحقائق والموجودات الخارجية وفي الجملة عن كل متعيّن وقد يخص المعقولات من الماهيات والحقائق والاعيان بالكلمة المعنوية والغينية

(۶۳)

والخارجيات بالكلمة الوجودية والمجردات المفارقات بالكلمة التامة *

(۱۴۸) كلمة الحضرة * اشارة الى قوله تعالى كن وقوله تعالى انما امرنا لشىء اذا اردناه ان نقول له كن فيكون فهى صورة الارادة الكلية *

(۱۴۹) الكنز الخفى * هو الهوية الاحدية المكنونة فى الغيب وهو بطن كل باطن *

(۱۵۰) الكنود * فى الشريعة تارك الفرايض وفى الطريق تارك الفضائل وفى الحقيقة من اراد شيئا لم يرده الله تعالى لانه ينازع الله فى مشيته فلم يعرف حق نعمته *

(۱۵۱) كون الفطور غير مشتت للشمل * ومعناه ان تكثر الواحد الحق بتمييز التعينات لا يوجب تفرق الجمعية الالهية ولا الاحدية الذاتية *

(۱۵۲) كوكب الصبح * اول ما يبدو من

(۴۴)

بمظهر ع | التجليات وقد يطلق على المتحقق بمظهرية النفس الكلية من قوله تعالى فلما جنّ عليه الليل رأى كوكبًا *

الكيماء ج | (۱۵۳) الكيمياع * القناعة بالموجود وترك التشوق الى المفقود قال اميرالمؤمنين علي

يغنى ج | رضى الله عنه القناعة كنز لا ينفد *

كيماء ج النفس ج | (۱۵۴) كيمياع السعادة * تهذيب الاخلاق باجتناب الرذائل و تركيبتها عنها واكتساب

تجليتها ج | الفضايل وتحليتها عٔبها *

كيماء ج | (۱۵۵) كيمياع العوام * استبدال المتاع الاخروي الباقى بالحُطام الدنيوى الفاني *

كيماء ج | (۵۶) كيمياع الخواص * تخليص القلب من الكون باستينار المكون *

* باب اللام *

(۱۵۷) اللائحة * هى ما يلوح من نور

ايضا ح | التجلي ثم يروح ويسمى بارقة و خطرة *

(۱۵۸) اللاهوت * هى الحيوة السارية

(۴۵)

ي الاشياء والناسوت هو المحل القائم به و ذلك الروح ؏

(۱۵۹) اللب ٭ هو العقل المنوّر بنور القدس الصافي عن قشور الاوهام والتخيلات ٭

(۱٦۰) لب اللب ٭ هو مادةُ النور الآلهي القدسي الذى يتأيّد به العقلُ فيصفو من القشور المذكورة ويدرك العلوم المتعالية عن ادراك القلب المتعلق بالكون المصونة من الفهم المحجوب بالعلم الرسمى و ذلك من حسن السابقة المقتضى بخير الخاتمة

(۱٦۱) اللبس ٭ هى الصورة العنصرية التي تلبس الحقائق الروحانية قال الله تعالى ولو جعلناه ملكا لجعلناه رجلا و للبسنا عليهم ما يلبسون و منه لبس الحقيقة الحقانية بالصُّور الانسانية كما اشير اليه في الحديث القدسي بقوله تعالى اوليائي تحت قبا بي لا يعرفهم فيرى ٭

القائم بذلك / ج / الروح

تارة / ج

المنقالية / ع / المناقلية / ظ

لحسن / ع

بالصورة / ج

(١٦٢) اللسن * ما يقع به الافصاح الالهى للآذان الواعية عمّا يريد ان يعلمهم ذلك اما على سبيل التعريف اللهى و اما على سبيل نبى او ولىّ او صديق *

(١٦٣) لسان الحق * هو الانسان المتحقق بمظهرية الاسم المتكلم *

(١٦٤) اللطيفة * هى كل اشارة دقيقة المعنى يلوح منها فى الفهم معنى لاتسعه العبارة

(١٦٥) اللطيفة الانسانية * هى النفس الناطقة المسماة عندهم بالقلب و هى فى الحقيقة تنزّل الروح الى رتبة قريبة من النفس مناسبة لها بوجه و مناسبة للروح بوجه و يسمى الوجه الاول الصدر والثانى الفؤاد

(١٦٦) اللوح * هو الكتاب المبين والنفس الكلية *

(١٦٧) اللوائح * جمع لائحة و قد تطلق على ما يلوح للحس من عالم المثال كمال

(٤٧)

سارية لعمر رضى الله عنه و هو من الكشف الصوري و بالمعنى الاول من الكشف المعنوي الحاصل من الجناب الاقدس *

(١٦٨) اللوامع * انوار ساطعة تلمع لاهل البدايات من ارباب النفوس الضعيفة الطاهرة فتنعكس من الخيال الى الحس المشترك فتصير مشاهدة بالحواس الظاهرة فيترآئ لهم انوار كانوار الشهب والقمر والشمس فتضيئ ما حولهم فهي اما من غلبة انوار القهر والوعيد على النفس فتضرب الى الحمرة و اما من غلبة انوار اللطف والوعد فتضرب الى الخضرة والفقوع *

(١٦٩) ليلة القدر * ليلة يختص فيها السالك بتجلٍ خاص يعرف به قدره و رتبته بالنسبة الى محبوبه و هي وقت ابتداء وصول السالك الى عين الجمع و مقام البالغين في المعرفة *

(٤٨)

* باب الميم *

(١٧٠) الماسك والمسوك به والمسوك لاجله * هو العهد المعنوية وهى حقيقة الانسان الكامل كما قال الله تعالى لولاك لما خلقت الافلاك قال الشيخ ابو طالب المكي قدس الله سره في كتاب قوة القلوب ان الافلاك تدور بانفاس بني آدم وقال الشيخ محيي الدين العربي قدس الله سره في استفتاح كتاب نسخة الحق الحمد لله الذى جعل الانسان الكامل معلّم الملك ولدار سبحانه و تعالى تشريفا وتنويها بانفاسه الفَلَك كل ذلك اشارة الى ما ذكر *

(١٧١) ماء القدس * العلم الذى يطهر النفس من دنس الطباع ونجس الرزائل او الشهود الحقيقي بتجلى القديم الرافع للحدث فان الحدث نجس *

(١٧٢) المبدايّة * اضافة محضة تلى الاحدية

باب الميم (٤٩)

باعتبار تقدم الذات الاحدية على الحضرة الواحدية التي هي منشأ التعينات و النسب الاسمائية والصفات والاضافات اعتبارات عقلية *

(١٧٤) مبادى النهايات * هي فروض العبادات اي الصلوة والزكوة والصوم والحج وذلك ان نهاية الصلوة هي كمال القرب والمواصلة الحقيقية ونهاية الزكوة هي بذل ما سوى الله لخلوص محبة الحق ونهاية الصوم هى الامساك عن الرسوم الخلقية وما يقويها بالفناء فى الله ولهذا قال فى الكلمات القدسية الصوم لى وانا اجزى به ونهاية الحج الوصول الى المعرفة والتحقق بالبقاء بعد الفناء لان المناسك كلها وضعت بازاء منازل السالك الى النهاية و مقام احدية الجمع والفرق *

الواصلة ع / بخلوص ج

فج / ج معرفته

(٥٠) باب الميم

التى ذكرها أبو محمد رُوَيم وهى التمسك بالفقر والافتقار والتحقق بالبذل والايثار و ترك التعرض والاختيار ❋

(١٧٦) المتحقق بالحق ❋ من يشاهده تعالى فى كل متعين بلا تعين به فانه تعالى وانكان مشهودا فى كل مقيد باسم اوصفة اواعتبار او تعين اوحيثية فانه لاينحصر فيه ولا يتقيد به فهو المطلق المقيَّد والمقيَّد المطلق المنزَّه من التقيد و اللاتقيد والاطلاق واللااطلاق ❋

(١٧٧) المتحقق بالحق والخلق ❋ من يرى ان كل مطلق فى الوجود له وجه الى التقيد وكل مقيد له وجه الى الاطلاق بل يرى كل الوجود حقيقة واحدة له وجه مطلق و وجه مقيد بكل قيد ومن شاهد هذا المشهد ذوقا كان متحققا بالحق وبالخلق والفناء والبقاء ❋

(١٧٨) المجذوب ❋ من اصطنعه الحق ❋

باب الميم (٥١)

تعالى لنفسه واصطفاه لحضرة أنسه وطهّره بماء قدسه فحاز من المنح والمواهب ما فاز به بجميع المقامات والمراتب بلا كلفة المكاسب والمتاعب ٭

(١٧٩) المجالي الكلية والمطالع والمنصّات ٭ هى مظاهر مفاتيح الغيوب التى انفتحت بها مغالق الابواب المسدودة بين ظاهر الوجود وباطنه وهي خمسة ٭ الاول هو مجلى الذات الاحدية وعين الجمع ومقام أو أدنى والطامّة الكبرى ومجلى حقيقة الحقائق وهو غاية الغايات ونهاية النهايات ٭ الثانى مجلى البرزخية الأولى ومجمع البحرين ومقام قاب قوسين وحضرة جمعية الاسماء الآلهية ٭ الثالث مجلى عالم الجبروت وانكشاف الارواح القدسية ٭ الرابع مجلى عالم الملكوت والمدبّرات السماوية والقائمين بالامر الالهى فى عالم الربوبية

باب الميم (٥٢)

* التخامس مجلى عالم الملك بالكشف الصورى وعجائب عالم المثال والمدبّرات الكونية فى العالم السفلى *

(١٨٠) مجلى الاسماء الفعلية * هى المراتب الكونية التى هى اجزاء العالم وآثار الافعال *

(١٨١) مجمع البحرين * هو حضرة قاب قوسين لاجتماع بحرى الوجوب والامكان فيها وقيل هو حضرة جمع الوجود باعتبار اجتماع الاسماء الالهية والحقائق الكونية فيها *

(١٨٢) مجمع الاهواء * هو حضرة الجمال المطلق فانه لا يتعلق هوى الا برشحة من الجمال ولذلك قيل * شعر * نقّل فؤادك حيث شئت من الهوى * ما الحب الا للحبيب الاول * وقال الشيبانى رحمة الله عليه * كل الجمال غدا لوجهك مجملا * لكنه فى العالمين مفصّل *

باب الميم

(١٨٣) مجمع الاضداد ※ هو الهوية المطلقة التي هي حضرة تعانق الاطراف

محبة ظ

(١٨٤) المحبة الاصلية ※ هي محبة الذات عينها لذاتها لا باعتبار امر زايد لانها اصل جميع انواع المحبات وكل ما بين اثنين فهي اما لمناسبة في ذاتيهما او لاتحاد في وصف او مرتبة او حال او فعل ※

زايد . ج

(١٨٥) المحفوظ ※ هو الذي حفظه الله تعالى من المخالفات في القول والفعل والارادة فلا يقول ولا يفعل الّا ما يرضى به الله ولا يريد الّا ما يريده الله ولا يقصد الا ما امر الله به ※

امره ج

(١٨٦) محو ارباب الظواهر ※ رفع اوصاف العادة والخصال الذميمة ويقابله الاثبات الذي هو اقامة احكام العبادة واكتساب الاخلاق الحميدة ※

الظاهر ج

(١٨٧) محو ارباب السرائر ※ هو ازالة العلل

الآفات و يقابله اثبات المواصلات وذلك بجميع اوصاف العبد و رسوم اخلاقه وافعاله بتجليات صفات الحق واخلاقه وافعاله كما قال كنتُ سمعَهُ الذى يَسمَعُ به الحديث

(١٨٨) محو الجمع ومحو المحقيقى ۞ فناء الكثرة فى الوحدة ۞

(١٨٩) محو العبودية ومحو عين العبد ۞ هو اسقاط اضافات الوجود الى الاعيان فان الاعيان شؤنٌ نفسيه ظهرت فى الحضرة الواحدية بحكم العالمية فهى معلومات معدومة العين ابدا الا ان الوجود الحق ظهر فيها فهى مع كونها ممكنات معدومة لها آثار فى الوجود بظاهر بها وبصورها المعلومة والوجود ليس الا عين الحق تعالى والاضافة نسبة ليس لها وجود فى الخارج والافعال والتاثيرات ليست الا تابعة للوجود اذ المعدوم لا يؤثر فلا فاعل ولا موجود الا

الحق تعالى وحده فهو العابد باعتبار تعينه
و تقيّده بصورة العبد التي هى شان من
شوئنه الذاتية و هو المعبود باعتبار اطلاقه و
عين العبد باقية على عدمها فالعبد ممحوّ
و العبودية ممحوّة كما قال الله تعالى وما
رميت اذ رميت ولكن الله رمى الا ترى
الى قوله تعالى ما يكون من نجوى ثلثة
الا هو رابعهم ولا خمسة الا هو سادسهم
و قوله لقد كفر الذين قالوا ان الله ثالث
ثلثة فاثبت انه رابع ثلثة ونفى انه ثالث
ثلثة لانه لو كان احدهم لكان ممكنا
مثلهم تعالى عن ذلك و تقدّس اما
اذا كان رابعهم فكان غيرهم باعتبار الحقيقة
عينهم باعتبار الوجود او غيرهم باعتبار
تعيناتهم عينهم باعتبار حقيقتهم *

(١٩٠) المحق * فناء وجود العبد فى ذات الحق
كما ان المحو فناء افعاله في فعل الحق د

باب الميم (٥٦)

الصفات ع
في الوجود وصفات

الطمس فناء صفاته في صفات الحق فالاول لا يرى في الوجود فعلا لشىء الا للحق و الثانى لا يرى لشىء صفة الا للحق والثالث لا يرى وجودا الا للحق *

(١٩١) المحاضرة * حضور القلب مع الحق في الاستفاضة من اسمائه تعالى *

(١٩٢) المحازاة * حضوره مع وجهه بمراقبة تذهله عمّا سواه حتى لا يرى غيره لغيبته عن كلهم *

كل مم ع

(١٩٣) المحادثة * خطاب الحق للعبد في صورة من عالم الملك كالنداء لموسى من الشجرة *

(١٩٤) المخترع * موضع ستر القطب عن الافراد الواصلين *

(١٩٥) المدد الوجودى * هو وصول كل ما يحتاج اليه الممكن في وجوده على الولاء حتى يبقى فان الحق يمدّه من النفس

ممكن ج

باب الميم (٥٧)

الرحماني بالوجود حتى يترجح وجوده على عدمه الذي هو مقتضى ذاته بدون موجده وذلك في التحلل وبدله من الغذاء والنَفَس ومدده من الهواء ظاهر محسوس واما في الجمادات والافلاك والروحانيات فالعقل يحكم بدوام رجحان وجودها من مرجحه والشهود يحكم بكون كل ممكن في كل آن خلقا جديدا كما يأتي *

(١٩٦) المراتب الكلية * ست مرتبة الذات الاحدية ومرتبة الحضرة الالهية وهي حضرة الواحدية ومرتبة الارواح المجردة ومرتبة النفوس العاملة وهي عالم المثال وعالم الملكوت ومرتبة عالم الملك وهو عالم الشهادة ومرتبة الكون الجامع وهو الانسان الكامل الذي هو مجلى الجميع وصورة جمعية وانما قلنا ان المجالي خمسة والمراتب ستة لان المجلى هو المظهر الذي

(٥٨)

يظهر فيه هذه المراتب والذات الاحدية ليست مجلى لشيء اذ لا اعتبار للتعدد فيها اصلا حتى العالمية والمعلومية فهى مرتبة اصلية ترتّب هذه المراتب بتنزلاتها وما عداها كلّها مجال باطنة او ظاهرة ولا مجلى لاحدية الذات الا الانسان الكامل *

رتبة ج تترتب ج

مجالي ع

يقيد ج

(١٩٧) مرآة الكون * هو الوجود المضاف الوحدانى لان الاكوان و اوصافها واحكامها لم تظهر الا فيه وهو يخفى بظهورها كما يخفى وجه المرآة بظهور الصور فيه *

يختفي ج
مختفي ج

(١٩٨) مرآة الوجود * هى التعينات المنسوبة الى الشؤن الباطنة التى صورها الاكوان فان. الشؤن باطنة والوجود المتعين بتعيناتها ظاهر فمن هذا الوجه كانت الشؤن مرايا للوجود الواحد المتعين بصورها *

الشيون ج الي ج

(١٩٩) مرآة الحضرتين * اعني حضرت

(٥٩) باب السين

الوجوب والامكان هو الانسان الكامل وكذا مرأة الحضرة الالهية لانه مظهر الذات مع جميع الاسماء *

(٢٠٠) المسامرة * محادثة الحق للعبد في سره لانها في العرف هى المحادثة ليلا *

(٢٠١) مسالك جميع الاثنية ع * هى ذكر الذاكر الذات بالاسماء الذاتية دون الوصفية والفعلية مع المعرفة بها وشهودها وذلك ان الذات المطلقة اصل جميع اسمائه تعالى فاجل وجوده تعظيمه واعظمها التعظيم المطلق المتناول بجميع اوصافه فان الذاكر اذا اثنى عليه بعلمه او جوده او قدرته فقد قيد تعظيمه بذلك الوصف اما اذا اثنى عليه باسمائه الذاتية كالقدوس و السبوح والسلام والعلي والحق وامثالها التى هى ابنية جميع الاسماء فقد عمّم التعظيم بجميع كمالاته *

جوامع الاثنية ع
فج

المطلق ع ج
وجوه ج
اوصافها ع

باب الميم (٦٠)

(٢٠٢) مُسْتَوَى الاسم الأعظم ٭ هو البيت المحرم الذي وسع الحق اعنى قلب الانسان الكامل ٭

(٢٠٣) مستتر المعرفة ٭ هى الحضرة الواحدية التى هى منشأ جميع الاسماء ٭

(٢٠٤) المستهلك ٭ هو الفانى فى الذات الاحدية بحيث لا يبقى منه رسم ٭

(٢٠٥) المسئلة الغامضة ٭ هى بقاء الاعيان الثابتة على عدمها مع تجلى الحق باسم النور اى الوجود الظاهر في صورها وظهوره باحكامها وبروزه فى صور الخلق الجديد على الآنات باضافة وجوده اليها وتعينه بها مع بقائها على العدم الاصلى اذ لولا بدوام ترجح وجودها بالاضافة والتعين بها لما ظهرت قط وهذا امر كشفي ذوقي ينبوع عنه الفهم ويأباه العقل ٭

(٢٠٦) المستريح ٭ من العباد مَن اطلعه

باب الميم (٦١)

الله تعالى على سر القدر لانه يرى ان كل مقدور يجب وقوعه فى وقته المعلوم وكل ما ليس بمقدور يمتنع وقوعه فاستراح من الطلب والانتظار لما لا يقع [لم تقع ع] والحزن والتحسر على ما فات كما قال الله تعالى ما اصاب من مصيبة فى الارض الآية ولهذا قال انس رضى الله عنه خدمته [خدمت رسول الله ج] صلى الله عليه وسلم عشر سنين فلم يقل لشيء فعلته لِمَ فعلته ولا لشيء تركته لِمَ تركته ولم يجد هذا الانسان الا الملائم ٭

(٢٠٧) مشارق الفتح ٭ هي التجليات [مشارف ع] الاسمائية لانها مفاتيح اسرار الغيب وتجلى الذات ٭

(٢٠٨) مشارق شمس الحقيقة ٭ تجليات الذات قبل الفناء التام فى عين احدية الجمع ٭

(٢٠٩) مشرق الضمائر ٭ من اطلعه الله [مشرف ع]

باب الميم

على ضمائر الناس وتجلّى له باسمه الباطن فيُشرف على البواطن وكان الشيخ ابو سعيد بن ابى الخير قدس الله روحه احدهم ¤

(٢١٠) المضاهاة بين الشؤن والحقائق ¤ هي ترتّب الحقايق الكونية على الحقايق الالهية التى هي الاسماء وترتّب الاسماء على الشؤن الذاتيه فالاكوان ظلال الاسماء وصورها والاسماء ظلال الشؤن ¤

(٢١١) المضاهاة بين الحضرات والاكوان ¤ هي انتساب الاكوان الى الحضرات الثلث اعلى حضرة الوجوب وحضرة الامكان وحضرة الجمع بينهما فكل ما كان من الاكوان نسبته الى الوجوب اقوى كان اشرف واعلى فكان حقيقة علوية روحية او ملكوتية او بسيطة فلكية وكل ما كان نسبته الى الامكان اقوى كان اخس وادنى

باب الميم (٦٣)

فكانت حقيقة سفلية عنصرية بسيطة او مركبة وكل ما كان نسبته الى الجمع اشد كانت حقيقة انسانية وكل انسان كان الى الامكان اميل وكانت احكام الكثرة الامكانية فيه اغلب كان من الكفار وكل من كان الى الوجوب اميل واحكام الوجوب فيه اغلب كان من السابقين الانبياء و الاولياء وكل من تساوى فيه الجهتان كان مقتصدا من المؤمنين وبحسب اختلافات الميل الى احدى الجهتين اختلف المؤمنون في قوة الايمان وضعفه ⁕

(٢١٢) المطالعة ⁕ توقيعات الحق للعارفين ابتداء وعن سوال منهم فيما يرجع الى الحوادث وقد يطلق على استشراف المشاهدة عند طوالعها ومبادي بروقها ⁕

(٢١٣) المَطْلَع ⁕ هو مقام شهود المتكلم عند تلاوة آيات كلامه متجليا بالصفة التي

باب الميم (۶۴)

هى مصدر تلك الآية كما قال الإمام جعفر بن محمد الصادق لقد تجلّى الله لعباده في كلامه ولكن لا يبصرون وكان (رضى الله عنه) ذات يوم في الصلوة فخر مغشيا عليه فسئل عن ذلك فقال ما زلت اكرر الآية حتى سمعتها من قائلها قال الشيخ الكبير شهاب الدين السهروردى قدس الله روحه كان لسان الإمام جعفر بن محمد الصادق في ذلك الوقت كشجرة موسى عليه السلام عند ندائه منها بأنّي انا الله ولعمرى انّ المطلع اعمّ من ذلك وهو مقام شهود الحق فى كل شيئ متجليا بصفاته الى ذلك الشيئ مظهرها لكن لما ورد فى الحديث النبوى ما من آية الّا ولها ظهر وبطن ولكل حرف حد ولكل حد مطلع خصّوه بذلك *

(۲۱۴) معالم اعلام الصفات * هي الاعضاء

كالعين والاذن واليد فانها المحال التى يظهر بها معاني الصفات و اصولها والمَعلَم محل الظهور كمعالم الدين ومعالم الطريق *

(٢١٥) المعلِّم الاول ومعلم الملائكة ع * هو آدم عليه السلام لقوله تعالى يا آدم انبئهم باسمائهم * [الملك ج]

(٢١٦) مغرب الشمس * هو استتار الحق بتعيناته والروح ع بالجسد * [للروح بالجسد ج]

(٢١٧) مفتاح سر القدر * هو اختلاف استعدادات الاعيان الممكنة فى الازل *

(٢١٨) المفتاح الاول * هو اندراج الاشياء كلها على ما هى عليها في غيب الغيوب الذي هو احدية الذات كالشجرة فى النواة يسمي بالحروف الاصلية *

(٢١٩) مفرِّع الاحزان ومفرِّج الكروب ع * هو الايمان بالقدر * [مفرج ج]

(٢٢٠) الْفَيِّض ٭ هو اسم من اسماء النبى عم لانه المتحقق باسماء الله و مظهر افاضة نور الهداية عليهم و واسطتها ٭

فائدة ج على الخلق ج

(٢٢١) المقام ٭ هو استيفاء حقوق المراسم فان من لم يستوف حقوق ما فيه من المنازل لم يصح له الترقي الى ما فوقه كما ان من لم يتحقق بالقناعة حتى يكون له ملكة لم يصح له التوكل ومن لم يتحقق بحقوق التوكل لم يصح له التسليم وهلمّ جرا في جميعها وليس المراد من هذا الاستيفاء ان لم يبق عليه بقية من درجات المقام السافل حتى يمكن له الترقي الى المقام العالى فان اكثر بقايا المسافل

الرفيعة ج

و درجاته الرفيعة انما يستدرك في العالى بل المراد تملّكه على المقام بالتثبت فيه بحيث لا يحول فيكون حالا وصدق اسمه عليه بحصول معناه بان يسمى

قانعا و متوكلا وكذا في الجميع فانه انما يسمى مقاما لاقامة السالك فيه *

(٢٢٢) مقام التنزل الربانى * هو النفَس الرحمانى اعنى ظهور الوجود الحقانى فى مراتب التعيُّنات *

(٢٢٣) المكانة * هى المنزلة التى هي ارفع المنازل عند الله وقد يطلق عليها المكان وهو المشار اليه بقوله تعالى فى مقعد صدق عند مليك مقتدر *

(٢٢٤) المكر * هو ارداف النعم مع المخالفة وابقاء الحال مع سوء الادب واظهار الآيات والكرامات من غير امر ولا حدّ *

(٢٢٥) الملك * عالم الشهادة *

(٢٢٦) الملكوت * عالم الغيب *

(٢٢٧) مالك الملك * هو الحق فى حال مجازاة العبد على ما كان منه مما امربه *

(٢٢٨) مُنبِّه الهمم هو النبي صلى الله عليه

وسلم لانه الواسطة في افاضة الحق الهداية على من يشاء من عباده و امدادهم بالنور والآيات *

(٢٢٩) المناصفت * هى الانصاف اعنى حسن المعاملة مع الحق و الخلق *

(٢٣٠) المنهج الاول * هو انتشار (الواحدية من الوحدة الذاتية و كيفية انتشاء) جميع الصفات والاسماء في رتب الذات وصن اشهده الله على ترتب الاسماء والصفات في جميع رتب الذات فقد دله على اقرب السبل من المنهج الاول *

(٢٣١) المنقطع الوحداى * هو وحضرة الجمع التى ليس للغير فيها عين ولا اثر فهى محل انقطاع الاغيار وعين الجمع الاحدية و يسمى منقطع الاشياء وحضرة الوجود وحضرة الجمع *

(٢٣٢) منتهى المعرفة * هى الحضرة الواحدية

(٦٩)

وقسمى منشأ السِّوى باعتبار انتشاء النفس الرحمانى الذى منه تظهر صور العالمى فانها تظهر بالوجود ومنزل التدلّى لتتنزّل الحق فيه الى صور الخلق ومنزل التدانى لدنو الخلق فيه من الحق ومُنْبَعَث الجود لابتداء فيضان جُود الحق منه الى غير ذلك من الاسماء *

(٢٣٣) المنا سبة الذاتية * بين الحق ومبده من وجهين أمّا بان لا يوثر احكام تعيّن العبد وصفات كثرته في احكام وجوب الحق ووحدته بل يتأثر منها وينصبغ ظلمة كثرته بنور وحدته وامّا بان يتصف العبد بصفات الحق ويتحقق باسمائه كلها فان اتّفق الامران فذلك العبد هو الكامل المقصود لعينه وان اتفق الامر الاول بدون الثانى فهو المحبوب المقرّب وحصول الثانى بدون الاول محال وفي كلا الامرين مراتب

كثيرة اما فى الامر الاول فبحسب شدة غلبة نور الوحدة. على الكثرة وضعفها وقوة استيلاء احكام الوجوب على احكام الامكان وضعفها واما. في الامر الثانى فبحسب استيعاب تحققه بالاسماء كلها وعدمه بالتحقق ببعضها دون البعض *

(٢٣٤) المُهَيَّمون * هم الملائكة المهيمة في شهود جمال الحق الذين لم يعلموا ان الله خلق آدم لشدة اشتغالهم بمشاهدة الحق وهَيَمانهم وهم العالون الذين لم يكلفوا بالسجود لغيبتهم عما سوى الحق و لهم بنور الجمال فلا يسعون شيأ مما سواه وهم الكروبيون *

(٢٣٥) الموت * باصطلاحهم قمع هوى النفس فان حيوتها به ولا تميل الى لذاتها وشهواتها ومقتضيات الطبيعة البدنية الا به واذا مالت الى الجهة السفلية جذبت القلب

لكريم قال كرمُك يا ربُّ وقال الشيخ لعارف محيى الدين ابن العربي هذا من باب تلقين الحجّة وفى الجملة لا يرى لذنوب جميع عباده في جنب كرمه تعالى وزنا ولا يرى لجميع نِعَمه تعالى عند فيض كرمه قدرا فيكون اكرم الناس لصدور فعله من كرم ربّه الذي تجلّي له ربّهُ به وقس عليه *

(٢٣٥) عبد الجواد * فانه مظهر اسمه الجواد وواسطةُ جوده على عباده فلا يكون اجود منه في الخلق وكيف لا وهو جاد بنفسه لمحبوبه فلا يتعلق بقلبه ما عداه *

(٢٣٦) عبد الرقيب * هو الذي يرى رقيبَه اقربَ اليه من نفسه ادراكا لغنائها وذهابها في تجلّي الاسم الرقيب فلا يجاوز حدّا من حدود الله تعالى ولا احد اشد مراعاةً لها منه لنفسه ولما يحضره من اصحابه فانه

رقبته ج

برتبهم ج يراقبهم برتبة الله تعالى *

(٣٣٧) عبد المجيب * هو الذي اجاب دعوة الحق واطاعه حين سمع قوله اجيبوا داعي الله فاجاب الله دعوتَه حتى تجلى له باسمه المجيب فيجيب كلَ من دعاه من عباده الى حاجةٍ لانه من جملة الاستجابة التي اوجبه عليه لاجابته تعالى له في قوله تعالى واذا سألك عبادى عني فاني قريب اجيب دعوة الداع اذا دعان فليستجيبوا لي الآية لانه يرى دعائهم دعاءَ بحكم القرب والتوحيد اللازم للايمان الشهودي في قوله وليؤمنوا بي *

(٣٣٨) عبد الواسع * هو الذي وسع كل شيء فضلا وطولا ولا يسعه شىء لاحاطته بجميع المراتب فلا يرى مستحقا الا اعطاه من فضله *

(٣٣٩) عبد الحكيم * هو الذي بصّره الله تعالى

(١٠٥)

بمواقع الحكمة في الاشياء ووفقه للسداد في القول والصواب في العمل فلا يرى خللًا في شيئ الا يسترة ولا فسادا الا يُصلحه *

(٣٢٠) عبد الوَدُود * من كملت مودته لله ولاوليائه جميعا فاحبه الله والقى محبته على جميع خلقه فاحبه الكل الآ جهال الثقلين قال النبي صلى الله عليه وسلم ان الله اذا احب عبدا دعا جبرئيل فقال اني احب فلانا فأحبَّه فيحبه جبرئيل ثم ينادى في السماء فيقول ان الله يحب فلانا فاحبوه فاحبه اهل السماء ثم يوضع له القبول في الارض *

(٣٢١) عبد المجيد * من مجّدة الله بين الناس لكمال اخلاقه وصفاته وتخققه باخلاق الله فيمجدونه لفضله وحسن خلقه *

(٣٢٢) عبد الباعث * من احى الله قلبة

اصلحه ح

(١٠٦)

بالحيوة الحقيقية بعد موته الارادى عن صفات نفسه وشهواتها واهوائها وجعله مظهرا لاسم الباعث فهو يحيي موتى الجهل بالعلم ويبعثهم على طلب الحق *

(٣٤٣) عبد الشهيد * هو الذي يشهد الحق شهيدا على كل شي فيشهده فى نفسه وفى غيره من خلقه *

(٣٤٤) عبد الحق * هو الذي تجلى له الحق فعصمه في افعاله واقواله واحواله عن الباطل فيرى الحق في كل شي لانه الثابت الواجب القائم بذاته والمسمى بالسوى باطل (زائل ثابت به بل يراه فى صور الحق حقا والباطل باطلا *

(٣٤٥) عبد الوكيل * من يرى الحق في صور الاسباب فاعلا لجميع الافعال التي ينسبها المحجوبون فيعطل الاسباب ويكل الامور الى من يوكلها منه ويرضى به

وكيلا *

(٣٤٦) عبد القوى * هو الذي يقوى بقوّة الله على قهر الشيطان وجنوده التى هي قوى نفسه من الغضب والشهوة والهوى ثم قوىَ على قهر اعدائه من شياطين الانس والجن فلا يقاومه شيٍ من خلق الله الا قهره ولا يناوئه احد الا غلبه *

(٣٤٧) عبد المتين * هو الصلب في دينه الذي لم يتأثر ممّن اراد اغواءه ولم يكن لمن ازله من الحق بشدّته لكونه امتن من كل متين فعبد القوي هو المؤثر في كل شيٍ وعبد المتين هو الذي لم يتأثر من شيٍ *

(٣٤٨) عبد الولىّ * من يتولاّه الله من الصالحين والمؤمنين فان الله تعالىَ وهو يتولى الصالحين الله ولىّ الذين آمنوا فهو يتولى بولاية الله اولياءَ من المؤمنين والصالحين *

(١٠٨)

(٣٤٩) عبد الحميد * هو الذى تجلى له الحق بأوصافه الحميدة فيحمده ويحمده الناس وهو لا يحمد الا الله *

(٣٥٠) عبد المحصى * من تحقق بهذا الاسم بمظهريته له فتجلى الحق له به فيعلم عدد ما وجد وما سيوجد ويحيط كل شىء علما ويحصى كل شىء عددا *

(٣٥١) عبد المبدئ * هو الذى اطلعه الله على ابدائه فهو يشهد ابتداء الخلق والامر فيبدى بازنه ما يبدى من الخيرات *

(٣٥٢) عبد المعيد * هو الذى اطلعه الله على اعادته (فهو يشهد اعادة) الخلق والامور كلها اليه فيعيد بازنه ما يجب اعادته اليه ويشهد عاقبته ومعاده فى عاقبيته وسعادة على احسن ما يكون *

(٣٥٣) عبد المحيى * من تجلى له الحق باسمه المحيى فاحيى قلبه به واقدره على

احياء الموتى كعيسى عليه السلام *

(٣٥٤) عبد المميت * من امات الله من نفسه هواه وغضبه وشهوته فحيى قلبه ونور مقله بحيوة الحق ونوره حتى اثر في غيره باماته قوى نفسه او نفسه بالهمه المؤثرة المتأترة من الله بتلك الصفة التي تجلّي بها له *

(٣٥٥) عبد الحيّ * من تجلى له الحق بحيوته السرمدية فحىى بحيوته الديمومية * فىى ج

(٣٥٦) عبد القيوم * هو الذى شهد قيام الاشياء بالحق فتجلّت قيوميته له فصار قائما بمصالح الخلق فيما بالله مقيما لاوامره في خلقه بقيّوميته ممدّا لهم فيما يقومون به من معاشهم ومصالحهم وحيوتهم * قيومته ج حيوته ج

(٣٥٧) عبد الواجد * هو الذي خصّه الله بالوجود في عين الجمع الاحدية فوجد الواجد الموجود بوجود الوجود الاحدي بالوجود ج فج

(١١٠)

فاستغنى به عن الكل لانّ الفايز به فائز بالكل فلا يفقد شيأ ولا يطلب شيأ *

(٣٥٨) عبد الماجد * هو الذى شرّنه الله باوصافه واعطاه ما استعدّه واطاق بحمله من مجده وشرفه كعبد المجيد *

تحمله ج

(٣٥٩) عبد الواحد * هو الذى بلّغه الله الحضرة الواحدية وكشف له من احدية جمع اسمائه فيدرك ما يدرك ويفعل ما يفعل باسمائه ويشاهد وجوه اسمائه الحسنى *

جميع الاشياء ج
وجود ج
اسماء ج

(٣٦٠) عبد الاحد * هو وحيد الوقت صاحب الزمان الذى له القطبية الكبرى والقيامُ بالاحد الاولُ *

المقام بالاحدية
الاولى ج

(٣٦١) عبد الصمد * هو مظهرا لصمديه الذى يصمد لدفع البليّات وايصال امداد الخيرات ويستشفع به الى الله لدفع العذاب واعطاء الثواب وهو محلّ نظر الله الى العالم

يصمده

في ربوبيّته له *

(٣٦٢) عبد القادر * هو الذي شاهد قدرة الله في جميع المقدورات بتجلى الاسم القادر له. فهو صورة اليد الآلهى الذي به يبطش فلا يمتنع عليه شيء و يشاهد مؤثرية الله تعالى في الكل ودوام ايصال مدد الوجود الى المعدومات مع عدميتها بذواتها فيرى نفسه معدومة بذاتها مع كونه مؤثرًا بقدرة الله في الاشياء وكذا *

(٣٦٣) عبد المقتدر * لكنه يشهد مبدأ الا يجاز وحاله *

(٣٦٤) عبد المقدّم * هو الذى قدّمه الله و جعله من اهل الصف الاول فيُقدِّم تجلى هذا الاسم له كل من يستحق التقديم باسمه وكلُّ ما يجب تقديمه من الافعال *

(٣٦٥) عبد المؤخّر * هو الذي اخّره الله عمّا عليه كل مفرط مجاوز عن حدوده تعالى

متعالٍ بالطغيان فهو يؤخِّر بهذا الاسم كل طاغٍ مادٍّ ويردّه الى حدّه ويردعه عن التعدى والطغيان وكذا كل ما يحب تأخيره من الافعال وقد يجمعهما الله لاقوام *

(٣٦٦) عبد الاول * هو الذي شاهد اوّلية الحق على كل شيئ وازليته فيكون هو الاول بتحققه بهذا الاسم على الكل في مقامات المسابقة الى الطاعات والمسارعة الى الخيرات وعلى كل من وقف مع الخالقية لتحققه بالازلية والخلقية الموسومة بسمة المحدوث *

(٣٦٧) عبد الآخر * هو الذي شهد آخريته تعالى و بقاءه بعد فناء الخلق وتحقق معنى قوله تعالى (كل شيئ هالك الا وجهه وقوله) كل من عليها فان ويبقى وجه ربك ذو الجلال والاكرام بطلوع الوجه

البافى عليه فيبقى ببقائه وامن الفناء بلقائه وقد يتّصف بهما بعض اوليائه اكثرهم *

(٣٦٨) عبد الظاهر * هو الذى ظهر بالطاعات والخيرات حتى كشف الله له عن اسمه الظاهر فعرفه بانه الظاهر واتصف بظاهريته فيدعو الناس الى الكمالات الظاهرة وائتمر بها ورجّح التشبيه على التنزيه كما كانت دعوة موسى عليه السلام ولهذا وعدهم الجنان والملاذ الجسمانية وعظم التورية بالعجم الكبير وكتابتها بالذهب *

(٣٦٩) عبد الباطن * هو الذي بالغ في المعاملات القلبية واخلص لله وقدّس الله سرّه فتجلّى له باسمه الباطن حتى غلبت روحانيته واشرف على البواطن واخبر من المغيبات فيدعو الناس الى الكمالات المعنوية والتقديس وتطهير السرّ و رجّح التنزيه على

التشبيه كما كانت دعوة عيسى عليه السلام الى السموات والروحانيات وعالم الغيب والتقشف في الملبس والاعتزال والخلوة *
(٢٧٠) عبد الوالى * من جعله الله واليا للناس بالظهور في مظهره باسمه الوالى فهو يلى نفسه وغيره في السياسه الالهية ويقيم عدله في عباده يدعوهم الى الخير ويأمرهم بالمعروف وينهاهم عن المنكر فاكرمه الله تعالى وجعله اول السبعة الذين يظلّهم الله في ظل عرشه وهو السلطان العادل ظل الله في ارضه و انقل الناس ميزانًا لان الحسنات الرعايا وخيراتهم توضع في ميزانه من غير ان ينقص من اجورهم شيأ اذ به اقام دينه فيهم وحملهم على الخيرات فهو يده وناصره والله مؤيّده وحافظه *
(٢٧١) * عبد المتعالى * المتعالى هو المتبالغ في العلو من ادراك الغير وعبده الذى هو

(١١٥)

مظهرٌ مَن لا يقف بكل كمالٍ وعلوٍّ حصل له بل يطلب بهمّته العالية الترقي الى اعلى منه لانه شهد العلوّ الحقيقى المطلق المقدّس عن عُلوى (المكان والمكانة وعن كل تقيد فلا يزال يطلب العلوّ) فى جميع الكمالات الا ترى اكرم الخلايق واعلاهم رتبة كيف خوطب بقوله وقل ربّ زدني علما ٭

(٣٧٢) عبد البرّ ٭ من اتّصف بجميع انواع البرّ معنى وصورة فلا يجد نوعا من انواع البرّ الّا اتاه ولا فضلا الا عطاءً ولكن البرّ من آمن بالله (دايما من نفسهٔ) واليوم الآخر الى آخر الآية ٭

(٣٧٣) عبد التوّاب ٭ هو الرجّاع الى الله دائما من نفسه وجميع ما سوى الحق حتى شهد التوحيد الحقيقي وقبِلَ توبة كل من تاب إلى الله عن جريمته ٭

(٣٧٤) عبد المستقيم * من اقامه الله لاقامة حدوده في عباده على الوجه المشروع ولا يرق لهم (ولا يرؤف بهم) كما قال تعالى ولا تأخذكم بهما رأفة في دين الله *

(٣٧٥) عبد العفو * من كثر عفوه عن الناس وقلّت مواخذته بل لا يجنى عليه احد الّا عفاء قال النبى صلى الله عليه وسلم ان الله عفو يحب العفو وقال حوسب رجل ممن كان (قبلكم فلم يوجد له من الخير شيي الا انه كان رجلًا موسرا وكان) يامر غلمانه بالتجاوز من المعسر قال الله تعالى نحن احق بالتجاوز منه فتجاوزوا عنه *

(٣٧٦) عبد الرؤف * من جعله الله مظهرًا لرأفته ورحمته فهو ارأف خلق الله بالناس الا فى الحدود الشرعية فانه يرى الحد وما اوجبه عليه من الذنب الذى اجرى الله

(١١٧)

على يده بحكم الله وقضائه رحمة منه عليه ... من ج
وانكانت ظاهره نعمة وهذا مما لايعرفه الا ... نقمة ج
خاصة الخاصة بالذوق فاقامة الحد عليه ... فاقامته ج ... فج
ظاهرا عين الرافة باطنا * ... به ... صح

(٣٧٧) عبد مالك الملك * من شهد مالكيته
تعالى لملكه فراى نفسه ملكا له خالصا ... فج
من جملة ملكه فتحقق بعبوديته حتى
اشتغل بعبوديته لمولاه عما ملكه اياه وعن
كل شيء فجازاه الله بجعله مظهرا لمالك
الملك اذ لا يملكه شيء حتى شغله عن
ربه وكان حرّا من رق الكون مالكا للاشياء
بالله لا بنفسه فانه عبد حقا * ... عبده ج

(٣٧٨) عبد ذو الجلال والاكرام * من اجلّه ... ذو ج
الله واكرمه لاتصافه بصفاته وتحققه باسمائه
وكما تقدست اسماؤه وعزت وتنزهت ... اسمائه ج
وجلت فكذلك مظاهرها ورسومها فلا يراه
احد من اعدائه الا هابه وخضع له بجلاله

قدره ولا احد من اوليائه الا اكرمه واعزه لاكرام الله اياه وهو يكرم اولياء تعالى ويهين اعداءه ⁂

(٣٧٩) عبد المقسط ⁂ هو اقوم الناس بالعدل حتى ياخذ من نفسه لغيره حقا له ولا يشعر به ولا يعرفه ذلك الغير لانه يعدل بعدل الله الذي تجلى له به فيوفي كل ذي حق حقه ويُزيل كل جور يطّلع عليه فهو على كرسي النور يخفض من يجب خفضه ويرفع من يجب رفعه كما قال عليه السلام المقسطون على منابر من نور ⁂

(٣٨٠) عبد الجامع ⁂ هو الذي جمع الله فيه جميع اسمائه وجعله مظهرا لجامعيته فجمع بالجمعية الالهية كل ما تفرق وتشتّت من نفسه وغيره ⁂

(٣٨١) عبد الغنى ⁂ هو الذي اغناه الله من جميع الخلايق واعطاه كل ما احتاج اليه

من غير مسئلة منه الا بلسان الاستعداد لتحققه بفقره الذاتي وافتقاره اليه بجوامع هممه *

(٣٨٢) عبد المغني * هو الذي جعله الله بعد كمال الغنى معنيا للخلق بانجاح حوائجهم وسدّ خلاتهم بهمته التي امدها الله تعالى من اغنائه بتجلى اسم المغني فيه *

(٣٨٣) عبد المانع * هو الذي حماه الله تعالى ومنعه مّن كل ما فيه فساده ان طلبه واحبه وظن فيه خيرة كالمال والجاه والصحة وامثالها واشهده معنى قوله تعالى عسى ان تكرهوا شيئاً وهو خير لكم وعسى ان تحبوا شيئاً وهو شرّ لكم وقد جاء في الكلمات القدسيّة ان من عبادي من افقرته ولو اغنيته لكان شرًّا له وان من عبادي من امرضته ولو عافيته لكان شرا له وانا أعلَم بمصالح عبادي أُدَبّرهم كما أشاءُ ومن تحقق

بهذا الاسم منع اصحابه عما يضرهم ويفسدهم ومنع الله به الفساد حيث اتي ولو حسبوا فيما منعوه خيرهم وصلاحهم *

(٣٨٤) عبد الضار والنافع * هو الذى اشهده الله كونه فعالا لما يريد وكشف له عن توحيد الافعال فلا يرى ضرا ولا نفعا ولا خيرا ولا شرا الا منه فاذا تحقق بهذين الاسمين وصار مظهرا لهما كان ضارا نافعا للناس بربه وقد خص الله تعالى بعض عباده باحدهما فقط فجعل بعضهم مظهرا للضر كالشيطان ومن تابعه وبعضهم مظهرا للنفع كالخضر ومن ناسبه *

(٣٨٥) عبد النور * هو الذى تجلى له باسمه النور فيشهد معنى قوله تعالى الله نور السموات والارض والنور هو الظاهر الذى يظهر به كل شيء كونا وعلما فهو نور في العالمين يُهتدى به كما قال عليه السلام

اللهم اجعلني نورا ٭

(٣٨٦) عبد الهادى ٭ هو مظهر هذا الاسم جعله الله هاديا لخلق الله ناطقا عن الحق بالصدق مبلّغا ما امره به و انزل اليه كالنبى صلى الله عليه و سلم بالاصالة و وَرَثَتُه بالتبعية ٭

(٣٨٧) عبد البديع ٭ هو الذي شهد كونه تعالى بديعا فى ذاته و صفاته و افعاله وجعله الله مظهرا لهذا الاسم فيبدع ما عجز عنه غيره به ٭

(٣٨٨) عبد الباقى ٭ من اشهده الله تعالى بقاءه وجعله باقيا ببقائه عند فناء الكل يعبده به بالعبودية المحضة اللازمة لتعيّنه فهو العابد و المعبود تفصيلا و جمعا و تعيّنا وحقيقة اذ لم يبق رسمه و اثره عند تجلّى الوجه الباقي كما ورد فى الحديث القدسى ومَن انا قتلتُه فعليّ ديتُه ومَن

ج دينه ج علي ديته فانا ديته *

(٣٨٩ عبد الوارث * هو مظهر هذا الاسم و هو من لوازم عبد الباقي لانه اذا كان باقيا ببقاء الحق بعد فنائه من نفسه لزم ان يرث ما يرثه الحق من الكل بعد فنائهم من العلم والملك فهو يرث الانبياء علومَهم و معارفهم وهدايتهم لدخولهم في الكل *

(٣٩٠) عبد الرشيد * من آناه الله رشده بتجلى هذا الاسم (فيه كما قال لابراهيم عليه السلم و لقد آتينا ابراهيم رشده ثم اقامه لارشاده الخلق اليه والى مصالحهم الدنيوية و الاخروية في المعاش و المعاد) *

(٣٩١) (عبدالصبور * هو المثبِّت في الامور بتجلى هذا الاسم) فيه فلا يعاجل في العقوبات والمواخذات ولا يستعجل في رفع المسلَّمات و يصبر في المجاهدات وما امره الله به من الطاعات وما ابتلاه

(١٢٣)

الله به ‖ من البليات وما يعتريه من الاذيات ٭

(٢٩٢) العبرة ٭ ما يعتبر به من ظواهر احوال الناس في الخير والشرّ وما جرى عليهم في الدنيا وما انتقلوا عليه منها الى الآخرة ودار الجزاء الى ما يؤول اليه حال المعتبر والى بواطن الامور وخفياتها حتى تبيّن له عواقب الامور ومعرفة الخفايا وما يجب عليه القيام به والعمل له قال النبي صلى الله عليه وسلم امرتُ ان يكون نطقى ذكرا وصمتى فكرا و نظرى عبرة و يدخل فيها العبور من روٴية الحكمة في ظواهر الخليقة الى روٴية الحكيم ومن ظاهر الوجود الى باطنه حتى يرى الحق وصفاته في كل شي ٭

(٢٩٣) العقاب ٭ يعبّر عندهم من العقل الاول تارة و من الطبيعة الكلية اخرى

و ذلك انهم يعبّرون عن النفس الناطقة بالورقاء والعقل الاول يختطفها من العالم السفلى و الحضيض الجسماني الى العالم العلوي و اوج الفضاء القدسى كالعقاب وقد تختطفها الطبيعة و تصطادها وتهوى بها الى الحضيض السفلي كثيرا فلهذا يطلق العقاب عليهما و الفرق بينهما فى الاستعمال بالقرائن *

(٣١٤) العلّة * عبارة من بقاء حظ العبد في عمل أوحالٍ او مقام اوبقاء رسم او صفة *

(٣١٥) العماء * الحضرة الاحدية عندنا لانه لا يعرفها احد غيره فهو فى حجاب الجلال وقيل هى الحضرة الواحدية التى هي منشأ الاسماء و الصفات لان العماء هو الغيم الرقيق و الغيم هوالحائل بين السماء والارض وهذه الحضرة هي الحائلة بين سماء الاحدية و بين ارض الكثرة

(١٢٥)

الخليقية ولا يساعده الحديث النبوي لانه سئل عليه السلام اين كان ربنا قبل ان يخلق الخلق فقال في عماء وهذه الحضرة تتعين بالتعين الاول لانها محل الكثرة فظهور الحقايق و النسب الاسمائية و كل ما يتعين فهو مخلوق فهي العقل الاول قال عليه السلام اول ما خلق الله العقل فاذا لم يكن فيه قبل ان يخلق الخلق الاول بل بعده والدليل على ذلك ان القائل بهذا القول يسمي هذه الحضرة حضرة الامكان و حضرة الجمع بين حضرة الوجوب و الامكان و الحقيقة الانسانية (وكل ذلك من قبيل المخلوقات و يعترف) بان الحق في هذه الحضرة متجلى بصفات الخلق و كل ذلك مقتضى ان ذلك ليس قبل ان يخلق الخلق اللهم الا ان يكون مراد السائل

الخلقية ج	ج
عماء ج	ج
وظهور ج	ج
	نح
احكام ج	ج
	نح
يقتضي ج	ج

الحق ج خلق ظ بالخلق العالم الجسماني فيكون العماء الحضرة الالهية المسماة بالبرزخ الجامع و
يقول ج تقويم انه سئل عن مكان الرب فان الحضرة الالهية منشأ الربوبية *

(٣٩٦) العمد المعنوية * هى التى يستمسك بها السموات المشار اليها بقوله رفع السموات بغير عمد ترونها فانه تلويح الى عمد لا ترونها وهى روح العالم و قلبه و نفسه وهى حقيقة الانسان الكامل الذي لا يعرفه الا الله كما قال تعالى اوليائى تحت قبابى لا يعرفهم غيري *

(٣٩٧) العنقاء * كناية عن الهيولى لا نها لا ترى كالعنقاء ولا يوجد الا مع الصورة فهى معقولة و تسمى الهيولى المطلقة المشتركة بين الاجسام كلها العنصر الاعظم فح

(٣٩٨) (العنصر الاعظم * هو العنقاء) * مع

(٣٩٩) عوالم اللبس * هي جميع المراتب

النازلة من الحضرة الاحدية لان الذات القدسية تتنزل بتعيناتها فيها و تتّصف بلباس الاسماء و بالصفات الروحانية و المثالية الى الحسية فيلتبس بها *

(٥٠٠) العين الثابت * هى حقيقة الشئ في الحضرة العلمية ليست بموجودة بل معدومة ثابتة في علم الله والمرتبة الثانية من الوجود الحقي *

(٥٠١) عين الشيء * هو الحق تعالى *

(٥٠٢) عين الله و عين العالم * هو الانسان الكامل المتحقق بحقيقة البرزخية الكبرى لان الله ينظر بنظره الى العالم فيرحمه بالوجود كما قالوا لولاك لما خلقت الافلاك و الانسان المتحقق بالاسم البصير لان كل ما يبصر في العالم من الاشياء فانه يبصر بهذا الاسم *

(٥٠٣) عين الحيوة * هو باطن الاسم الحى

(١٢٨)

الذي من تحقق به شرب من ماء عين الحيوة الذي من شربه لا يموت ابدا لكونه حيّا بحيوة الحق وكل حي في العالم يحيي بحيوة هذا الانسان لكونه حيوته حيوة الحق *

(٥٠٤) العيد * ما يعود على القلب من التجلي او وقت التجلي كيف كان *

* باب الفاء *

(٥٠٥) الفتق * ما يقابل الرتق من تفصيل المادة المطلقة بصورها النوعية او ظهور كل ما بطن في الحضرة الواحدية من النسب الاسمائية و بروز كل ما كمن في الذات الاحدية من الشؤون الذاتيه كالحقايق الكونية بعد تعينها في الخارج *

(٥٠٦) الفتوح * كل ما يفتح على العبد من الله تعالى بعد ما كان مغلقا عليه من النعم الظاهرة و الباطنة كالارزاق والعبادة والعلوم والمعارف والمكاشفات وغير ذلك *

(١٢٩)

(٤٠٧) الفتح القريب * هو ما انفتح على العبد من مقام القلب وظهور صفاته و كمالاته عند قطع منازل النفس وهو المشار اليه بقوله تعالى نصر من الله وفتح قريب *

(٤٠٨) الفتح المبين * هو ما انفتح على العبد من مقام الولاية و تجليات انوار الاسماء الالهية المغنية لصفات القلب وكمالاته المشار اليه بقوله تعالى انا فتحنا لك فتحا مبينا ليغفر لك الله ما تقدم من ذنبك وما تاخر يعنى من الصفات النفسية و القلبية *

المغنية بصفات ج

(٤٠٩) الفتح المطلق * هو اعلى الفتوحات و اكملها و هو ما انفتح على العبد من تجلى الذات الاحدية والاستغراق في عين الجمع بفناء الرسوم الخلقية كلها و

الالهية ج

ورايت الناس لاية ضج هو المشار اليه بقوله تعالى اذا جاء نصر الله والفتح ٭

(٤١٠) الفترة ٭ خمود حرارة الطلب اللازم للمبتدى ج للبداية ٭

(٤١١) الفرق الاول ٭ هو الاحتجاب بالخلق عن الحق وبقاء الرسوم الخلقية بحالها ٭ كليها ضج

(٤١٢) الفرق الثانى ٭ هو شهود قيام الخلق بالحق و رؤية الوحدة فى الكثرة والكثرة فى الوحدة من غير احتجاب صاحبه باحدهما عن الآخر ٭

(٤١٣) الفرقان ٭ هو العلم التفصيلي الفارق بين الحق والباطل والقرآن هو العلم اللدني الاجمالي الجامع للحقائق كلها ٭ ج

(٤١٤) فرق الجمع ٭ هو تكثر الواحد بظهوره فى المراتب التي هي ظهور شؤون الذات الاحدية وتلك الشؤون فى الحقيقة اعتبارات محضة لا تحقق لها الا عند

بروز الواحد الحق بصورها *

(٤١٥) فرق الوصف * ظهور الذات الاحدية باوصافها فى الحضرة الواحدية *

(٤١٦) الفرق بين المتخلق والمتحقق * ان المتخلق هو الذى يكتسب فضائل الاخلاق والاوصاف الحميدة تكلفا وتعملا و يجتنب الرزائل والذمائم فله من الاسماء الالهية آثارها والمتحقق بها هو الذى جعله الله مظهرًا لاسمائه واوصافه وتجلى فيه بها فنعما رسوم اخلاقه و اوصافه *

(٤١٧) الفرق بين الكمال والشرف والنقص والخسة * هو ان الكمال عبارة عن حصول الجمعية الالهية والحقائق الكونية فى الانسان وكل من كان حظه من الاسماء الالهية والحقائق الكونية اوفر و ظهوره بها اتم والجمعية الالهيه بجميع صفاته واسمائه فيه اكثر كان اكمل وكل من كان حظه منها اقل كان انقص وعن مرتبة

الخلافة الآلهية ابعدَ و اما الشرف فهو عبارة عن ارتفاع الوسائط بين الشيئ و موجدِه او قلتها فكلما كانت الوسائط بين الحق والخلق اقلّ و احكام الوجوب على احكام الامكان اغلب فيه كان الشيئ اشرف وكلما كانت الوسائط بينه و بين الحق تعالى اكثر كان الشيئ اخس فعلى هذا يكون العقل الاوّل والملائكة المقرّبون من الانسان الكامل اشرف وذلك الانسان منهم اكمل *

(٤١٨) النَّطور * هو تمييز الحق عن الخلق بالتعين و توابعه *

(٤١٩) النهوانة * خطاب الحق بطريق المكافحة في عالم المثال *

* باب الصاد *

(٤٢٠) صاحب الزمان و صاحب الوقت والحال * هو المتحقق بجمعية البرزخية الاولى

المطّلع على حقائق الاشياء الخارج عن
حكم الزمان وتصرفات ماضيه ومستقبله
الى الآن الدائم فهو ظرف احواله وصفاته لاحواله ج
وافعاله فلذلك يتصرف فى الزمان بالطى
والنشر و فى المكان بالبسط والقبض
لانه المتحقق بالحقائق والطبائع والحقائق
فى القليل والكثير والطويل والقصير و
العظيم والصغير سواء ان الوحدة والكثرة
والمقادير كلها عوارض وكما يتصرف فى فكما ج
الوهم فيها كذلك فى العقل فصدق و فكذلك ج
افهم تصرفه فيها فى الشهود والكشف فهم ج
الصريح فان المتحقق بالحق المتصرف
بالحقائق يفعل ما يفعل فى طور وراء طور الطوار ج
الحس والوهم والعقل ويتسلط على
العوارض بالتغيير والتبديل *

(٤٢١) مبيح الوجه * هو المتحقق بحقيقة
الاسم الجواد و مظهريته و لتحقق رسول الله

(۱۳۴)

مع شناع ج ‌ صلى الله عليه وسلم به. روى جابر رضي الله
استشفع ج ‌ عنه ان الله ما سُئِل عنه عليه السلام شئ قط
‌ قال لا و من استشفع به الى الله لم يرد
‌ سؤاله كما اشار اليه امير المؤمنين علي
‌ رضي الله عنه اذا كانت لك الى الله
المسئلة ج ‌ سبحانه حاجةٌ فابدأ بمسألة الصلوة على
النبي صلى الله عليه و سلم ثم اسأل
حاجتك فان الله اكرم من ان يسأل
حاجتين فيقضي احدهما ويمنع الاخرى
والمحقق بوراثته فى جوده عليه الصلوة والسلام
هو الاشعث من الاخفياء. الذي قال فيه
عليه السلام رب اشعث مدفوع بالابواب
لو اقسم على الله لابرّه و انما سمي صبيح
الوجه لقوله صلى الله عليه وسلم اطلبوا
الحوائج عند صباح الوجوه ٭
(۲۲م) الصَبا٭ هي النفحات الرحمانية الآتية

(١٣٥)

من جهة شرق الروحانيات والدواعي الباعثة على الخير ۞

(٤٢٣) الصدّيق ۞ مبالغة في الصدق وهو الذي كمل في تصديق كل ما جاء به رسول الله صلى الله عليه وسلم علماً وقولاً وفعلاً بصفاء باطنه و قربه لباطن النبي صلى الله عليه وسلم لشدّة مناسبته له ولهذا لم يتخلل في كتاب الله تعالى مرتبة بينهما في قوله تعالى اولئك الذين انعم الله عليهم من النبيين والصديقين والشهداء والصالحين و قال صلى الله عليه وسلم انا و ابو بكر كفرسي رهان فلو سبقني لآمنت به ولكن سبقته فآمن بي ۞

(٤٢٤) صدق النور ۞ هو الكشف الذي لا استتار بعده شبّه بالبرق الذي امطر فسمّي صادقاً اذ الذي لم يمطر سمّي كاذباً فان الانسان اذا تعاقب عليه التجلي والاستتار

النور ع — اشبهته حاله فانا بلغ الكشف به مقام الجمع سمي صدق التنوّر اذ لا استتار بعده ولا اختفاء ٭

(٤٢٥) الصَّدأ ٭ ما ارتكب على وجه القلب من ظلمة هيئآت النفس وصور الاكوان ع
الامكان ج — فحجبه من قبول الحقائق و تجليات الانوار ما لم تبلغ غاية الرسوخ فاذا بلغ في ع
واذا ج —
الحجر بان ج الكلي ج — الرسوخ حدّ الحرمان و الحجاب الكلّ سمي رينا ورانا كما ذكر ٭

(٤٢٦) الصعق ٭ هو الفناء فى الحق بالتجلي الذاتي ٭

(٤٢٧) الصفوة ٭ هم المتحققون بالصفاء من كدر الغيرية ٭

(٤٢٨) صورة الحق ٭ هو محمد صلى الله عليه وسلم لتحققه بالحقيقة الاحدية و الواحدية
قع بالصاد ج — و يعبّر عنه ايضًا بصاد كما لوّح اليه ابن عباس رضى الله عنهما حين سئل عن

معنى ص فقال جبل بمكه كان عليه عرش الرحمن

(٦٢٩) صورة الازل ٭ هو الانسان الكامل لتحققه بحقائق الاسماء الالهية — الآلهية ج

(٦٣٠) مواقع الذكر ٭ هي الاحوال الالهية والمواطن المعنوية التي تصون الذاكر من التفرق عن مذكوره وتجمع همة عليه بالكلية — مته ج نج

(٦٣١) صون الارادة ٭ هو انقطاع النفس من رؤية وقوع شيئ بارادة غير الله و شهود وقوع جميع الاشياء بارادة الحق تعالى — صورة ج مي ج

٭ باب القاف ٭

(٦٣٢) القابلية الاولى ٭ هي اصل الاصول وهو التعين الاول

(٦٣٣) قابلية الظهور ٭ هي المحبة الاولى المشار اليها بقوله احببت ان اعرف

(٦٣٤) قاب قوسين ٭ هو مقام القرب الاسمائي باعتبار التقابل بين الاسماء في

الامر الآلهي المسمى دايرة الوجود كالابداء والاعادة والنزول والعروج والفاعلية والقابلية وهو الاتحاد بالحق مع بقاء التميز والاثنينية المعبر عنه بالاتصال ولا اعلى من هذا المقام الا مقام او ادنى و هو احدية عين الجمع الذاتية المعبر عنه بقوله تعالى او ادنى لارتفاع التميز والاثنينية الاعتبارية هناك بالفناء المحض والطمس الكلي للرسوم كلها

معلم مع

(٥٣٥) القيام بنيه ٭ هو الاستيقاظ من نوم الغفلة والنهوض من سنة الفترة عند الاخذ في السير الى الله

(٥٣٦) القيام بالله ٭ هو الاستقامة عند البقاء بعد الفناء والعبور على المنازل كلها والسير من الله في الله بالانخلاع من الرسوم بالكلية

بالله في الله ج

(٥٣٧) التبخ ٭ هو اخذ الوقت القلب بوارد يشير الى ما يوحشه من الصد

فخ

والهجران و امثال ذلك وقد مرّ ذكره في ما يقابله من البسط والقبض اكثر ما يقع عقيب البسط لسؤ ادب يصدر من السالك في حال البسط والفرق بينهما و بين الخوف والرجاء انّ تعلّق الخوف والرجاء بالمكروه والمرغوب المتوقّع في مقام النفس والقبض والبسط انما يتعلقان بالوقت الحاضر لا تعلّق لهما بالاجل

(۶۳۸) القَدَم * هى السابقة التى حكم الحقُّ بها للعبد ازلا ويُختصّ بما يكمل ويتم به الاستعداد من الموهبة الاخيرة بالنسبة الى العبد لقوله عليه السلام لا يزال جهنم تقول هل من مزيد حتى يضع الجبّار فيها قدمه فتقول قطنى قطنى و انما يكنى عنها بالقدم لان القدم آخر شئ من الصورة وهى آخر ما يقرب به الحق الى العبد، من اسمه الذى اذا اتصل به و تحقق كمل

(۱۸۰)

(۴۳۹) قدمُ الصدق ٭ هى السابقة الجميلة والموهبة الجزيلة التى حكم بها الحق تعالى لعبادة الصالحين المخلصين من قوله تعالى و بشِّر الذين آمنوا ان لهم قدم صدق عند ربهم والصدق هو الخيار من كل شيء

(۴۴۰) القرب ٭ عبارة عن الوفاء بما سبق فى الاول من العهد الذى بين الحق والعبد في قوله تعالى الست بربكم قالوا بلى وقد يخص بمقام قاب قوسين

الازل ج

(۴۴۱) القشر ٭ كل علم ظاهر يصون العلم الباطن الذى هو لبّه عن الفساد كالشريعة للطريقة والطريقة للحقيقة فان من لم يصن حاله و طريقته بالشريعة فسد حاله وآلت طريقته هَوَسًا و هوى و وسوسة ومن لم يتوسَّل بالطريقة الى الحقيقة ولم يحفظها بها فسدت حقيقته و آلت الى الزندقة والالحاد

مع

(٤٤٢) القطب * هو الواحد الذى هو موضع نظر الله تعالى من العالم فى كل زمان و هو على قلب اسرافيل عليه السلام

(٤٤٣) القطبية الكبرى * هى مرتبة قطب الاقطاب و هو باطن نبوة محمد عليه الصلوة والسلام فلا يكون الاورثته لاختصاصه عليه الصلوة والسلام بالاكملية فلا يكون خاتم الولاية وقطب الاقطاب الا على باطن خاتم النبوة

(٤٤٤) القلب * جوهر نورانى مجرد يتوسط بين الروح والنفس. و هو الذى يتحقق به الانسانية ويسميه الحكيم النفس الناطقة والروح باطنه والنفس الحيوانية مركبه وظاهره المتوسطة بينه و بين الجسد كما مثل القلب فى القرآن بالزجاجة والكواكب الدرى والروح بالمصباح فى

قوله تعالى مثل نوره كمشكوة فيها مصباح (المصباح في زجاجة الزجاجة كانها كوكب دري توقد من شجرة مباركة زيتونة لا شرقية ولا غربية) والشجرة هى النفس والمشكوة هي البدن وهو الوسط فى الوجود ومراتب التنزلات بمنابة اللوح المحفوظ فى العالم

(٦٢٥) القوامع * كل ما يقمع الانسان من مقتضيات الطبع والنفس والهوى ويردّه عنها وهى الأمداد الاسمائية والتأييدات الآلهية لاهل العناية فى السير الى الله والتوجه نحوه.

(٦٢٦) (القيامة) * الانبعاث بعد الموت الى الحيوة الابدية وذلك على ثلثة اقسام اولها الانبعاث بعد الموت الطبيعى الى حيوة فى احدى البرازخ العلوية او السفلية بحسب حال الميت فى الحيوة الدنيوية لقوله ثم كما

(١٤٣)

تعيشون تموتون وكما تموتون تبعثون وهي القيامة الصغرى المشار اليها في قوله صلعم من مات فقد قامت قيامته و ثانيها الانبعاث بعد الموت الارادي الى الحيوة القلبية الابدية في عالم القدس كما قيل من مات بالارادة يحيى بالطبيعة وهي القيامة الوسطى المشار اليها في قوله تع افمن كان ميت فاحييناه فجعلنا له نورا يمشى به في الناس الاية وثالثها الانبعاث بعد الفناء في الله في الحبوة الحقيقية عند البقاء بالحق وهي القيامة الكبرى المشار اليها بقوله تعالى اذا جاءت الطامة الكبرى)

* باب الراء *

(٦٦٧) الرامى * هو المتحقق بمعرفة العلوم السياسية المتمكنُ من تدبير النظام الموجب لصلاح العالم *

(٦٦٨) الران * هو الحجاب الحائل بين

القلب وبين عالم القدس باستيلاء الهيأت الجسمانيه عليه ورسوخ الظلمات الجسمانية فيه بحيث يحتجب من انوار الربوبية بالكلية ❊

انوار ج ‾

(٩٤) الرب ❊ اسم للحق عزّ اسمُه باعتبار نسب الذات الى الموجودات العينية ارواحا كانت او اجسادا فان نسب الذات الى الاعيان الثابتة هي منشاء الاسماء الآلهية كالقادر والمريد ونسبها الى الاكوان الخارجية هي منشاء الاسماء الربوبية كالرزاق والحفيظ فالرب اسم خاص يقتضى وجوب المربوب وتحققه والآله يقتضى ثبوت المألوه وتعينه وكل ما ظهر من الاكوان فهو صورة اسم ربانى بربّه الحق به ياخذ وبه يفعل ما يفعل واليه يرجع فيما يحتاج اليه وهو المعطي اياه ما يطلبه منه ❊

تعالى ج ‾

بهمنه بالفعل ج ‾ ج ‾ ج ‾

(٤٥٠) ر ب الارباب ❋ هو الحق باعتبار الاسم الاعظم والتعين الاول الذى هو منشأ جميع الاسماء وغاية الغايات اليه يتوجه الرغبات كلها وهو الحاوي لجميع المطالب النسبية واليه الاشارة بقوله وان الى ربك المنتهى لانه عليه الصلوة والسلام مظهر التعين الاول فالربوبية المختصة به هي هذه الربوبية العظمى ❋

(٤٥١) رتب الاسماء ثلثة ❋ ذاتية و وصفية وفعلية ❋ لان الاسم انما يطلق على الذات باعتبار نسبة وتعين وذلك الاعتبار اما امر عدمي نسبي محض كالغني والاول والآخر او غير نسبي كالقدوس والسلام ويسمى هذا القسم اسماء الذات او معنى وجودي نعتبره العقل من غير ان يكون زايدا على الذات خارج العقل فانه محال وهو اما ان لا يتوقف على تعقل الغير كالحي

والواجب واما ان يتوقف على تعقل الغير دون وجوده كالعالم والقادر وتسمى هذه اسماء الصفات واما ان يتوقف على وجود الغير كالخالق والرازق وتسمى هذا اسماء الافعال لانها مصادر الافعال *

(٦٥٢) الرتق * اجمان المادّة الوحدانية المسماة بالعنصر الاعظم المطلق المرتوق قبل خلق السموات والارض المفتوق بعد تعينهما بالخلق وقد يطلق على نسب الحضرة الواحدية باعتبار لا ظهورها وعلى كل بطون وغيبة كالحقائق المكنونة فى الذات الاحدية قبل تفاصيلها فى الحضرة الواحدية مثل الشجرة فى النواة *

(٦٥٣) الرحمن * اسم للحق باعتبار الجمعية الاسمائية التى فى الحضرة الآلهية الفائض منها الوجود وما يتبعه من الكمالات على جميع الممكنات *

(٤٥٤) الرحيم * اسم له باعتبار فيضان الكمالات المعنوية على اهل الايمان كالمعرفة والتوحيد *

(٤٥٥) الرحمة الامتنانية * هي الرحمانية المقتضية للنعم السابقة على العمل وهي التي وسعت كل شيء *

الرحمة ج
المفيضة ج

(٤٥٦) الرحمة الوجوبية * هي الرحيمية الموعودة للمتقين والمحسنين في قوله تعالى (فسأكتبها للذين يتّقون) وفي قوله تعالى (ان رحمة الله قريب من المحسنين) وهي داخلة في الامتنانية لان الوعد بها على العامل محض المنّة *

الرحمة ج

ج

العمل ج

(٢٥٧) الرِدى * بكسر الراء هو ظهور صفات الحق على العبد *

الورد ى ج

(٤٥٨) الرَدى * بفتح الراء هو اظهار العبد صفات الحق بالباطل كما قال تعالى سأصرف عن اياتي الذين يتكبرون في

(۱۵۸)

الارض لغير الحق منقول عن الردي بغير ج
الذي هو الهلاك قال الله تعالى الكبرياء
ردائي والعظمة ازاري فمن نازعني واحدا واحد ج
منهما قصمته * ادخلته النار ج

(۴۵۹) الرسم * هو الخلق وصفاته لان
الرسوم هي الآثار وكل ما سوى الله آثاره
الناشية من افعاله واياه عني من قال
الرسم نعت يجري في الابد بما جرى في كما ج
الازل لان الخليقة وصفاتها كلها بقدر الخلقة ج
الله تعالى *

(۴٦۰) رسوم العلوم ورقوم العلوم * هي
مشاعر الانسان لانها رسوم الاسماء الآلهية
كالعليم والسميع والبصير ظهرت على
ستور الهياكل البدنية المرخاة على باب دار صور ج المرضاة ج
القرار بين الحق والخلق فمن عرف نفسه لمن ع
وصفاتها كلها بانها آثار الحق وصفاته ورسوم
اسمائه وصورها فقد عرف الحق * صفاتها ج

(٦١ ٢) الرّعونة * الوقوف مع حظوظ النفس ومقتضى طباعها *

(٦٢٢) الرقيقة * هي اللطيفة (الروحانية وقد تطلق على الواسطة اللطيفة) الرابطة بين الشيئين كالمداد الواصل من الحق الى العبد ويقال لها رقيقة (النزول كالوسيلة التى يتقرب بها العبد الى الحق من العلوم والاعمال واخلاق السنية والمقامات الرفيعة ويقال لها رقيقة) العروج ورقيقة الارتقاء. وقد تطلق الرقائق على علوم الطريقة والسلوك وكل ما يلطّف به سرّ العبد ونزول كثافات النفس *

(٦٣٢) الروح * في اصطلاح القوم هي اللطيفة الانسانية المجرّدة وفي اصطلاح الاطبّاء هو البخار اللطيف المتولد فى القلب القابل لقوة الحيوة والحسّ والحركة ويسمى هذا في اصطلاحهم النفس فالمتوسط بينهما المدرك

(١٥٠)

للكليات والجزئيات القلب ولا يفرق الحكماء بين القلب والروح الاول ويسمونها النفس الناطقة ✽

(٦٦٤) الروح الاعظم والاقدم والاول والاخر ✽ هو العقل الاول ✽

القلوب ج

(٦٦٥) روح اللقاء ✽ هو الملقى الى القلب علم الغيوب وهو جبرئيل عليه السلام وقد يطلق على القرآن وهو المشار اليه في قوله تعالى ذو العرش يلقى الروح من امره على من يشاء من عباده ✽

✽ باب الشين ✽

(٦٦٦) الشاهد ✽ ما يحضر القلب من اثر المشاهدة وهو الذى يشهد له بصحة كونه محتظيا من مشاهدة مشهودة اما بعلم لدني لم يكن له فكان او وجد او حال او تجل او شهود ✽

تجلى ج

(٦٦٧) شعب الصدع ✽ هو جمع الفرق

(١٥١)

النرقي عن الحضرة الواحدية الى الحضرة الاحدية ويقابله صدع الشعب وهو النزول من الاحدية الى الواحدية حال البقاء بعد الفناء للدعوة والتكميل ٭

(٤٦٨) (الشطح ٭ لغة الحركة ويقال للطاحونة الشطاحة لكثرة تحرك الرحى ويقال شطح الماء فى النهر اذا فاض من حافتيه لكثرة الماء وضيق النهر وعرفا حركة اسرار الواجدين اذا قوي وجدهم بحيث يفيض من اناء استعدادهم) ٭

(٤٦٩) الشفع ٭ هو الخلق وانما اقسم بالشفع والوتر لان الاسماء الالهية انما يتحقق بالخلق فما لم ينضم شفعية الحضرة الواحدية الى وترية الحضرة الاحدية لم تظهر الاسماء الالهية ٭

(٤٧٠) الشهود ٭ رؤية الحق بالحق ٭

(٤٧١) شهود المفصل فى المجمل ٭ رؤية

الكثرة في الذات الاحدية *

الاحدية ج — (٤٧٢) شهود المجمل في المفصل * رؤية الاحد في الكثرة *

(٤٧٣) شواهد الحق * هي حقايق الاكوان فانها تشهد بالمكون *

(٤٧٤) شواهد التوحيد * تعينات الاشياء

بتعين ج — فان كل شيء له احدية يتعين خاص يمتاز بها عن كل ما عداه كما قيل ففي كل شيء له آية تدل على انه واحد *

الاشياء ج — (٤٧٥) شواهد الاسماء * اختلاف الاكوان
فع فع — بالاحوال والاوصاف والافعال كالمرزوق يشهد
الرزق ج — على الرازق والحي على المحيي والميت على المميت وامثالها *

الشيون ج — (٤٧٦) الشُّون * الافعال *

(٤٧٧) الشُّون الذاتيّة * اعتبار نقوش الاعيان والحقائق في الذات الاحدية كالشجرة واغصانها و اوراقها وازهارها

وثمارها الى النواة وهى التى تظهر فى الحضرة الواحدية وينفصل بالعلم *

(٤٧٨) الشيخ * هو الانسان الكامل في علوم الشريعة والطريقة والحقيقة والبالغ الى حدّ التكميل فيها لعلمه بآفات النفوس وإمراضها وادوائها ومعرفته بدوائها وقدرته على شفائها والقيام بهداها ان استعدت وُ وتقفت لاهتدائها *

* باب التاء *

(٤٧٩) التاء * يكنى بالتاء عن الذات باعتبار التعينات والتعددات *

(٤٨٠) التأنيس * هو التجلي في المظاهر الحسية تانيسا للمريد المبتدي بالتزكية والتصفية ويسمى التجلي الفعلى لظهوره في صور الاسباب *

(٤٨١) التجلّى * ما يظهر للقلوب من انوار الغيوب *

(٤٨٢) التجلى الاول * هو التجلى الذاتى وهو تجلى الذات وحدها لذاتها وهي الحضرة الاحدية التي لا نعت فيها ولا رسم ان الذات التي هي الوجود (الحق المحض وحدتُه عينُه لان ما سوى الوجود) من حيث هو وجود ليس الا العدم المطلق وهو اللّاشيء المحض فلا يحتاج في احديته الى وحدة وتعين يمتاز به عن شيء اولا اذ لا شيء غيره عن غيره فوحدته عين ذاته وهذه الوحدة منشأ الاحدية والواحدية لانها عين الذات من حيث هي اعنى لا بشرط شيء اى المطلق الذي يشمل كونه بشرط ان لا يكون شيء معه وهو الاحدية وكونه بشرط ان يكون معه شيء وهو الواحدية والحقائق في الذات الاحدية كالشجرة في النواة وهي غيب الغيوب * (٤٨٣) التجلى الثاني * هو الذي يظهر به

(١٥٥)

اعيان الممكنات الثابتة التى هى شوُن الذات لذاته تعالى وهو التعين الاول بصفته العالمية والقابلية لان الاعيان معلوماته الاول والذاتية القابلية للتجلى الشهودى وللحق بهذا التجلى تنزل من الحضرة الاحدية الى الحضرة الواحدية بالنسبة الاسمائية ٭

(٤٨٤) التجلى الشهودىّ ٭ هو ظهور الوجود المسمى باسم النور وهو ظهور الحق بصور اسمائه فى الاكوان التى هي صورها وذلك الظهور هو نفَس الرحمن الذي يوجد به الكل ٭

(٤٨٥) التحقيق ٭ شهود الحق في صور اسمائه التى هي الاكوان والاعيان فلا يحتجب المحقق بالحق عن الخلق ولا بالخلق عن الحق ٭

(٤٨٦) التصوّف ٭ هو التخلق بالاخلاق الالهية (٤٨٧) التلوين ٭ هو الاحتجاب عن احكام او حال او مقام سَنِي بآثار حال او مقام دني وعدمه على التعاقب وآخرة التلوين في مقام تجلى الجمع بالتجليات الاسمائية في حال البقاء بعد الفناء وانما قال الشيخ محيى الدين قدس الله روحه انه عندنا اكمل المقامات وعند الاكثرين مقامٌ ناقصٌ لانه اراد بالتلوين الفرق بعد الجمع اذا لم يكن كثرة الفرق حاجته عن وحده الجمع وهو مقام احدية الفرق في الجمع وانكشاف حقيقة معنى قوله تعالى كل يوم هو في شان ولا شك انه اعلى المقامات وعند هذه الطائفة ذلك نهاية التمكين ٭ واما التلوين الذي هو آخر التلوّنات فهو عند مبادي الفرق بعد الجمع حيث يتحجب الوجد بظهور آثار

(١٥٧)

الكثرة عن حكم الوحدة *
* ولم يوجد فيها ما اوّله ثاء *
* باب الخاء *

(٩٨٨) الخاطر * ما يرد على القلب من الخطاب او الوارد الذي لا تعهد للعبد فيه وما كان خطابًا فهو على اربعة اقسام ربانى وهو اول الخواطر ويسميه السهل السببَ الاول ونَقر الخاطر و لا يخطىء ابدا ويعرف بالقوة والتسلط وعدم الاندفاع بالدفع * ومَلَكى وهو الباعث على مندوب او مفروض وفى الجملة على كل ما فيه صلاح ويسمى الهاما * ونفسانى وهو ما فيه حظ النفس ويسمى هاجسا * وشيطانى وهو ما يدعو الى مخالفة الحق قال الله تعالى الشيطان يعدكم الفقر ويأمركم بالفحشاء وقال النبي صلى الله عليه وسلم لمة (الملك تصديق بالحق ووعد بالخير ولمة

الشيطان تكذيب بالحق وإيعاد بالشر ويسمى وساوسا ويعبّر بميزان الشرع فما فيه قربة فهو من الاولين وما فيه كراهة او مخالفة شرعا فهو من الآخرين ويشتبه في المناجاة فما هو اقرب الى مخالفة النفس فهو من الاولين وما هو اقرب الى (الهوى وموافقة النفس) فهو من الآخرين والصّادق الصّافي القلب الحاضر مع الحق سهل عليه الفرق بينهما بتيسير الله وتوفيقه *

المباهات ج

مخالفة الحق ج

(٤٨٩) الخاتم * هو الذي قطع المقامات بأسرها وبلغ نهاية الكمال وبهذا المعنى يتعدّد ويتكثر *

(٤٩٠) خاتم النبوة * هو الذي ختم الله به النبوة ولا يكون الا واحدا وهو نبينا محمد صلى الله عليه وسلم وكذا *

فج

(٤٩١) خاتم الولاية * وهو الذي يبلغ به صلاح

الدنيا والآخرة نهاية الكمال ويختل بموته نظام العالم وهو المهدى الموعود في آخر الزمان * (۴۹۲) فرقة التصوف * هي ما يلبسه المريد من يد شيخه الذي يدخل في ارادته و يتوب على يده لامور * منها التزيي بزي المراد ليتلبس باطنه بصفاته كما يلبس ظاهره بلباسه وهو لباس التقوى ظاهرا وباطنا قال الله تعالى قد انزلنا عليكم لباسا يوارى سوآتكم وريشا ولباس التقوى ذلك خير * ومنها وصول بركة الشيخ الذي لبسه من يده المباركة اليه * ومنها نيل ما يغلب على الشيخ في وقت الالباس من الحال الذي يرى الشيخ ببصيرته النافذة المتورة بنور القدس انه يحتاج اليه لرفع حجبه العايقة وتصفية استعداده فانه اذا وقف على حال من يتوب على يده علم بنور الحق ما يحتاج اليه فيستنزل من الله ذلك حتى يتصف

يلبس ج نع

ببصرته ج
لدفع ج

(١٦٠)

قلبه به فيسري من باطنه الى باطن المريد ۞ ومنها المواصلة بينه وبين الشيخ به فيبقى بينهما الاتصال القلبى والمحبة دائما ويذكره الاتباع على الاوقات فى طريقته سيرته واخلاقه واحواله حتى يبلغ مبلغ الرجال فانه اب حقيقى كما قال عليه الصلوة والسلام الآباء ثلثة اب ولدك واب علمك واب ربّاك ۞

(٩٣) الخضر ۞ كناية عن البسط والياس من القبض ،واما كون الخضر عليه السلام شخصا انسانيا باقيا (من زمان موسى عليه السلام الى هذا العهد او روحانيا) يتمثل بصورته لمن يرشده فغير محقق عندى بل قد يتمثل معناه له بالصفه الغالبة عليه ثم يضمحلّ وهو روح ذلك الشخص او روح القدس ۞

(٩٤) الخطرة ۞ داعية تدعو العبد الى ربه

بحيث لا يتمالك دفعها *

(٤٩٥) الخِلّة * تحقق العبد بصفات الحق بحيث تخلله الحق ولا تخلّى منه ما يظهر عليه شيء من صفاته فيكون العبد مرآة للحق *

يخلى ج

(٤٩٦) الخلوة * محادثة السر مع الحق بحيث لا يرى هذا غيره هذا حقيقة الخلوة ومعناها واما صورتها فهي ما يتوسل به الى هذا المعنى من التبتّل الى الله والانقطاع عن الغير *

مع

(٤٩٧) خلع العادات * هو التحقق بالعبودية موافقة لامر الحق بحيث لا يدعوه داعية الى مقتضى طبعه وعادته *

موافقا ج

(٤٩٨) الخلق الجديد * هو اتّصال امداد الوجود من نفَس الرحمن الى كل ممكن لانعدامه بذاته مع قطع النظر عن موجده وفيضان الوجود عليه منه على التوالي

ايصال ج

غميضان ج

(١٦٢)

حتى يكون في كل آن خلقا جديدا لاختلاف نسب الوجود اليه مع الآنات واستمرار عدمه في ذاته ٭

٭ باب الذال ٭

(٤٩٩) زخائر الله ٭ قوم من اوليائه تعالى يدفع بهم البلاء عن عباده كما يدفع بالذخيرة بلاء الفاقة ٭

(٥٠٠) الذوق ٭ هو اول درجات شهود الحق بالحق في اثناء البوارق المتوالية عند ادنى لبث من التجلي البرقي فاذا زاد وبلغ اوسط مقام الشهود يسمى شربا فاذا بلغ النهاية يسمى ريّا وذلك بحسب صفاء السر من لحوظ الغير ٭

(٥٠١) ذو العقل ٭ هو الذي يرى الخلق ظاهرا والحق باطنا فيكون الحق عنده مرآة الخلق لاحتجاب المرآة بالصورة (الظاهرة فيه احتجاب المطلق بالمقيد ع) ٭

(١٦٣)

(٥٠٢) ذو العين ٭ هو الذي يرى الحق ظاهرا والخلق باطنا فيكون الخلق عنده (مرآة الحق لظهور الحق عنده واختفاء الخلق فيه) اختفاء المرآة بالصورة ٭

(٥٠٣) ذو العقل والعين ٭ هو الذي يرى الحق في الخلق والخلق في الحق ولا يحتجب باحدهما عن الآخر بل يرى الوجود الواحد بعينه حقا من وجه وخلقا من وجه فلا يحتجب بالكثرة عن شهود الوجه الواحد الاحد بذاته ولا (يزاحم في شهود كثرة الظاهر) احدية الذات التي يتجلى فيها ولا تحتجب باحدية وجه الحق عن شهود الكثرة الخلقية ولا يزاحم في شهوده احدية الذات المتجلية في المجالى كثرتها والى المراتب الثلث اشار الشيخ الكامل محيى الدين ابن الاعرابى في قوله ٭

نبه ج —

فج —

يتحجب ج —
الوجود ج فج مع يزاحمه في شهوده كثر مظاهر ج

كثرة ج —

※ شعر ※

ففى الخلق عين الحق ان كنت ذا عين
وفى الحق عين الخلق ان كنت ذا عقل
وان كنت ذا عين وعقل فما ترى
سوى عين شيء واحد فيه بالشكل

※ باب الضاد ※

(٥٠٤) الضّنائن ※ هم الخصائص من اهل الله الذين يضنّ بهم لنفاستهم عنده كما قال عليه الصلوة والسلام ان لله ضنائن من خلقه البسهم النور الساطع يحييهم في عافية ويميتهم في عافية ※

(٥٠٥) الضّياءُ ※ رؤية الاشياء بعين الحق عين الحق ※

※ باب الظاء ※

(٥٠٦) ظاهر الممكنات ※ هو تجلّي الحق بصور اعيانها وصفاتها وهو المسمى بالوجود الاضافي وقد يطلق عليه ظاهر الوجود ※

الضفائن ع

(٥٠٧) الظّل ٭ هو الوجود الاضافي الظاهر بتعينات الاعيان الممكنة واحكامها التي هي معدومات ظهرت باسمه النور الذي هو الوجود الخارجي المنسوب اليها فيستر ظلمة عدميتها النور الظاهر بصورها صار ظلا لظهور الظل بالنور وعدميته في نفسه قال الله تعالى الم تر الى ربك كيف مدّ الظل اي بسط الوجود الاضافي على الممكنات فالظلمة بازاء هذا النور هو العدم وكل ظلمة فهو عبارة عن عدم النور عما من شانه ان ينوّر ولهذا سمي الكفر ظلمة لعدم نور الايمان عن قلب الانسان الذي من شانه ان يتنور به قال تعالى الله وليّ الذين آمنوا يخرجهم من الظلمات الى النور الآية ٭

بظهور مد ج

يتنور ج

(٥٠٨) الظلّ الاوّل ٭ هو العقل الاوّل لانه اوّل عين ظهرت بنوره تعالى وقبلت صورة الكثرة التي هي شؤون الوحدة الذاتية ٭

(١٦٦)

(٥٠٩) ظل الآلٰه * هو الانسان الكامل المتحقق بالحضرة الذاتية *

* باب الغين *

(٥١٠) الغراب * كناية عن الجسم الكلي لكونه في غاية البعد من عالم القدس والحضرة الاحدية ولخلوّه عن الادراك والنورية والغراب مثل في البعد والسواد *

(٥١١) الغشاء والغشاوة * ما يركب وجه مرآة القلب من الصداء ويكلّ عين البصيرة و يعلو وجه مرآتها *

(٥١٢) الغنى * الملك التام فالغني بالذات ليس الا الحق اذ له ذات كل شيء والغني من العباد من استغنى بالحق من كل ما سواه لانه اذا غني بوجوده فاز بكل شيء بل لا يرى لشيء وجودا ولا تاثيرا وظفر بالمطلوب واستبشر بشهود المحبوب *

(٥١٣) الغوث * هو القطب حين ما يلتجأ

اليه ولا يسمى فى غير ذلك الوقت غوثا *

(٥١٤) غيب الهوية والغيب المطلق * هو ذات الحق باعتبار اللاتعين *

(٥١٥) الغيب المكنون والغيب المصون * هو سر الذات وكنهها الذي لا يعرفه الا هو ولهذا كان مصونا عن الاغيار مكنونا عن العقول والابصار *

(٥١٦) الغين دون الرين * هو الصداء المذكور فان الصداء حجاب رقيق يتجلى بالتصفية ويزول بنور التجلي لبقاء الايمان معه واما الرين فهو الحجاب الكثيف الحائل بين القلب والايمان بالحق والغين ذهول عن الشهود او احتجاب عنه مع صحة الاعتقاد *

———